Sage

Salvia Divinorum

and the

Entheogenic Experience

by

Martin W. Ball, Ph.D.

Sage Spirit – Salvia Divinorum

and the Entheogenic Experience

Martin W. Ball
© 2007

Kyandara Publishing
ISBN 978-0-6151-5708-5

Cover and artwork by Martin W. Ball

kyandara@yahoo.com

Dedicated to all those who use *Salvia divinorum* in a safe and responsible manner and who strive to keep this sacred herb legal and available for those of us who choose the shamanic path of entheogenic spirituality.

Special thanks to Daniel Siebert for his careful review of this work and his comments and corrections.

This is a book that truly contains much "sage" wisdom. Dr. Ball regards *Salvia divinorum* as a sacred herb and treats it with tremendous respect. He describes many of his personal experiences, shares meaningful insights, and provides helpful advice on using this herb as a tool for cultivating practical spirituality. *Sage Spirit* should be read by all who seek to understand the nature of *Salvia divinorum,* especially as it relates to human consciousness, personal growth, and spiritual development.

— Daniel Siebert

Table of Contents:

A Note on "Entheogen"

What is an entheogen? Is it the same thing as a psychedelic? And is that the same as a hallucinogen?

The answers to these questions will likely vary depending on precisely who is asked. In one sense, the terms entheogen, psychedelic, and hallucinogen are interchangeable when they are used to refer strictly to a substance, plant, or chemical. In another sense, these terms are all quite different from each other, significantly so, and are not interchangeable at all.

Hallucinogen strictly means *something that produces or gives rise to hallucinations*. Hallucinations are, by definition, false and erroneous sense impressions of things that are fundamentally non-existent. In other words, to hallucinate is to see, hear, smell, taste, or otherwise perceive or experience something as real that is actually not. To hallucinate is to be mistaken about our perceptions. There is a fundamental discrepancy between what we think we perceive and what actually exists.

1

Psychedelic, by contrast, has a very different connotation and reflects a deep philosophical disagreement with the term *hallucinogen*. Coming from the root word *psyche*, or mind, psychedelic means *mind manifesting*. Something that is psychedelic therefore manifests "mind" or "consciousness" or "awareness," or by extension, makes the mind more fully aware of itself, its contents, and its processes. A psychedelic "opens the mind," and "cleanses the doors of perception." A psychedelic reveals a deeper, more fundamental level, or levels, of perception and brings to conscious light things that were unknown or previously unperceived, secret, and hidden. It is easy to see that there are very different connotations between hallucinogen and psychedelic.

Both of the above terms have been used to refer to certain plants, fungi, and even animal-produced chemicals that have a direct impact on a person's perceptual and cognitive abilities. These terms are generally equally well known in popular culture. Often the terms are used interchangeably, though given the philosophical differences between them, this can be problematic. Psychedelic has also become a key word for describing certain genres and styles of music and art, often associated with "the 60's" or artwork inspired by that period of cultural history.

The term *entheogen* is a bit more mysterious and enigmatic, however, and though increasingly in use, it is still relatively unknown outside the subcultures that see this as the term of choice when referring to substances that alter our consciousness through expanding and enlivening our perceptions, thought processes, and spiritual sensitivities.

A Note on "Entheogen"

Literally, *entheogen* means *generating god within*. *Theos* is Greek for *god*, and *entheos* is *god within*. *Gen* means *becoming* or *coming into being*. Coined by enthnobotanical researchers in the 70's, Gordon Wasson and others introduced *entheogen* as a more accurately descriptive term to indicate the very special places that these unique plants and fungi hold in the cultures of many of the world's indigenous peoples. In many indigenous cultures, these sacred substances have been held in reverence for generations and entheogens have a foundational role in countless religious and spiritual traditions. In contrast with Western counter-cultural practices, entheogens are used in indigenous contexts not for diversion and entertainment, but for healing, spiritual revelation, and shamanic practice.

Taking inspiration from Gordon Wasson and his work on psilocybin mushrooms in Mexico with Maria Sabina, the Mazatec shaman, and Wasson's hypothesized role of *Amanita* mushrooms in the Vedic *Soma*, entheogen has become the term of choice for those who choose to use mind-altering plants and substances for the purpose of spiritual growth and development. In the contemporary West, the use of the term *entheogen* is meant to make a statement that is in clear contrast to *hallucinogen* and even *psychedelic*.

Entheogen is therefore a term that implies not just a physical thing. Rather, it places the emphasis on how that physical thing is treated, appreciated, contemplated, and used. With that in mind, it is perhaps better to say that entheogen means *a substance that is used primarily for spiritual, ceremonial, religious, or shamanic purposes with the intent of communing with a wider spiritual reality.*

Something important to emphasize with this definition is that the primary focus is not necessarily on the *theos* portion of the word, despite its literal translation. "God" is a highly loaded concept in Western and Near Eastern discourse, having clear connections to the monotheistic traditions of Christianity, Judaism, and Islam. There is a great deal of cultural and historical baggage to the use of this term, and for some, implies a long struggle against cultural and social imperialism.

This is not necessarily the "god" that is implied in the term *entheogen*. Certainly, most of the traditional cultures that have used these substances for millennia were not of the three monotheistic traditions. Here "god" must be taken in a much broader sense of indicating a deeper spiritual reality that lies behind, within, and surrounding the reality of our everyday perceptions. I can also be taken to mean the particular "god" or "gods" of any given indigenous tradition that might be associated with any particular plant or mushroom.

Furthermore, it is important to emphasize that many entheogens were and are used for shamanic practice, which can be very different from otherwise "religious" or "spiritual" practice, at least as these terms are commonly understood in the contemporary West. Shamanism, while a spiritual practice, is also extremely practical. An entheogen-using shaman might be consulted to help find a lost object, for example. This is not seeking enlightenment, communing with the Absolute, or visiting with God. It's about using the profound perception-altering properties of a unique substance to find a lost object through supra-sensory means. Indeed, the Mazatec mushroom-using shaman, Maria Sabina, was purportedly puzzled by the visits she received by young Westerners asking her to share the mushrooms so that they might find God. For Maria Sabina, mushroom use was about shamanizing – finding practical cures to peoples' ailments – not about having a mystical experience.

In traditional cultures, entheogens are universally regarded as both teachers and as tools. They impart knowledge, guide visionaries on journeys of discovery, and bring one to deep states of spiritual awareness and realization. And they are tools in that they are used to achieve specific aims, whether it be to perform a shamanic healing, communicate with plants and spirits to learn cures, initiate youth into the full mysteries of adulthood and mature consciousness, or divine the past or future.

Contemporary use of entheogens in a Western context is not necessarily identical to traditional or indigenous uses, though the adoption of the term indicates a desire to treat these unique substances with respect and reverence and use them in a way that is spiritually fulfilling, however we might define that. In neo-shamanic contexts, entheogens are often used by solo journeyers or small groups for the purpose of personal discovery, insight, and spiritual experience. Neo-shamanic practitioners also use entheogens for shamanic healing sessions that often incorporate aspects of indigenous traditions, as many neo-shamanic practitioners have had opportunities to study with indigenous shamans. Entheogens are also an integral ingredient in the cutting-edge nexus of spirituality, art, and creative expression in many underground and "outsider" art circles such as Burning Man.

For this work, I have chosen to use *entheogen* and *entheogenic experience* as my terminology of choice. I have a deep and profound respect for *Salvia divinorum*, and I would hope that others would share this as well. Philosophically, I am perfectly comfortable with the term *psychedelic,* and at times, I use it interchangeably with *entheogen.* From a philosophical perspective, I am of the view that these substances do in fact open our minds, broaden our awareness, and give us access to states of consciousness normally inaccessible to our waking minds. I feel that the term *hallucinogen,* somewhat ironically, is a rather gross distortion. On the contrary to being hallucinatory, in some respects, what is revealed in psychedelic states can be considered to be fundamentally more "real" and "true" than our ordinary perceptions.

Choosing the terms *entheogen* and *entheogenic experience* is intended to show a level of respect and reverence for these substances, and to encourage others to treat them and appreciate them similarly. Entheogens are serious, and working with them should be undertaken with dedication, humility, and an open mind and heart. They can be profoundly spiritually fulfilling, but they can be immensely challenging as well. My book, *Mushroom Wisdom: How Shamans Cultivate Spiritual Consciousness,* was my attempt to help bring the contemporary use of psilocybin mushrooms into the context of entheogenic practice. My goal here is to do the same for *Salvia divinorum* with this book.

Salvia divinorum, in particular, is such a unique plant that it deserves some special respect. The sage experience can range from mild, dreamy, and subtle, to an otherworldly journey into hyper-dimensional space in a matter of seconds. It can fill one with a deep sense of awe and fathomless wonder. It is deeply personal, intimate, and also alien and transcendent. It is *Salvia divinorum*.

Does *Salvia divinorum* reveal "God," "The Absolute," or even "The Sage Goddess" to the user? That is for each person to contemplate for him or herself. Salvia is what it is. How we understand and appreciate it will always be an individual choice, for it is only our own personal experience that can determine what the salvia experience is for us.

For those who choose to open that door and step through into the strange and fantastical world that is the Sage, I offer you this book as a guide to the entheogenic and psychedelic experience that is *Salvia divinorum*.

Take a deep breath, and let go . . .

Salvia divinorum

S alvia divinorum, the "diviner's sage," an incredibly powerful psychoactive plant originating in indigenous Mexico, is now widely available as a "shamanic" herb that is sold over the internet and at some herb stores. While it has been made illegal in some locations, for the most part, *Salvia divinorum* is legal to use, remains mostly unregulated, and is easily accessible. A once obscure and little-known herb has now entered the psychedelic mainstream and is being consumed by seasoned psychedelic and shamanic explorers, as well as inexperienced youth.

Among entheogen enthusiasts, *Salvia divinorum* is afforded special respect due to the unique nature of the sage experience, its rapid onset (particularly in smoked form, especially when the leaves have been potentiated or enhanced), and the profound vistas of the salvia journey. It can engender deeply mystical and shamanic states of consciousness and is efficacious for mediation, healing, shamanic journeying, and psychic insight. Its use can leave one feeling deeply empowered and connected to a wider, magical reality. It can also launch one into profoundly different realities where one loses sense of one's body and normal awareness, albeit briefly. Space and time ebb and flow into hyper-dimensional eddies and cosmic currents course through one's sense of being in body, mind, and spirit.

Salvia divinorum is therefore not an herb to be trifled with. Anything this powerful should be respected and approached with a sense of humility and wisdom. *Salvia divinorum* is in no way a party drug and has virtually no "recreational" value. And though legal and largely unregulated, it also is not an herb that adolescents should be playing with. While I do not support criminalizing *Salvia divinorum* or its use in any way, legally regulating *Salvia divinorum* to minimize its availability to young people is entirely reasonable.

As with all entheogens and psychedelics, the worlds that salvia opens up can be profoundly difficult and challenging to manage, navigate, and integrate into our normal, waking consciousness and life. It is my view that all such substances should be used by mature, responsible, and ideally, spiritually aware, adults, and not by minors. It is also my view that as a culture and society, we would benefit immeasurably were we to create structured and supervised entheogenic initiation rituals for our young people so that they can learn how to work with these powerful and profoundly valuable substances in a responsible and meaningful way.

Psychedelics in the West

Though mind-altering substances have been a part of human cultures and history since the dawn of time, psychedelics re-emerged onto the contemporary cultural scene in the West in the mid 1900's where countless numbers of young people took on the mantel of "hippies" and followed Timothy Leary's call to "turn on, tune in, and drop out," helping to inspire the indiscriminate use of LSD, and to a lesser degree, psilocybin mushrooms. This in turn led to the criminalization of many "psychedelic" substances and ultimately, gave birth to the "war on drugs," a severe and reactionary over-reaction to "drug" use that has been entirely ineffective and does far more social harm than good. Indeed, the "war on drugs" serves the purposes of politicians and those in power far more than it serves to protect citizens from the harm of illicit drug use.

For a time, psychedelics seemed to recede from the cultural background as the "just say no" era took over American culture and the federal government began a worldwide program of drug eradication, incarcerating thousands of non-violent drug "offenders" in prison, the majority being marijuana users (as is still true today). Other drugs such as ecstasy and methamphetamine came to the fore, each representative of different subcultures.

The seed was planted, however, and even though many associate psychedelics with "The 60's," there is currently a widespread and renewed interest in psychedelics substances.

The contemporary fascination with psychedelics is somewhat different from the interests of the "hippie" days. Today, there is far more information readily available in print and on the internet for experts and laypersons alike about the traditional and historical use of psychedelic and entheogenic plants, fungi, and even animals, than there was at the time of Leary. We now know that such plants and fungi have been used by countless cultures around the world for millennia, and there is good reason to believe that many of the major, and countless minor, religions and spiritual traditions have actively used such plants for religious and ceremonial purposes. Indeed, in the Americas in particular, we now know that many, if not the majority, of indigenous cultures, have used, and in many cases, continue to use, these plants for shamanism, healing, ceremony, and spiritual growth and empowerment.

Thus our collective knowledge of the practices of other people in other places and other times is far more abundant now than when psychedelics first re-emerged in Western cultures and societies. Inspired by such knowledge, many have desired to approach these plants in ways that are similar to their use in indigenous contexts, treating them as sacred, as powerful plant teachers, as shamanic allies, and as mystical sacraments. Many see the use and consumption of such substances as a matter of constitutional rights and as integral to the pursuit of spiritual and religious practice in free and open societies.

Neo-Shamanism and Entheogens

Though loosely defined, the "neo-shamanic" movement seeks to incorporate the use of entheogenic sacraments into contemporary contexts for the purposes of healing, personal insight, and spiritual growth and mystical experience. Neo-shamanic practice ranges from individual entheogenic explorers to those who study and learn from traditional indigenous shamans. Others are busy creating new traditions and ceremonies of their own, where entheogens are a fundamental component of their practice and experience.

Despite these changes in the way that psychedelics are appreciated and used by contemporary Westerners, there is still something of a shortage of good, experientially based writings on how such plants, fungi, and magical foods can be approached, worked with, and integrated into spiritual or creative practices from a contemporary view point. Books and Internet sites abound with information on entheogens and some writers have become psychedelic celebrities for their personal explorations, such as the late Terence McKenna and the insightful and observant Daniel Pinchbeck, and are considered shamanic characters in their own unique ways. These figures represent more of a heroic/adventurer approach to entheogens, however, and while entertaining and provocative, are not grounded in practical advice or specific spiritual teachings.

What we currently seem to be lacking, from a practical perspective, is work on how to approach these unique plants and fungi in ways that are personally authentic and spiritual meaningful, but not necessarily in an attempt to recreate a hypothetical past or appropriate methods, symbols, and traditions from indigenous peoples. In other words, we are missing our own guides for approaching entheogens as spiritual and creative catalysts. There is still the common perception that the use of these plants is hedonistic, escapist, and potentially dangerous and mind destroying as we are lacking in positive and constructive guides to their use. We need more than just experiential and cultural information on entheogens. We need practical information on their spiritual use as well.

The fact that many of these substances remain illegal, often for completely irrational reasons, makes the open and honest discussion concerning their use and value difficult, as it is still something of a taboo subject. Conducting scientific research is profoundly difficult to manage with these substances, and the personal exploration of such plants is fraught with the danger of being arrested and having one's life destroyed – not by the plants themselves, but by the society that condemns one's personal choices and personal spiritual or religious practices.

Yet the desire for greater understanding is there. Websites abound that sell many of the legal entheogens, often with names indicating shamanic or spiritual use of such plants. The best ones come with experiential advice, cautions, and even requirements that customers use these plants responsibly, such as the personal oath at Daniel Siebert's

Sagewisdom.org site. Now more than ever we need good guides and models for how to approach and work with these plants, given the resurgence of interest and use of such substances. And now, with a new generation growing up with easy access to such plants, we need to collectively discuss how to overcome the totally irrational "war on drugs" approach, and envision new and sustainable ways of appreciating and learning from the entheogens.

Such was my personal motivation in writing my book, *Mushroom Wisdom*. Inspired by my own experiences of having worked with psilocybin mushrooms for a number of years, and having successfully integrated them into my own personal spiritual practice and insight, I chose to write a book with some basic advice for what I understand the mushroom experience to be, how one can work with it, and how it contributes to spiritual growth, mystical awareness, and basic shamanic practice.

Many have expressed an interest in seeing a similar book written about *Salvia divinorum*. Daniel Siebert is offering *Mushroom Wisdom* at Sagewisdom.org, where he specifically recommends it for salvia users. I found this to be quite fitting, for even though I hadn't specifically discussed salvia in *Mushroom Wisdom*, my personal experiences with salvia were certainly influential in writing the book. Also, when participating in an interview for *Mushroom Wisdom* with Timothy White of *Shaman's Drum* magazine, he suggested that a guide for salvia users might be even more useful at this point in time, given the widespread use of *Salvia divinorum*, especially among young people.

The result of these suggestions and others is this book here. It is intended as a clear account of what one can expect from *Salvia divinorum*, as well as how to work with it as a spiritual and creative tool, Primarily, it is my hope that this work will help to dispel some misunderstandings about *Salvia divinorum*, encourage its responsible and mature use by adults, as well as help with the ongoing cultural discussion of how to integrate these substances and the experiences they engender into authentic and meaningful spiritual and creative traditions and practices.

My first Salvia Experience

I first visited with *Salvia divinorum* at Burning Man in 2001. I had recently finished graduate school in Religious Studies, earning my Ph.D. through my work on Mescalero Apache ceremonial traditions. I was familiar with *Salvia divinorum* through my studies of shamanism and ethnobotany and had read accounts from Richard Evans Schultes and Gordon Wasson about its traditional use among the Mazatec people of Mexico, where *Salvia divinorum* has been grown as an entheogen for countless generations. Among the Mazatecs, both salvia and psilocybin containing mushrooms are used for shamanic healing and insight. Some Mazatecs prefer mushrooms, some salvia, and some will use either. For some, salvia is primarily a substitute for mushrooms, but other Mazatec healers may prefer salvia to mushrooms. The Mazatecs have grown salvia for so long that the plant is domesticated to the point where it only very rarely produces viable seeds and is primarily grown from cuttings. It is likely that there are only a few genetic variants of this unique plant, though there maybe genetic variants that have not been scientifically identified as of yet in some Mazatec gardens.

Like most contemporary salvia users, my first experience with salvia had nothing to do with the Mazatecs, their culture, their traditions, or their indigenous understanding of salvia and how to use it. An article in 2001 in the LA Times caught my attention with the title of a "legal hallucinogen." The article was about *Salvia divinorum*, conveniently giving Daniel Siebert's website address. I quickly ordered some and brought my small package of enhanced salvia leaf with me to my first Burning Man adventure a couple of weeks later.

I had read through all the advice on Sagewisdom.org carefully, so I knew that salvia would come on quickly, and strong. As neither my friend nor I had any experience with this herb, we didn't know what to expect and approached it very cautiously.

It was late in the week when we finally decided to try it. We were alone in our camp, with most of our neighbors having gone out for the night to explore and enjoy the wonders that only Burning Man can offer. We sat in our dome with a small pipe and our salvia.

We each tried one round, to very little effect. Having read that only a small amount of enhanced leaf could be very powerful, we were timid about how much to take in. I went first, and then my friend. Since neither of us experienced much, I packed a larger bowl for a second round and smoked it.

I knew instantly, before I exhaled, that I had taken a sufficient amount to launch me into a full psychedelic experience. The sage enfolded me into its peculiar reality of ebbing and flowing psychedelic energy. I could feel it coursing through me in psychedelic fractal waves, like some cosmic serpent gently pushing and squeezing me through its enormous, multidimensional coils. It was an overwhelming experience of power. Needing to let my friend know, I blurted out. "It's here!"

"Where?" my friend asked.

"All around me – everywhere – I'm 'Shrooming – no – Saging!"

Use of mushrooms, having been my only point of comparison at that time, prompted my comment, but really the sage was something else entirely. While sharing certain characteristics with the psilocybin mushroom experience, it was undoubtedly something unique unto itself.

I was enveloped into the strange, hyper-dimensional world of the sage. It flowed through me and I easily left my normal sense of body behind, with my awareness drawn into this bizarre, in between space, a space that is neither here nor there. Like dreams that slip in between the cracks between worlds, the sage was a portal into other places, other times, other dimensions, and these dimensions were filled with energetic power, always flowing, moving, swirling into fractal pools of inter-dimensional portals.

It was profound and deeply empowering. After I returned from my brief journey, I jumped up out of my chair, rushing out into the empty street in the silvery moonlight proclaiming, "Now I understand!" and I felt that I did. An intimacy with the sage had been established in those fleeting moments. A healthy respect had also been established. Salvia was so overwhelmingly powerful, and so deeply interior, that I knew that it was not something to be played with. And its overwhelming nature certainly humbled me too. This was nothing to be cavalier or casual about. This was a deeply powerful entheogen that could launch one deep into psychedelic space. It was not something for partying, or even really engaging with others. It was so interior that the outside world was of little significance when under the influence of the salvia, and in fact, it could be a distraction from the fleeting perceptions of the inner vistas the salvia opened up.

Interestingly, my friend had nearly the opposite reaction to the sage. After my experience, he was ready to give it another try. We packed him a larger bowl than before, and he launched into his visit with the sage. Whereas I felt profoundly empowered by the experience, my friend felt largely spent (especially given it was already late in the week at Burning Man and we'd seen plenty of late nights and not much sleep at that point). He went to lie down in his tent and there he remained until the next morning. I, however, was very happy when some friends stopped by and I spent the next few hours enraptured in deep discussion.

That was my first experience with *Salvia divinorum*. At the time, my only other experience with entheogens was with psilocybin mushrooms, which I had been working with for several years in my own spiritual and shamanic practice. While my experience of working with

18

Salvia divinorum has grown and deepened since that first voyage, my basic impressions have largely remained unchanged. Sage is powerful, it flows, it is hyper-dimensional, and it produces radical experiences that appear to both transcend our normal perceptions of space and time as well as simultaneously enter one into a psychedelic topography of flowing organic fractal structures that are imbued with a living, conscious awareness.

In the years since that first experience, I have visited with the sage many times. Sometimes the visits have been brief, lasting only a matter of minutes. Other sessions have been extended through smoking additional sage at regular intervals, or through using oral forms of salvia consumption, which slows and lengthens the experience. I have saged individually, on my own for meditation, insight, and musical expression, as well as with others in improvised ceremonial contexts. The result is that I am extremely fond of *Salvia divinorum* and I have a deep love and respect for this very special plant. It is my hope that through sharing some of my experiences and thoughts about this powerful entheogen that others come to appreciate and enjoy this plant with a similar respect, both for those who are new to salvia as well as those who are familiar with its special and magical qualities.

The Salvia divinorum Experience

There are several methods available for consuming *Salvia divinorum*. The various methods in turn make for somewhat different *salvia* experiences, primarily affecting the duration and strength of the experience.

Mazatec Salvia Methods

Traditionally, *Salvia divinorum* has been used by the Mazatec peoples of Mexico either by making a liquid leaf infusion from the fresh leaves or by eating the fresh leaves. Salvinorin A, the active component of *Salvia divinorum,* is not easily absorbed in the digestive tract. Therefore, despite the fact that the Mazatecs might consume the leaves by swallowing them, it is the absorption in the mouth that really produces the entheogenic effects, and actual swallowing of salvia is not necessarily effective.

Taking *Salvia divinorum* as a liquid leaf infusion is the least effective method of delivery. Large quantities of leaves must be used in order to make an infusion that is strong enough to have a noticeable effect. And it is only the time that the infusion is actually in the mouth that is truly effective in producing a psychedelic state as it is through the oral mucosa in the mouth cavity where salvinorin A is absorbed. The possible advantage to this method is that the experience will be slower in onset and somewhat longer in duration, but it will tend to be mild. Many contemporary salvia users actually prefer the rapid onset of smoked enhanced leaf, and therefore this method of use among neo-salvia users is probably rare.

Another traditional method of salvia consumption on the part of the Mazatecs is simply to eat fresh leaves. As salvinorin A is not easily absorbed through the digestive tract, there is no need to swallow the leaves when salvia is consumed with this method, however. Thanks in large part to Daniel Siebert's research, it is now known that to be most effective, the leaves should be chewed and kept under the tongue, where salvinorin A is most easily absorbed. This sub-lingual delivery is slow and bitter, but effective.

There are various strains of *Salvia divinorum*. One strain, collected by Brett Blosser, is known as the "palatable" or "Blosser" strain. The "palatable" name is derived from the fact that this particular strain of salvia is reported to be slightly less bitter than other strains, and therefore somewhat more palatable. However, even the "palatable" strain tastes something like strong, bitter spinach, and it is debatable whether it is really is any more palatable than any other strain of salvia. Regardless, it isn't a bad taste, but it isn't exactly a good taste either.

When consumed as a quid, the leaves should be periodically chewed, swished about the mouth, and then put back underneath the tongue. Using this method, the effects of salvia come on slowly, generally within about 15 minutes, and can last longer than when using a smoked delivery method.

On his website, SageWisdom.org, Daniel Siebert reports that the leaf chewing method may be potentiated for better salvinorin A absorption by using a tooth brush to scrub out one's mouth prior to chewing the leaves. This may clean out any dead cells, possibly allowing for greater contact between the oral mucosa in the mouth and the leaves. Furthermore, he recommends rinsing with menthol mouthwash prior to chewing, as the menthol seems to improve salvinorin A absorption.

Liquid Sage Elixir

A somewhat similar method of delivery is through the use of liquid sage extract. This is less common simply for the fact that quality liquid sage extract is not as prevalent in the salvia market as raw leaf or enhanced leaf.

Liquid sage can either be used undiluted or diluted. Undiluted, the extract produces a fairly strong burning sensation in the mouth that can linger for several days, but is also the most effective and strongest method of delivery. However, diluting the elixir with hot water can mitigate this effect. This makes the sensation in one's mouth easier to tolerate, but it also does somewhat lessen the effects of the elixir.

For the liquid sage to be active, it must be held under the tongue, either for an entire 15 minutes, or using the staggering method recommended by Daniel Siebert of taking three consecutive doses of sage elixir every four minutes, which allows for a stronger and more powerful experience.

When consumed in this form, the effects of the salvia begin to come on within the first five to eight minutes. The effects will continue to build up after that point, eventually reaching a peak and then fading away over the next hour or more, depending on the amount originally consumed. Consuming additional doses of the elixir can also extend the experience.

These longer acting methods of salvia consumption are probably best for extended shamanic work with *Salvia divinorum*. For example, when engaged in a healing or performing some other kind of shamanic intervention, the longer duration of these methods is more conductive to doing extended shamanic journeying or healing work. By comparison, the smoked delivery methods produce a much faster, and generally more intense experience. Such experiences, while profound and provocative, move very quickly and can be disorienting, making sustained shamanic work more challenging.

Smoked Salvia

The most common delivery method for neo-salvia users is through smoking *Salvia divinorum* leaves. Websites that sell salvia generally have a variety of options from which to choose, ranging from raw leaves to various levels of potentiated leaves, usually labeled as "5x", "10x" and "20x" enhanced leaves, referring to the quantity of extracted salvinorin A that has been added to the raw leaves to bring them up to higher state of potentiated effect.

Raw leaves must be smoked in far greater quantities than potentiated leaf and is not recommended for those who do not want to engage in extended rounds of smoking. Multiple, relatively large, hits are required, taken in rapid succession, in order to produced the desired effects. However, given that it is more difficult to reach really deep states of sage space when using this method, those who are inexperienced with *Saliva divinorum* and are a bit more cautious about using it might prefer it.

Enhanced leaf, especially that which has been potentiated at the higher levels, such as "20x" enhanced leaf, does not require much smoking at all in order to achieve profound and extremely powerful effects, and therefore should always be used with caution, and especially for those unfamiliar with enhanced leaf, should be used in the presence of a "sitter."

There are a variety of reasons for using a sitter, especially when experimenting with salvia by unfamiliar users. The effects of enhanced leaf come on extremely quickly, and can be overwhelmingly powerful. If a big hit is taken, by the time one begins to exhale the full effects of salvia can be coming on. However, it will often take a few smaller hits to produce such a strong effect, as the smoke can burn very hot in the back of the throat, making smoking too much at once potentially uncomfortable.

The rapid onset of the effects of smoked enhanced leaf can quite literally knock one over. At especially high doses, a user might fall right over, losing all effective physical control over one's body. Such strong doses can also produce a blackout like experience where the user might not be able to recall the actual onset of the experience. However, this effect is only produced by deep explorations into sage space and through careful monitoring of the use of smoked enhanced leaf, can easily be avoided if it is deemed undesirable. People might also get up and move around, unaware of their immediate physical environment. Therefore, having a sitter, someone who is not under the influence of salvia who can help look out for the user, is generally sage advice.

Though having a sitter or journey partner is important for novice users, more experienced users will generally come to an understanding of how much salvia needs to be consumed to reach the desired state of entheogenic rapture, and the strongly debilitating effects of really powerful doses can easily be avoid. If however, that is the effect that one is going for, then a sitter could be the best option for even an experienced user who intends on journeying very deep into sage space.

Vaporizing Salvia

*S*alvia can also be consumed via vaporizing so that no smoking need be involved. Vaporizing is the act of heating a plant substance to the point where the active ingredients are turned into vapor without actually bringing the plant material to the point of combustion. For *Salvia divinorum* to be activated through vaporizing, the plant material must be brought to an extremely high temperature, and some commercial vaporizers might not be able to effectively activate the sage. However, successful vaporization can produce an even stronger effect than smoked enhanced leaf and therefore should be undertaken only with the proper precautions and attention to safety.

The Sage Experience

I have personally tried most of the methods of salvia delivery discussed above, with the majority of my experiences being with smoked enhanced leaf. I will therefore focus most of what follows on this method, with a few comments on the other methods.

Smoking enhanced salvia leaf is truly a profound and radical experience. If it is big enough, only one hit is needed for a powerful and rapid journey into the strange and fantastical world of sage space. With a big hit, by the time one begins to exhale, the effects are already coming on, sweeping one away into the experience.

A notable aspect of the salvia experience is that it has a very strong physical component to it. At lower doses, salvia produces a caressing feeling that moves through one's entire being. This is especially true of the slower delivery methods, such as chewed leaf or liquid extract. The power of the sage softly moves through, around, and within one's body and it can be a very sensual experience.

With smoked enhanced leaf, this physical effect comes on very rapidly and is very pronounced. There is a distinct sense of flow to the experience, which I personally liken to the sensation of wind, moving leaves, flowing water, or even an undulating serpent. Especially when eyes are closed, this sense of flow has a visual and synaesthetic aspect in that one can perceive and observe the flowing patterns of the sage.

Entry into Sage Space

As this strange experience begins to unfold, there can be a few moments of disorientation. Space and time seem to slip and bend around one another and the ordinary, linear sequence of time seems to fold in on itself, mobius strip-like. Images and impressions pass quickly through one's awareness, almost like suddenly being thrown into a dream and a sense of déjà vu is common. Personally, I often experience the desire to immediately communicate my sudden awareness of this strange reality to others, even if no one else is present. When conducting sage ceremonies with others, I've found that such a desire is common. As the sage first comes on, it is not unusual for those saging to make a brief comment or blurt something out which may or may not be intelligible. Most, however, do not try and expand on their exclamations and simply let themselves pass into the sage experience without further commentary, which they might try and take up later as the experience wanes.

The rapid entry into sage space is so strange and unusual that our minds struggle to sort out the flood of impressions and thoughts that rush through as the sage takes hold. At stronger doses, one's ordinary perception of one's body quickly passes away, and the infinite horizons of sage space quickly open up and enfold the visionary into the psychedelic state.

The flood of sage moves over, around, and through one. It has currents, eddies, whirlpools and undertows. It sweeps through one's awareness, enticing one to join in and go with the flow. It moves so quickly, however, that there is often the impression that the visionary is not quite either here or there. It is like being in some strange, in between realm. One is definitely not in ordinary reality, but might not be fully immersed in a completely articulated or defined alternate reality. It is somewhere in between.

I often have the experience when the sage is first coming on that it wants me to take more. I like to refer to this as the impish nature of salvia. Though not necessarily directly personified, it is not uncommon to experience the sage as an entity that entices you to come deeper into its realm – as though it wants you to journey even further. It can almost be teasing or playfully taunting. "Smoke more!" it tells you. "Just a little farther!" Many people I have spoken to about salvia report having such experiences and impressions immediately upon the onset of the sage.

Once one has consumed the desired amount of sage, one need only let go and flow with the experience. I find that the most interesting experiences are had when one lets awareness of the outside world simply fade away. For this reason, I recommend using salvia in a dark place, free from outside distractions. Closed, or partially closed eyes are the best, and one might even want to invest in eye covers so that extraneous light can be blocked out completely, letting one's inner sight fully engage the sage experience.

Within sage space, the undulating flow of the sage can begin to take on form as psychedelic alien landscapes, strange architectural structures, and hypnotic dream images. Often there is the impression of other presences within the sage space, though these presences might be more felt and intuited than necessarily "seen" directly. However, complete scenes can unfold with rather distinct images, personages, or entities in relatively well-defined spaces or places.

Transpersonal Awareness

Shape shifting or transpersonal experiences are also common when entering into sage space. Other personas or energetic patterns may seem to take one over one's personal sense of self, temporarily shifting the visionary into a different state of being. These forces might seem to have a will of their own with their own intentions and desires. For a few brief moments, they may seek expression through the visionary's person, manifesting through their physical movements, sounds, actions, or voice. Sage visionaries, for example, might find themselves signing or speaking with a voice that they would not necessarily consider to be their own.

Given the very physical nature of the salvia experience, this shape-shifting factor can have a very physical aspect to it. For me, given the close relationship between sound and vibration and my salvia experiences, such sensations often center on my throat. I can feel a distinct shift in my throat, and when I begin to sing, the sound both feels and sounds distinctly different, at least to my ears. In fact, I have been working with throat and overtone singing techniques that I have learned directly while in sage space.

Sound and Sage

I personally feel that importance of the use of sound as a driver for sage experiences cannot be overstated. I will regularly make use of a rattle, drum, didjeridu, and throat and overtone signing to structure and drive my sage experiences. Sage opens up a deep and profound level of awareness of the nature of sound and vibration, and there is a strong synaesthetic synthesis across the senses and awareness that takes place when sound is used as a sonic driver. Simply put, one can easily "get inside" the sound, and it can create amazing psychedelic structures within one's experience, giving the impression that true sound is hyper-dimensional. By comparison, sound as experienced in normal states of awareness is two dimensional, at best. When in sage space, sound and vibration can give rise to what I've taken to calling "soundstructures in hyperspace" in that the sound creates multidimensional structures and organic environments. Through synchronizing with the sage flow, we can enter into the various energetic patterns made accessible to us, and explore the sound worlds that the vibrations create and open up to our awareness.

The awareness of hyperdimensional sound structures is also a key in transpersonal experiences with sage. One's personal sense of identity and being can stretch out and merge with the landscape and structure of the vision, erasing the boundaries between self and world or self and the hyperdimensional object of one's perception.

Levels of Awareness

*A*nother common characteristic of the *salvia* experience is that of opening up to deeper, and somehow more fundamental, levels of consciousness and awareness. The sage itself can seem like a subterranean level of consciousness, as though it exists just beneath our ordinary awareness. This consciousness pervades all things and seems to exist in an in between state, as though it enters one into a hyper-dimensional nexus, the crack between worlds. There is often a transpersonal component to such an experience. This sage consciousness *just is*, and our awareness and participation in it is not necessarily personal. As is common for entheogenic experience, there is an unresolved paradoxical sense of both the objective and intimately subjective nature of the experience. Even though it is experienced in a highly subjective state, there is also the impression that this level of awareness is *just there*, whether we experience it directly or not. It is like entering a pre-existing, transpersonal, state of awareness.

All of this passes very quickly, especially with smoked enhanced leaf. Using sound as a driver can extend and stabilize the experience, but even then, smoked salvia will come and go within about 10 – 15 minutes. Rhythmic, patterned sound can help extend awareness of the patterned flow of salvia, however, and those who use sound will generally experience a more intimate awareness of salvia's effects for a slightly longer amount of time.

Returning from Sage Space

The sage experience will eventually fade away, however, and one's consciousness will return to "normal." Interestingly, emerging from a sage session can be profoundly quiescent, especially if it was a more meditative and introspective experience, or conversely, the return from a sage journey can be deeply empowering, giving one a sense of spiritual vigor and vitality. This empowering quality might even need to be expressed right away through musical or creative expression or through prayer or song.

Many emerge from a salvia experience feeling profoundly touched. The salvia experience is so unique, so personal, and when approached with a good mind, so intimate. There is a sense of having gone far out into the reaches of the entheogenic state and having returned with a sense of inner peace, balance, and empowerment.

Truly, *Salvia divinorum* can be a moving and deeply special experience.

In the Presence of the Sage

The following notes are from my personal journals of my *Salvia divinorum* experiences. Though all of my sage experiences have had their unique qualities, there are many consistent themes that I have encountered when working with *Salvia divinorum*. Direct accounts of entheogenic experiences can be useful to give someone unfamiliar with such experiences some idea of what they are like, yet one must also recognize that these are linguistic reconstructions of imaginative, deeply subjective states that, like dreams, shift and fracture into inconsistencies and non-linear progressions. These accounts here were all made relatively soon after the actual experiences with the longest time between experience and writing being the first account. They are presented in chronological order, though they are not meant as a comprehensive account of all my *Salvia divinorum* experiences.

I was so impressed by my early experiences with sage that I took copious notes and wrote detailed journals. As I became more familiar with *Salvia divinorum,* my journals became less focused on capturing all the details of the experience and instead gave attention to the features that were new, unique, or otherwise fascinating. Many experiences have gone unwritten in my personal journals, especially more recently.

My first visit with the sage was at my first journey to Burning Man in 2001.

Meeting the Sage at Burning Man

2001

Sitting in our wizard's hut, I packed a much larger bowl than before and consumed most of it in the first hit. I could feel the Sage start to pass over me as I peered into the bowl with my lighter. There I saw ash balled up into a seemingly intelligent entity, offering itself, wanting me to smoke it, whereupon I quickly consumed the remainder of the Sacred Herb. Instantly the Spirit of the plant began its work and I could see that the preliminary hits had been nothing in comparison to this powerful movement. It passed over me, through me, around me, like an eddy or tide of soft, velvety leaves in a gentle wind. All I could do was bow down before the power of the Spirit of the Sage, which quickly came right upon me and showed Its face of green complexion and soft gaze. It was immensely wise and powerful and I prayed to It that It would pass through me in wisdom and beauty. I had to breathe with It, to feel It, to be with It. It was strong medicine and It made Itself known in this way. For healing, for prayer, for ritual, for journeying, for wisdom and insight. I could feel how It showed you things in the body, patterns, illness, energy, strength, weakness. It flowed and flowed, moving continually, rushing in the soft liquid wind, streaming through, around, and over. It pushed around and through my body and being, making all things flow with It. It was a spirit on a river, a river of time, space, spirit, fluidity, flux. Many spirit voices echoing down endless canyons and waters flowing of deep blue and red, bottomless, fathomless, endless. To catch the Spirit and ride with It, to journey into insight, healing, blessedness. This was healing, this was power, this was knowledge.

I rushed from the wizard's hut into the moonlight, the luminous glaze that filled the world. Standing face to face with the moon, in sheer ecstasy, proclaiming "That's so interesting! Now I understand!"

Back in the wizard's hut I packed and consumed another large bowl after the Spirit had come upon Damon. Again the Spirit of the Sage passed over and through me, rolling, streaming, flowing in power beyond words. This time I was consumed in Beauty. It was all around me, above, below, in body, heart, mind, and spirit. It came from the four directions in Beauty. It came on the wind in Beauty. It came in the sand in Beauty. It came in the sky in Beauty. It came from the four mountains in Beauty. It came with the eagle in beauty. It came in all things in Beauty.

This was at Burning Man, August 31, 2001. It was our 5th day at the Burn. That morning I had seen an eagle flying powerfully against the strong westward winds as it surged towards East Mountain near our camp and it felt like the right time. I had decided to bless the sage and say a few prayers with my medicine bag before we consumed it, and once it came on I was thankful that I had, as I was overwhelmed with the sacredness of the Sage's power. The comparison to Mushrooms was immediate and obvious. It was also distinctly different, however. It rushed over me so quickly, in comparison to the slow fungal build of waves that eventually peak and then gradually fade away. The Sage came like a quick wind, powerful and strong, like Mushrooms at their peak. I felt that the Mushrooms and Sage were natural allies and could easily be used together.

The shamanic nature of the Sage was also immediately clear. It was something to be prayed with. It wasn't for places filled with distractions, noise, and the possibility of rude interruption. This was especially obvious when I took my second strong hit as a careless bike-rider crashed into our neighbor's tent, completely collapsing one side. I called out "Careful! That's my tent back there!" not knowing exactly where he had crashed. Damon quickly told me that it was fine and not to worry as the man tried in vain to rebuild the structure. I let it drift out of my attention, but it was very distracting to have this intrusion while the Sage was first flowing. And I was happy that Damon was there as a "sitter" at that moment.

Unlike myself, Damon didn't take another hit. After it passed him he said that he needed to go lie down for ten minutes. He went into his tent and quickly fell into a very deep sleep from which I could not rouse him later that evening when I was ready to accompany some neighbors out onto the playa.

Comments

*M*y general impressions of *Salvia divinorum* have not changed since that very first encounter with the sage. This experience, as are most of the others recounted here, was with enhanced salvia leaf, which only requires a couple good hits to fully enter one into the sage experience.

As can easily be seen by my choice of capital letters when referring to the sage, this first impression was a strong one. Primarily I was overwhelmed by the sheer power and rapidity of the sage experience. It was all encompassing and complete. There was no part of me that was not consumed by the sage as it flowed through me with its strange force, coursing through my entire being. Though I felt there was a similarity, none of my experiences with psilocybin could compare to the rapid onset and pure power of the *Salvia divinorum* experience.

I was certainly grateful that I had approached the sage as an entheogen and worked with it ritually before consuming it, which helped to set my mind and heart in the right place to truly appreciate the sage's power.

Something else that is very common for my sage experiences, which is reflected in this passage, is the deep feeling of empowerment that comes from being in the presence of the sage. I almost always come away enlivened and invigorated by the sage with a deep and personal sense of spiritual satisfaction from having undergone the experience. It fills me with a profound sense of gratitude and of having been in the presence of a truly powerful essence with a pure spiritual quality.

However, this is not the case for everyone. As can be seen with the case of my friend, he was largely overwhelmed by the sage experience and was unable to stay awake afterwards. Sage will affect different people differently, as will also be seen in the examples that follow.

Lastly, I would also point out that my second full sage experience described in this initial visit was significantly more powerful than the first. I consumed relatively the same amount of sage each time, but as is often the case, a second or third round of sage can be quite stronger than the initial dose. *Salvia divinorum* has something of a cumulative effect, so the same amount, when consumed relatively shortly after an initial dose, can be of a different order of experience entirely, as is also reflected in cases below. I find it continually fascinating, though not necessarily surprising, that there appear to be many deeper and deeper levels to the experience.

Feathers and Blessings

At 12:30 in the afternoon, I got out my medicine bag and prepared myself for another Saging.

I sat on the floor on my zafu with my medicine bag and feathers before me with some cedar incense filling the air. As was the case at Burning Man, it took a couple smokings before the Spirit of the Sage showed its face, but when It did, It was unmistakable. The first couple hits I could feel It begin, but It wasn't flowing. At the third It flowed like a strong river and I was once again overwhelmed by Its sacredness. I felt that It should be used as part of deep prayer and meditation. Mushrooms have this quality as well, but it feels much more dominant in the Sage. With the Sage I feel as though I have to pray. It almost demands it.

The Beauty was all around me again, and flowing, flowing through me. I could feel It press and pass through me, pushing my arms as I held my abalone shell. I sat with It and felt that It was there to give power to bless things. I saw eagle feathers, healings, bodies. My feathers were brilliant and radiant with power and magic, as was the abalone and stones and medicine within. I understood that objects should be put there to be blessed, or to make an offering.

I took another large hit and the Sage blew strongly once more, flowing, flowing. All things moved and passed in motion, through the body, through space.

I picked up my abalone and went to the balcony door where I sat and prayed to the directions, the mountains, the sky, the trees, the birds, the fish, insects, all things around me and with me. I saw more feathers and blessings and how the Sage can be used in ritual for healing and insight. Ritual is key – it brings out the power.

In time the Sage wind passed. I returned to my zafu. I tried to meditate but my lower back hurt, and I felt quite hot, like energy was running through me. So I lay down and listened to some soft Cocteau Twins.

Comments

This visit with the sage was dominated by impressions of ritual activity connected with the use of *Salvia divinorum*. No doubt my experience was influenced by the fact that I had various ritual objects about me that I made use of both before and throughout the sage experience. This is only natural as the context in which entheogens are used greatly influences the nature of the experience that will unfold. When one treats psychedelic substances as entheogens, that is what they become.

In *Mushroom Wisdom*, I discuss the use of entheogens as being a "spiritual mirror" in that they reflect back to us our spiritual and mental states. This is certainly true for *Salvia divinorum*, and many of the experiences recounted here can be seen to have this quality. There is a sense of the existential subjective that appears in such experiences so that these spiritual reflections can be experienced as profoundly personally meaningful.

In the above account, I was primarily focused on the ritual use of salvia as that was how I was structuring my experience and giving it a foundation in my own sense of spiritual practice. As this was the setting for my experience, it played a direct role in influencing the actual content of my experience.

The next account comes from shortly after the description given above. About an hour passed and then my good friend, Mark, arrived. I had told him of my sage experience at Burning Man and he was keen to give the sage a try. Mark and I got together several times in September of 2001 to visit with the sage, with the following account being the first.

I have included my descriptions of Mark's experiences and our subsequent discussions concerning our experiences here as Mark's experiences show a very interesting contrast with my own visits with *Salvia divinorum*. For whatever reason, Mark had a far more difficult time becoming comfortable with the *Salvia divinorum* experience, despite having a good deal of experience with other entheogens and various spiritual disciplines. He struggled with it all along, and eventually decided at the end of these sessions that sage wasn't for him, though he has visited with the sage again more recently, with several years passing between these early experiences and his later ones.

In some sense, I think that our contrasting experiences highlight the fact that *Salvia divinorum* is not necessarily for everyone, and also makes clear that despite the fact that we are both consuming the same plant, very different experiences can manifest depending on the person. Entheogens are a deeply personal experience and are always reflective of our own personal states. They function as spiritual mirrors in that they reflect our thoughts, intentions, and patterns of manifestation back on our selves. Therefore it is perfectly reasonable that two people in the same place using the same entheogen will have two totally different experiences, and the contrasts between Mark's experiences and my own are clear examples of this.

Mark's Energetic Body

Not long after this Mark arrived. I invited him in and he immediately expressed his interest in partaking of the Sage. Though he had never tried it, I had told him about it and he was eager to see for himself. I told him that I wanted to bless him first. I got my medicine bag back out and prayed with it and blessed Mark with the Pollen. He was then ready to take the Sage. I gave him several hits and then he began to describe energy as flowing around him and as sitting like a large ball in his lap. He later said that it wasn't really visual for him, despite the very physical feeling of the flow.

After It had mostly passed over him, I packed a good hit for myself. Immediately the wind began to blow and I meditated my way into the flow as eyelids were pushed into a half-closed position. My attention focused on Mark as he stretched out his arms into the space above him. I saw him as a twisted organ in the system of this unimaginably large organism, stretching out into cosmic space. There was energy flowing through channels of different deep colors. Mark, the organ, with long tentacle-roots, feeding on the cosmic life force, needed to expand. To grow, to moisten, to become as a sponge. It was as if the power was flowing through the organ but not as strongly as it could, as if the organ needed more, or to unbind itself, to unfold, to unfurl. It was twisted in on itself.

Mark's physical boundaries flowed like water in the wind. He shook himself and the energy dripped off him like watercolors. The energy continued to flow into his abdomen and out from behind him. We discussed it some and he agreed that it was concentrated in that area. I suggested that he needed to "fatten up" and "become a sponge."

The Sage quickly began to pass and Mark expressed some disappointment that the Sage hadn't fully come over him.

Comments

In this passage we see how *Salvia divinorum* functions to bring shamanic insight and perception into people's energetic selves. Here, my friend Mark appears to me as being somehow blocked in his energy, as though something is wanting to manifest or flow more freely, but is unable to express itself fully. This is accented by my friend's lanky body type, but the visual impression is more than just his physical body – it is also a perception of energetic flow, its connection to forces outside of the body, and its circulation through the body.

Significantly, it was not long after this that Mark started working as a spiritual healer, more fully manifesting talents and passions that had not been completely articulated in his life before. He began to work energetically to heal and help those in need, becoming a quite successful professional spiritual healer. This sense of emerging into a new sense of being and purpose is not surprising at all, given the impression of blocked energy in this salvia experience that needed to manifest itself more fully in his being. It was as though he was preparing for a metamorphosis and transformation that has now come to pass.

Terror and Healing

Two days after 9/11

$\mathcal{M}$ark and I visited with the Spirit of the Sage today. Mark came over around 2:00 pm to join me in the Saging. After the proper blessings and prayers I served Mark up a large bowl of sage. He smoked it and seemed to be somewhat affected as he quickly glanced over to his right as if the Sage had suddenly manifested there, and occasionally glanced my way with an inquisitive look on his face. Overall, I don't believe that he was too affected, however, and he was not completely overcome by the Sage Wind, which was surprising given the size of the bowl.

I was going to go next, but decided to give Mark another round. This time I packed probably the largest bowl yet. This had a much more profound effect on Mark. He began to rock back and forth while sitting cross-legged on the couch, at one time almost even lifting himself up. His hands twitched and he grabbed oddly at his pant legs. He was holding my book of Huichol yarn paintings, which he dropped at one point and wasn't really capable of placing on the table, so I helped him.

A few minutes later Mark began to comment on the energy that he could feel, and again commented on feeling as if the energy was a ball in his lap (I find this recurring theme somewhat odd and suggested that perhaps he needs to "crack" the egg . . .). He also commented on the visual quality of the Sage and said the he was energetically drawn to the image on the book cover.

After this Mark wanted to place the book by my medicine bundle and he went and sat in the east before the abalone and placed the book on the ground. He seemed to be compelled to do this by inner direction, an experience that I can relate to, having had many inspirations for symbolic manipulation. Mark asked if the energy he was feeling was his own or the Sage.

I joined him with a large bowl.

I could feel the Spirit of the Sage quickly. Unlike other times, instead of coming at me, the Wind blew from behind, with the leaves pushing through me. This time I closed my eyes, and kept them that way for the duration of the experience, except to smoke more from the bowl and to get a rattle later in the experience.

After the first hit the Sage seemed to want me to smoke more, so I lifted the pipe to my gaze to find that the sage had exposed unburned portions, as if offering itself. I smoked and again closed my eyes with my right hand clasping my feather.

I prayed and meditated my way into the Saging, the Wind blowing softly through me. Behind closed eyelids the Spirit presented a rush of subtle images and physical sensations. Though the order is somewhat difficult to reconstruct, one of the first impressions in my mind was Mark remarking how the energy felt and asking if it was him or the Sage. I saw, through the feeling in my own body, that the flow was the Sage but that the energy, the power, was Mark's and that he could direct it with his intention. As for myself, the power filled my entire being, which was greatly enhanced by prayer and concentration. There was no part of my being that was not filled with the Saging (which seems to be in contrast to Mark's experience where he's feeling more constricted and cut off from the full manifestation of the experience).

When I opened my eyes to take my additional hits the Sage subtly shifted to lower intensities that could be renewed by closing my eyes and refocusing on the inner experience of the Sage.

After the second and third hit my mind shifted away from thinking about Mark to other dimensions. The colors before my eyes and the shapes continually shifted in a shamanic dream-flux of organic, and somewhat alien, images, textures, and scenes. My own shape shifted and transformed with the subtle flow of the Spirit as It traveled. I stood on the edge of a cliff, overlooking a vast forest with a river and mountains, sky and clouds. My shoulders arched over as I called to the Eagle and transformed and took flight, soaring through the air above the vast scene below. Then all turned green and I was enveloped in emerald green power-substance. The Sage pushed as it surrounded me and lifted me up from the ground of this shamanic/alien/organic space.

And then the scene shifts. All is red and orange. There seem to be temples, like Aztec and Mayan pyramids. The sunlight streams down in golden light. There are others here, but they are difficult to see in detail, though they have the aura of aliens, of something beyond or from elsewhere. Are these offerings or sacrifices? The world is being made beautiful.

I take one more small hit and finish the bowl. I have the urge to shake a rattle, so I grab the nearest one available. I return to my seat and begin rattling. This driving sets off a rapid shamanic journey. I'm rushing through the trees, up the canyons, through the creeks. I pass over a waterfall, deep in a dark place. I enter the mountain, following some spirit, some guide. I look for the Master of the Mountain. There's confusion. I find my medicine stones. I take them in my hand. There seems to be fire.

Suddenly I'm at the beach. I'm in the water. I am the water. I touch the sand . . .

I'm an eagle. I circle a few times above the ocean on the breeze and then I begin to rush over the mountains. Faster, faster. Suddenly I'm flying over New York. I have my medicine. I pray. I pray for the dead. I pray for the living. I pray for the terrorists. I pray for the world and for beauty. Healing light comes in from the four directions in the four colors. All is beauty.

Next, the same in Washington.

Then, white, pure light, spreading from the middle of the earth and shining across the globe, encircled in a rainbow. It is Beauty, Compassion, Peace, Wisdom.

All the while I'm looking, looking, looking, so hard, so directed. My eyes search behind my closed eyelids. I feel the concentration on my brow. The rattle propels me. It breathes. It lives. I follow the Spirit where It goes. See what It shows me. It is all so subtle, but all so clear. Like a dream, softly behind the eyes. Thought and action are one. It is Seeing. I have a body, many bodies, in this Seeing. All is rapid transformation and flux, and the continuous Sage flow and Wind moves on, pushing me, leading me.

Gently I let the rattle fade as I return into my body. Mark had been meditating through all this. I had briefly considered whether my rattle would disturb him, but quickly decided that I was going to do what I felt moved and directed to do.

When Mark saw me come out of my trance, he wanted me to tell him about what I had experienced. I wasn't ready to talk yet and though most of the Sage had passed, I still felt an outflowing. I felt supremely good and filled with Beauty and satisfaction. It was strong medicine, strong prayer. Its sacred power was just overwhelming.

Comments

The following commentary comes directly from my journals and was written as a reflection on my sage experiences up to the point of having saged at Burning Man, and now several more sessions soon afterwards as recounted in these journals.

I think that it is important to emphasize the ultimately positive nature of all of these experiences that I have now had with the sage. I'd also like to emphasize that it is an experience that you *do* something with, which is why I've highlighted its prayerful nature. Saging is not just about the experience itself, but what you do with it, where you put your thoughts, prayers, and intentions. This is related to the concentration aspect of the experience – the Sage goes where you concentrate on it. The trick is to let It flow without trying to control It, yet still directing it with one's intention. I'm not sure if Mark has been able to actualize this aspect of the Sage as he has repeatedly commented that it hasn't fully enveloped him in the experience. He attributed this to his firm, "unmovable," spiritual center, but I don't know if I fully agree. I personally think that his own intentions have stopped him from having experiences similar to mine. He described the sage as not quite getting "up" to his head, as if it "stopped" before going all the way and that his own intention pushed it back. As I thought the other day, when contemplating the Sage, the shaman is both master of his domain (through intention and concentration) yet also mastered by the domain, as the shaman must literally and figuratively, "go with the flow" in order to have a productive experience. I think Mark's been fighting it, in some sense, and keeping himself from having a fully rewarding sage experience.

Overall, my experience yesterday was deeply rewarding for the fact that it gave me a visceral and direct experience of extending blessings and prayers out in response to the tragedy of this week's terrorist attacks. Through the Saging, I was able to express my feelings and desire to perform a ritual of beauty and compassion for the situation.

It made me think of how the sage can be used for shamanic healing in two complimentary ways. The first way is through the body and direct sight: with the Sage one can both see and feel the energies and flows within the body and it thus gives insight into one's psychophysical nature. This can be used for working on patients directly.

In addition to this bodily experience, there's also the inner visionary nature. This is the shamanic realm itself. In this dimension one can work on the subtle and spiritual energies that are experienced only in shamanic insight. This is the realm of soul retrieval, of power, and spirit allies. In this realm I was able to call upon my ally of the Eagle, and even transform into the Eagle. This is where the deep and subtle spiritual information is. I can't overemphasize how shamanic the experience is – especially when I used the rattle. It was very similar to my "core shamanism" experiences of 6 or so years ago now (using Michael Harner's shamanic drumming method). At times, the sound itself was a little distracting if I thought of it too much, but once I allowed it to slip into the landscape of the experience, the sounds became a powerful driver, at times frenetic, at others, calm. Ultimately, it provided a vehicle through which I could "return" to my body and the present experience of sitting cross-legged on the floor.

At one point in our later discussion after the sage had passed, Mark asked if my experience of the sage was an experience of God. He was quite surprised when I answered in the negative. As I described it, the Sage is a shamanic spirit. It reflects on the sacred and the Totality, but It is a Spirit – a character, an ally. It is a being. It is not necessarily "God."

In this sense Sage is also very similar to Mushrooms in that they are not necessarily God either, but they do open one to the experience of the organic totality of existence. However, they are power. That much is clear and irrefutable. They both are mind, body, heart, and spirit power (though I would tend to characterize mushrooms as more heart medicine than the sage, which seems to flow more outwardly to ecstatic shamanic experience).

I read a couple accounts of the sage on the Internet that said that the salvia experience is ultimately atheistic. From my own experience, I would not necessarily agree with that view either. While the Sage is not an experience of God, it is an experience of sacredness, prayer, beauty – in other words, those qualities that one might use to describe "God," however one may understand this. In that sense, at least for me, the Sage is a deeply spiritual and sacred experience. It engenders prayer, reverence, and awe. As with my experience on Friday, when I was returning, all I could do was say "Thank you, thank you, thank you," as my heart poured out of me in genuine gratitude. I suppose that one might call this an experience of grace.

If one describes God as life force, energy, power, consciousness, etc., then perhaps one may call the Sage an experience of God, or a reflection of God. However, one must recognize that the Sage is its own spirit – it has its own quality and character. The Sage is not the

Mushrooms and vice-versa. They are different Spirits, but they both open you to the same reality.

This reality is the reality of symbols that transform themselves in the spiritual world. As I thought the other day, there's no such thing as something being "only" a symbol. Symbols are the true reality. Symbols are real power. The Sage, and probably most mind-manifesting substances, opens one to the unfathomable depths of symbols. In the contemplation of symbols there is gnostic revelation. The Saging is a revelation of things hidden, of things below the surface, of things felt but not understood, of dream images flowing from the psyche, from the collective. It is the Mind of Mind. It is Sage!

To this original commentary, I would also like to highlight the perception of alien presences in this sage experience. By "alien" I mean to invoke a sense of otherness and strangeness, and not necessarily little grey men with large dark eyes. At higher doses, impressions of strange otherness, both in the environment and the sense of presences populating these alien landscapes, can be quite common.

Another somewhat common feature in my experiences of *Salvia divinorum* is the appearance of pyramids and architectural structures. On several occasions I have seen pyramids of various make, or pyramid-like temple structures. Often there is a sense of ceremony or ritual connected to these pyramid visions.

Cosmic Serpents Born of Fire

I had the opportunity to visit with the Spirit of the Sage again yesterday with Mark up at his place. We met after work specifically for this purpose. I had suggested that we give it a try at his place, as that would allow us to comfortably be outside without worry of being intruded upon.

We set up a small table on Mark's patio with various symbolic and powerful objects to create an altar and ritual space. I performed my usual blessings with my medicine bag and gave Mark the first bowl.

He seemed to really struggle with his first smoke. Sweat broke out all over his body and his hands again began to twitch as they had done previously. Mark's intention was to keep his eyes closed, which he mostly managed to do. Again he described the same feelings as before, with the Sage "not coming all the way around," as if it wouldn't completely envelop him.

As I took my first hit and the Sage began to come on my first thought was "I don't understand how this can be for Mark," as the Sage filled all aspects of my being – there was no place in me where the Sage wasn't.

With that first hit it was like a fire started to burn in my body. It wasn't painful in any way – it was just a fire. I kept my eyes closed and the fire seemed to begin in my chest, or more specifically, in my ribs. From there it moved deeper into my being and then began to rush up my torso, through my neck and throat and then emanated, almost out of my mouth. I tilted my head back and just went with the flow of the experience. Behind my closed eyes I saw yellow, orange, and red, dancing in the characteristic leaf like structure of the Sage's visual nature.

Then there was a change. It was as if an immensely large, almost cosmic, snake moved through my body with astounding speed and power. It came from behind me in a rush of green scales, again shaped like the sage leaves. It passed directly through my body on the left with green on one side and the red, yellow and orange of the fire on the right. The cosmic snake undulated and pulsed with power as it flowed, infinitely long in a parade of deep green with subtle hints of purple and deep blue.

At this point I took another hit and finished off the bowl. The scene behind my eyelids began to shift and now I was seeing blue ocean to the right and a shoreline on the left. I groped for my rattle but had to open my eyes to find it. I then rattled for a minute but I seemed to be loosing the visual quality of the experience.

At this point my attention shifted more to the sounds in the space around me. To flow with the sounds I picked up my didjeridu, and began to play what seemed a perfectly fitting drone to the experience. With the didjeridu I was joined by a crow, which seemed a spirit messenger, who came and sat on a nearby tree and called out into the afternoon air. I matched the crow with my own calls and then again matched the didjeridu to the sound of an insect flying nearby. It was like all the sounds coalesced into one concert, one great symphony of life and spirit power. The symphony reached a crescendo with the piercing call of two red tail hawks and the Sage faded away.

Comments

*A*gain in this experience my friend Mark seemed to be fighting against the sage and the full expression of the experience. Something to note is that he began to perspire quite significantly, and this is something that I've noticed among others who are having a difficult time with the sage. My own experience evoked a sensation of fire, though this did not result in my perspiring or becoming overheated.

This was my first experience of fully associating the *Salvia divinorum* experience with the sensation or impression of a cosmic snake. At the time, I felt as though I were between the coils of a massive, infinitely long serpent that writhed about, pushing and squeezing me (not uncomfortably) between its massive coils. Experiences of tunnels or "wormhole" like structures are also very common and very similar to this impression of a cosmic snake.

Sound became a very interesting factor in this particular sage experience and this was my first attempt at using the didjeridu while under the influence of the sage. The effect was quite profound, with a feeling of having participated in a larger movement of vibration, sound, and "music" that was the larger nature surrounding and encompassing me and my experience. The peculiar vibratory nature of the didjeridu had the effect of synchronizing many aspects of the experience into one uniform movement of sound, harmonizing different energies and currents together into a complete whole.

This was not the end of this particular sage session, and continued as follows.

Welcome to Sage Space

*A*fter some brief discussion, Mark was ready for another round with the sage. I suggested that he try and not fight and control the experience so much and just be with the Sage. His breathing techniques had been very labored in all his previous experiences as he would tend to gulp and really force the smoke into his lungs. He decided that he would take a more receptive attitude this time and try and relax into it more. This seemed to produce better results for him as for the first time after the Sage had begun to pass he commented that he could direct the Sage power with his consciousness.

My own second round was far more powerful than the first. At the first round I had thought to myself "Here It is," but with the second my thought was, "No, HERE IT IS." I find this second experience very difficult to describe. Ultimately, it was an experience of Power. My mind felt confused and I had difficulty maintaining clarity in the experience. First let me say that the presence of the Sage came this time in a multiplicity. It was a profound experience of Many, and these Many were in the Spirit world of the Sage itself. It was as though the Sage is its own spiritual dimension. It is not necessary the underlying reality (which I often feel is revealed by Mushrooms) but rather it was its own personal realm of power. It was the Sage dimension. And this dimension was heavily populated by Spirit powers. I find this very hard to describe. It wasn't really as though I was seeing figures, as I wasn't. For example, Mark had later asked, "Were they people?" and my answer was that no, they weren't. It was more the presence of multiple consciousnesses, multiple awarenesses, other beings, other intentions.

Physically I again had the feeling of snakes: infinite snakes of cosmic proportions. There were two of them and my own physical being was between them with one on my right and the other on my left. They writhed and undulated and I could feel their immense cosmic bodies pushing me first to one side and then to another. It was a great pulsing of waves of unimaginable power. This was not painful, or frightening. Rather, I wanted more, much more. I was on the very edge of being totally taken into the experience, so close to not even being in my body or in my physical place at all. I was on the precipice of completely entering into this Sage dimension. It was as if I was being shown the veil of a completely other world of mystical and shamanic power. I wanted to go but there was something that kept saying, "Wait, we can't go yet." But this other world was a world of magic. A magic forest with incredible plants, animals, and spirit beings. It was so complete. So immense. Unfathomable. I felt that if I could sit with the Sage longer then I could fully immerse myself in the reality and just leave my body behind. It was fundamentally different from my previous experiences of imaginative seeing with the Sage for this was fully the Realm of the Sage, not the realm of my own inner vision. This distinction is profoundly difficult to articulate, but it was different. This Realm was the being of the Sage itself. I knew that to fully enter this Realm that I would need a powerful Sage experience of longer duration.

Comments

The above description contains many elements that I have found to be very common with strong sage experiences. There is this peculiar sensation of not quite either being here or there. One is certainly not in the ordinary world, but there is often the impression that one is not fully embodied in the "other" world, whatever it may be. It is as though the veil between worlds is pulled back just long enough to look inside, but fully entering that space is elusive.

Significantly, this experience was my second round of sage for this particular session. A second or third round is often a much stronger experience, even when the same amount of sage is used. In this case, I was so impressed by the different quality of the experience that in my later reflections, as recounted in my journal, I tried to really distinguish this experience from my previous forays into sage space.

At lower doses, it is easy to let one's imagination take flight in the flow of the sage and see inner visions, vistas, and scenes. These can seem both self-generated and as something that is viewed objectively in sage space. The stronger experiences have a very different quality, however, in that the unfolding visions seem far less self-generated or directed and take on an even more objective sense, despite the fact of subjectively entering deeper into the experience.

In these stronger experiences, there are often a few moments of disorientation as the sage comes on. As is recounted in the account above, feelings of multiple agencies or awarenesses are common – as though one's mind has been split into pieces that are disassociated from each other, where certain aspects appear to be "other" and "not me." This creates the impression of presences that may be more felt than necessarily seen or experienced directly.

In these stronger experiences there is also often the sense of a dominating presence in the sage experience. This presence, which feels like the spirit of the sage itself, will often give instructions or make judgments about the experience, such as to smoke more, or now is not the time, or remember this, or think about that, etc. Whether the actual spirit of the sage or not, the impression is that these thoughts are coming from "outside" and that the one under the influence of the sage is merely picking up on transmitted information or communication.

The above experience also highlights the fleeting and transitive nature of strong sage experiences with enhanced leaf. There is often the feeling that if one had more time, then one could more fully enter this other world. However, smoking more sage will not necessarily achieve this result, as stopping to smoke more sage often launches one into a new experience and not necessarily a continuation of the previous experience. In a sense, it is like waking from a dream and then trying to go back to sleep and pick up the previous dream in the same spot.

This was my last sage experience for some time. After this, I took up a lecture position at UC Berkeley where I was teaching two graduate seminars in Native American Studies, commuting back and forth between Berkeley and Santa Barbara, where my wife was, pregnant, and preparing to give birth. My next sage experience didn't come until after the birth of our daughter, which also inspired the birth of my series of spiritual fantasy novels, *Tales of Aurduin*. After these significant changes in my life, I wanted to see what the sage would reveal and the following account was my first sage experience after those earlier sessions recounted above. Several months had passed, accompanied by major life changes.

Returning to the Sage

*L*ast night I Saged. I wanted to visit with the Spirit of the Sage as I felt it was a good time for me to see what it would reveal, given the current state of things in my life with job, family, writing, and general spiritual and physical health (getting over an extended bought of severe insomnia). Much had changed since those early sessions and I wanted to see what might be different, or similar, with my experience with the Sage.

As always, I got out my medicine bag to pray with the Sage and sit with It. I've been carrying my bag around with me back and forth between Berkeley and Santa Barbara (home and family). I've often thought of the sage, knowing it was in my bag, but haven't gone to it. Now, the time felt right. There had been so many rapid changes in my life, and my insomnia had been so severe. Having mostly recovered, I wanted to see what would be shown to me.

I cleared a space in my living room by setting aside chairs and a table. I sat upon my poncho on the floor and laid my medicine out before me. After praying with the pollen and everything else I smoked a single, large hit of the sage. By the time I exhaled I could feel the Sage coming on. At first It came from my right sweeping to the left. My first thought was almost a dismissive "It's just like before," but by the time that thought had left my mind a great sweep of the Sage overcame me. It was like a rushing wind of leaves fist curling over me from the side and then rushing at me from the front. It swept over me and through me and I could feel It in every aspect of my being.

My first response was that I felt overwhelmed and could only breathe through the experience as I felt my pulse quicken with the Sage rushing on. In my mind echoed the thoughts, "I don't understand," "You caught me off guard," I said Willeto's benediction "I he he I'la," "thank you, thank you," and "Beauty is before me, Beauty is before me." For a moment I had the image of myself curling up as a ball on the ground, huddled in the fetal position, waiting for the Sage to pass. But my reaction was to reach down and pick up a small feather and hold it up to my forehead as a protection from the vast onslaught of pure Sage. The feather, in combination with the medicine lying out before me made me feel some measure of protection from the absolutely overwhelming power of the Sage.

All the while thoughts rushed through my mind that I had been caught off guard, somehow not really prepared for the rush of the Sage, as though I hadn't devoted myself to the proper preparations. Searching deeper I saw how I haven't really stopped to pray and be with the mountains, the plants, and the land the way that I should. I thought of my medicine and the thought came that I had not given more time and thought to it in a reverential way, that I hadn't paid proper respect, or that my mind had perhaps been elsewhere.

So I thought of where else my attention has been and if there were things that were out of place. All felt good, but still with the feeling that more reverence was needed. I was glad at the thought that I'll be getting two trips out to New Mexico soon. I also thought about my music, my story, my family, and things felt good. The feeling of truly being caught off guard was still with me, however, it all happening so quickly and in such a rush of everything.

I asked the Sage what I needed to do, asked to be shown. Upon asking this question the small feather in my hand suddenly felt like it should go down towards the abalone shell before me. Lightly, ever so lightly, it floated my hand down away from my forehead where I could see it before me. It became so light in my hand that I couldn't even feel it, as if it weren't there at all. In all this it seemed and felt powerful and I thought how the feather needs to be carried lightly, lovingly, and with care. Not something to be played with. Walk lightly. Walk with respect and recognition of the powers and the mountains. So good to be going to Mescalero.

Just meditating was good, to be there, to feel the Sage flow through my being, through my body and mind. The medicine before me moved and flowed with the Sage wind, feather light in my hand. It shimmered and waved lightly in the air above the colorful and flowing abalone shell, a well of Beauty. A prayer, being with It and the flow of life.

Comments

*A*s is often the case with entheogens, my experience was a reflection of my state of mind at the time that I chose to visit with the sage. The account above has many of the same themes of power, flow, and awe, but in this experience I was not so much empowered by it as I was overpowered by it.

Certainly, I was in a very different stage of life. In the earlier accounts, I had just returned from my first trip to Burning Man, a truly joyous, liberating, and transformative experience. In the account above, I was working as a lecturer at UC Berkeley, commuting between Berkeley and Santa Barbara, my first child had just arrived, and I had just begun working on a monumental creative writing undertaking of my fantasy series. There had been many significant changes in my life and I was feeling the strain of various pressures.

Strangely, perhaps the greatest disruption in my life at that time was having started my first novel, *Orobai's Vision.* The story so quickly became so immense in my mind with such an elaborate plot, and I had so little time to work on it, given the other factors in my life at that time, that I went through about three weeks of almost complete insomnia, with only a few hours of sleep a night, at best.

In many ways, my experience of taking up the challenge of writing this story was mirrored in my experience of the sage in this particular session. I certainly was not prepared for how overwhelming the task of writing my story would be and how consuming it would be of my attention and thoughts. In short, I was caught off guard, and had a very difficult time managing processing the story, like a backlog in my mind of things that needed so desperately to get into written form.

What I needed, and what the sage showed me through the physical sensation of the feather in my hand, was that lightness was needed. Lightness, care, a gentle touch. I needed to let go of some of the pressures I was building up around myself and release into the experience.

Going into this experience, I asked for a reflection on my current state, and that is what I received.

This was the last time I used *Salvia divinorum* for some time and was my last journal entry regarding salvia until 2005. In the intervening time period I continued to attend Burning Man, where I enjoyed sage several more times. I incorporated some of my salvia experiences into my writing for *Orobai's Vision*, and even created a character in the second novel of my series, *The Fate of Miraanni*, based on the cosmic serpent aspect of my salvia experiences.

At Burning Man in 2003 my friends and I created a theme camp called "The God Box," where we offered equal opportunity mystical experiences for supplicants of the Mystic Toad. I created a long, looped recording of myself performing various styles of throat and overtone singing that I originally called the "Toadian Chant," which we play as atmospheric music in our camp. The following account tells of a very profound experience I had with *Salvia divinorum* while listening to this droning piece of music and another I call "Didjscape," a long didjeridu, flute, and throat singing piece. Using sound as part of my *Salvia divinorum* experiences was integral by the time of this account, regularly using didjeridu and rattling to drive and shape my experiences. Curious to see what it would be like on a more passive side of listening to sound, I decided to listen to some of my own recordings while saging.

Soundstructures in Hyperspace

I had the opportunity to spend an hour with the sage yesterday. I sat in the garage in front of my computer, listening repeatedly to "Didjscape," and "Toadian Chant," and also a couple other songs for comparison.

The first couple hits of the enhanced leaf seemed very mild. I could tell that the sage was there, but it seemed weak. I took another big hit. This time, I had the impression that there were beings, up and behind me, almost cheering me on – "Yeah, go for it! Smoke some more! You're almost there! Smoke some more!"

So I did.

This was similar to the time at Burning Man that I felt a female spirit entity urge me on, but that was more seductive. This was humorous and jovial.

As I've experienced before, it felt as though I was on the verge of being in an alternate dimension. I smoked the rest of what was in the bowl and then packed another bowl, smoking the entire thing. This was some of the most I've ever had in immediate succession.

I found that I was within a fantastic architectural structure that was also the structure of an alternate dimension. It ebbed and flowed with the sage flux, but it also had remarkable stability (by this point I was listening to the Toadian Chant, which gave the world of the sage space greater stability). The architecture of this dimension cuts through ours so that it both exists simultaneously with it, and parallel to it. In this sense, my mind seemed perfectly balanced between the two. I knew I was in the garage, sitting there with my eyes shut, and the computer was playing music, and outside was the tree, and sunlight, and the birds. But I was inside this fantastic structure, and there were others there (something I've experienced before as well – so many similar elements – yet different!) – more felt than actually seen – just knowing that they're there.

Then, inside the structure this lesson began to unfold about how sound in our dimension, which, by comparison, is one-dimensional, in "their" dimension creates three-dimensional architectural structures. The Toadian chant seemed to be sustaining this structure that I was in now. Our sounds create landscapes and structures for these hyper-dimensional beings to enjoy. They liked it. They wanted it. It was pleasurable for them and they were applauding.

A scene then began to unfold within the architecture of the vision. There was the image of a man and a woman, making sounds, singing, inside the same structure that I was in with the other beings up and behind me (almost on a balcony – watching the show?). The man and woman were signing and making unique vibrations. As they sang, a three dimensional pyramid-like structure formed in the organic space between them. The more energy they added to their voices, the higher the pyramid grew, stacking up, layer upon layer, with each layer a different band of energy and vibrational substructure.

What I didn't realize at first was that this scene was very similar to the ending of *Tales of Aurduin,* and when it finally occurred to me, it seemed obvious that the man and woman figures were related to my characters, Ashi and Jao. I thought a lot about book 4 once I realized this. I considered the possibility that I might have written parts of the end wrong – or at least some things that I should add to make it more realistic (imagine the possibility of making it *more realistic!*—fantastic!) I'll have to go back and check what I've already written.

It also made me think of my friend, Marianne. Instantly I thought that I had to tell her that this was how to do it – this was how to create structures in hyperspace – with sustained sound. I wanted to tell her right away, but then smiled, knowing that I had just sent her the same music that I was listening to now. I had already sent her the message – all she needed to do was tune in. It all made perfect sense with Marianne's quest for sacred sounds and the symbols in the sand.

I saw that to create stable structures in hyperspace, you need sustained sound – there can't be a break (like a drone). You also need different layers of sound to extend and build up the structure. And you need lots of energy in the system! Lots of people or animals or spirits sustaining it all – holding it together.

And the spirits in this dimension will help too. We can invite them to come through voices or instruments – they can reside within a song or a chant, and they can add their energy to it – because they want us to succeed. They get to travel through the music and it creates "stuff" for them.

At some point I packed the bowl for a third time and took several more hits.

This time, as the experience began, I thought of how I *should have created a balcony for myself to go out on to look at the fantastic birds*. What a thought to have! I'm not sure how I would have done it, but I had the distinct impression that I could sculpt this space and its organic architecture – again, all through sound.

I thought that this balcony experience was going to last, but it quickly swept on, like the coursing serpent. *The serpent is the larger structure of this dimension – one is inside the serpent.* This big organic flow rushed on like an undulating landscape, like a living roller coaster. It seemed like this time the structure was changing more rapidly, and I was being pulled along. I think I was listening to Didjscape at this point.

I thought again of the structures of this dimension. I changed the song back to the Toadian chant, as it had more permanent structure. It didn't quite have the same effect as before. I stayed with it for a little while, but then changed to listening to a song with electronic instruments and didjeridu and flute.

It seemed that only organic instruments can really build the structure of this dimension – it has to do with the resonant vibrations – the voice of the instrument.

The electronic aspects of the song didn't really build structure. Rather, with this song, I had the impression that the Sage Spirits expressed themselves through the organic instruments, like the flute and especially the didj. The spirit only comes through when it's really strong, though, when it's really flowing pure and clean with super resonant vibrations and overtones.

This was similar to a saging at Burning Man. I was playing my didj. I was tunneling through reality, inside the sage spirit. It was moving through me and the didj. The didj was playing me. Afterwards, I proclaimed to Rod and Damon, "that was a sage spirit!"

I changed to another song with didj and throat signing. Interestingly, this song didn't quite make it for me. In the voices (my voices) there wasn't the proper resonance. I thought of how this song sounded so different here in the sage space. It wasn't what I thought it might have been – not nearly as effective as the Toadian Chant.

I started to think of how if our sound creates structures in "their" dimension, and they can be invited into our dimension to make sound. The shaman can use the sound to change structures in this dimension. I thought of how one could sing the shape of a person to make them whole – sing their health, their physical form (I thought of book 1 and Miraanni and Orobai healing Sto'orn). You'd have to find the right spirit to do it – the one that had that form. There has to be the right vibration. In the vibration the spirit can manifest, but it has to be just right. It's hard to explain. In listening to recordings of my own voice, I could see the difference between moments when the right kinds of vibrations were there and when they weren't.

Overall there's a strong correspondence between these hyper-dimensional spirits, three dimensional architecture, and powers of manifestation.

Comments

$\mathcal{I}$ still think of this experience quite often and ponder over the significance of this session. Since that time I have learned to work with vibrations even more, learning various throat and overtone singing techniques from the sage, as is discussed later.

But this experience was quite startling for me. It was very strong, for one, and was deeply structured by the music, especially the chant of throat and overtone singing, in a way that was more profound and apparent than other sage sessions. I think that this is largely due to the layered structure of the songs I was listening too, with multiple layers of harmonics and overtones, giving the music a deep, hyper-dimensional sound.

At the time, I was very surprised by the appearance of male and female forms in the flux of the sage space in this session. As I commented above, once they began to sing and thereby build the pyramid structure, I was immediately reminded of the conclusion of my series, as this scene is very reminiscent of events at the end of the fourth book, *The Fifth Temple*. I had finished writing this book not long before Burning Man that year, bringing my *Tales of Aurduin* to a conclusion. However, that had been several months prior to this experience, and I hadn't been thinking of my books going into this experience. In other words, I do not think it was simply the contents of my thoughts that determined this experience. As for exactly how this relates to my novel, I'll leave that for the readers of those books.

In recounting experiences like this, it is difficult to articulate precisely what is meant by referring to other beings and spirits. This particular experience was significantly stronger than many other sage experiences and was a bit more drawn out than others as well, so the entire visionary experience had a very real sense to it, but "real" in sage space is an enigmatic thing.

Ultimately what I really learned from this strange experience is that there are infinite layers to vibratory sound and that sage is the ideal entheogen for exploring these vibrations and the psychedelic structures they create in the medium of consciousness and inner awareness. In some sense, I do think that "sage spirits" can pass into our sounds, our vibrations, our instruments, and our voices. Perhaps it is best to think of it as a very deep level of inspiration.

Feeling thus inspired, I decided to visit again with the sage soon and explore some of these ideas further, and in many respects, this relationship between sage and vibration has been the primary focus of my association with *Salvia divinorum* ever since.

Disassociated Sage Spirits

I had the opportunity to visit with the sage this afternoon. I was out in the garage and it was relatively dark, with the sun having gone down with a faint glow to the evening sky and the multicolored ambiance of Christmas lights outside. I said a quick statement of intention. I felt a little awkward verbalizing my intentions, there in the garage by myself. I raise this now, as my hesitation to verbalize is in stark contrast with later in the experience. Then, I burned up a bowl.

There was an immediate sense of the familiar to the experience. Desiring to go deeper, I made sure to smoke the entire bowl.

Wanting to explore some of the ideas form last time, I had the intention of exploring musical sounds and vibrations. For this first round, I went with my frame drum and chanting/overtone singing/throat singing. As I had felt was part of the lesson last time, I found that it was certain vibrations that really worked with the sage. This time, there was an interface between the vibrations of the drum and my different kinds of chanting and intoning. The drum made my voice quiver oddly. I experimented with different sounds, holding the drum at different angles, and trying different tones.

It was quite strange, the way all the aspects of the sound were interacting with each other – very difficult to put into words. I got the impression that when three levels of vibration are harmonized a powerful overtone develops – this is when the sage can really express itself – or better to say, different aspects of the sage can express itself, as the tone groups can be high, medium, low, whatever, and they all seem to have different personalities and qualities.

I also felt that my throat singing wasn't nearly as good as it should be to really access this sage vibration. I had the sensation at one point of almost shape-shifting into a frog/amphibian-like entity that was producing this fantastic deep-throat frog chant, but it was very difficult to sustain for long. At several points I said out loud, "Sing through me! Use my voice!" This helped a little, but I was still insufficient.

Eventually the sage wound down. It was very interesting, and intense, but also mild, in some respects – milder than the previous session of "soundstructures in hyperspace." This was probably because I was controlling all the sound rather than listening to the continuous loops of my recorded music. As it was all happening I thought of how utterly bizarre it must have sounded to anyone outside – like some otherworldly shamanic session going on in my garage – even stranger than the usual noises I'm making out there!

Packed another bowl and smoked that one up.

I grabbed a didj and began to play – or, should I say, tried to begin to play.

This is when the real disassociation came. It felt like whatever entities were with me in that first round were back, but this time, they were all interested in the didj. At first, it was like the flow of the sage dimension was flowing through me at the wrong angle, and I couldn't get the didj to make any sound. Then the experience shifted in that the entities, or personalities of the sage spirits, all wanted a turn playing the didj.

Was it me, disassociating different configurations of myself? Was I overly objectifying different moments of playing? Were there actually spirits working through my body playing the didj? All of the above? Probably some mixture, I suppose.

The point is, the didj took on such different qualities as I felt different entities were having a go at it. At first, I couldn't play. Then another one came, and I forgot to breathe, just pushing out as much air as possible. Then several came doing different rhythms. They were different tones, however. Of course, the pitch of the didj doesn't change (this was my D didj), but it varied between higher and lower bass tones, which was really strange. It was like the bass tone moved with different spirits, adjusting to their range of interlinked tones. It was when three tones joined together was when the fourth overtone emerged that was the most powerful – that's when the sage spirit was really there – just like with the singing and drumming earlier, but through the didj. Within the sage experience, this had a distinct three-dimensional sense to it – as though the tones were building harmonic relationships in space in a geometric sense.

Now, I've known about the difference between when a didj is just the basic drone and when it's really vibed in to get the really crisp high tones/overtones, but this seemed different. When it was *just right*, all the tones were so pure, so crisp, so well defined and distinct. It was an order beyond ordinary good playing (or at least, that's how is *sounded* and *felt* to me).

That went on from some time, but it was ultimately hard to maintain sustained didjing, so as the sage was wearing off, I set it down.

In the darkness, I saw my rattle. I picked it up and started rattling. Though the sage was wearing off and this was the tail end, this was definitely the most powerful part of the experience. Feeling empowered, I stood up. I considered my experience, almost like possession (though more intuited than really strongly felt – I don't want to overstate this), and the shape shifting earlier, and decided that I needed to use my words.

I started speaking to the sage and the four directions and the above and the below as I rattled. The words came out strong and moving. I felt like I was on stage in some sense – as though I were being watched and perceived. Perhaps by the sage itself. I let the sage know that I was inviting it to use my voice, my body, my instruments, but if I was going to let it in, it was for compassion, wisdom, humility, beauty, and more. I started naming different plants and animals and insects and I could see them all in my mind. The sage was just flowing, and so were the words.

The rattle was so important. Much more so than with the drum and didj, I felt in control of the rattle. I was directing the sound – not some disassociated part of myself. It was sharp and percussive. I created a circle around me and enlivened the space. It cut through my dimension and the sage dimension.

In the end, I felt very empowered, prayerful, and centered. I thought of how different my words were at the end versus the beginning. I was confident, empowered, authentic.

Wow!

Comments

$\mathcal{A}$s is clear from my earlier accounts, I had already experienced using sound as an integral part of my sage experiences, through rattling and using the didjeridu. This session was different, however, as it came on the heals of the prior, very moving and very powerful, experience of "soundstructures in hyperspace." In a sense, I was attempting to work from a more specific theory of how sound interacts with *Salvia divinorum* and sage space.

This was my first real foray into attempting chanting and overtoning while experiencing *Salvia divinorum*. I had been using throat and overtone singing in my recorded music for several years by this point, but my experience of throat singing was certainly different in this sage session. In the account above, I speak of having this deep, frog-like throat singing. At the time, I found it very difficult to sustain and also had trouble breathing. It was as though the sound and vibration wanted so much to get out that I just had to keep signing out and there didn't seem to be room to breathe. Not being able to sustain this, only naturally, I found the technique difficult and found myself "unworthy" to make it, despite my pleas.

I have since explored these techniques of throat and overtone signing with far greater success, though it wasn't until Burning Man of 2006 that I really returned to this intentional sonic exploration.

Also since this time I have become much more attuned to using my frame drum to accompany my throat and overtone signing, and in fact, find that the singing is greatly enhanced by the sonic stimulation of the drum, as I began to experience but not fully understand in the above account.

In some respects, the two accounts given above mark a turning point in my relationship to *Salvia divinorum*. While I still greatly enjoy a meditative session in quiet with *Salvia divinorum*, my overwhelming urge is to express the sage tones and sing all the way through my sage sessions. It takes me from being a passive observer of the experience to being a co-creator of my sage experience, something I find deeply and endlessly fascinating.

From my own perspective, there are definite patterns and rhythms within my sage experiences. When my eyes are closed, I can easily get inside these patterns and ride with them with my drum and throat singing. The feeling is one of pure power. It is like completely pure spiritual energy just flowing through me, as though my body and voice become an empty vessel for the expression and manifestation of Spirit. I find it deeply rewarding and empowering.

It wasn't until the following summer that I returned to the *Salvia divinorum* experience, however, so I did not fully incorporate my vibratory lessons until some months later at the 2006 gathering for Burning Man, as is recounted in another account below. In the intervening time, I did have the opportunity to try liquid *Salvia divinorum* for the first time. The account of that experience follows. It was originally written as a series of emails to a friend.

Sage Goddess

I wanted you to know that the Sage Goddess emerald essence is truly divine.

I've had my vial of "emerald essence" for two years now, and it's been through the heat extremes of Burning Man twice (it says to always store it in a room temp location), so I was a little worried that it would be a dud by now, but not so! The info that came with it recommended four droppers full for a first time, so that's what I went with. Heated some water, made the right combo in a shot glass, and in it went. Oh how it sparkles and tingles! It's like magic fireworks on the tongue.

So you keep this sparkling gooey green mix in your mouth under your tongue for 14 minutes. I started at 8:40 and kept it in till 8:55. By about 10 minutes I could feel it coming on. I've definitely had stronger from smoking enhanced leaf as I officially took a "moderate" dose. I could also easily go stronger with the essence, and was even about to add another dose when I read the instructions and saw that after the first dose, unless you stagger it within the first fifteen minutes, it will only increase the duration of the experience and not the strength, so I decided to just ride with the experience as it was.

And it was magical!

The Sage Goddess is VERY smooth. Rather than the torrent and rush that comes with smoked sage, this was gentle, caressing, soft, intimate and very smooth. I went outside and watched the stars twinkle overhead and the trees wave in the wind – just beautiful!!! Then I went back inside. I got my rattle and rattled and called to the spirits and then sat and meditated and rattled for probably 40 minutes to an hour with eyes closed, journeying through the sage space.

It was definitely more subtle than a good smoked bowl, but the duration makes it much more open to really getting inside of it and working with. To use sage for shamanizing, I'd definitely say that this was the way to go. It would profoundly enhance any ritual or ceremony and it carries huge potential or intimate work. And it was so gentle! Sometimes mushrooms can be brutal, but this was full of love, humility, compassion, play, laughter, and was just this beautiful caress. Really, I can't recommend it enough.

I'm definitely interested in going stronger. I think that it would be even more interesting. This was enough for me to get visuals, feel the flow, and really know that the sage was there, but you know the sage – she always wants you to take more, and I think that a stronger dose would be a great experience.

At the level that I had of four drops, it was so deeply sensual and expressive. I've gotten the impression before and felt it again with this sage that touch can be so profound in that state.

I was a little concerned going into it that it would be an intense onslaught, but it certainly wasn't. I just can't emphasize how gentle and loving it was. The Sage Goddess is kind! It was such a good experience – so positive! And funny too – just this sense of levity and joy to the whole thing.

Comments

*M*y remarks as expressed to my friend in the email accounts given above do a good job of summing up my feelings about that particular experience. There were no profound visions or deep revelations – just a profound sense of peace, joy, and completeness. This was an extremely positive experience for me. I even went for another round the next night of the same dose and had a beautiful time doing Tai Chi out in the breezy summer night, under the sparkling stars. Both experiences, while mild in terms of the effect of the salvia, were just tremendously beautiful and positive. It was a great blessing for me to be in the presence of the sage for those two sessions and I came away, as is so often the case, with a deep spiritual satisfaction and sense of joy, empowerment, and blessings. It also shows that deeply rewarding experiences do not need to be particularly strong salvia experiences as even moderate doses can leave a deep impression when approached with the proper mindset and in the right environment.

At Burning Man that year my campmates and I all tried liquid *Salvia divinorum* together at roughly the same dose as the account given above. Not surprisingly, we got very different results in the sense that my friends were not nearly as impressed by the experience as my tales of liquid sage led them to think they would be. I attribute this primarily to the fact that my private sage sessions were in the context of a deeply meditative and introspective setting, whereas our session of liquid sage at Burning Man was a very different environment with a very different mindset. No one had a bad experience with the liquid sage at Burning Man – they were only disappointed that they didn't journey further into sage space and it felt like a let down, given the expectations generated by my own account and everyone's experience with smoking enhanced salvia leaf.

We did have a couple sessions with enhanced leaf at Burning Man 2006, where we followed our standard procedure for a salvia ritual, which has grown up naturally over the previous Burning Man gatherings among my friends and myself.

It was at these enhanced leaf sessions that I returned to my exploration of overtones and sound with *Salvia divinorum*.

Overtones at Burning Man, 2006

It must have been Wednesday when Marianne, Damon, Rod and I all took some sage.

Marianne smoked up her bowl as I rattled for her. She closed her eyes, opened them, and laughed. Typical Marianne.

Damon was next. I watched Damon closely. I didjed for him. He got all clammy and all the hair on his arms and legs stood up on end. He didn't say anything about his experience.

Rod went next and I rattled for him. Then it was my turn.

I smoked the sage. Reality swirled and the sage rippled through space and time. This was a deep sage experience. I closed my eyes and started rattling.

I thought back to Alex Grey's painting at Entheon Village of the person meditating with the white light in the third eye and the cosmic grid stretching out over the mountainous landscape of the painting. I thought of seeing Alex Grey sitting there, painting, infinitely patient with a deep sense of spiritual equanimity. Could I ever have that level of patience, I wondered.

The sage vision started to unfold before my inner eye. I felt like I was at a perspective that was outside of the great cosmic taffy stretcher of reality. I know that sounds funny, but that's about the best description I could give. Behind closed eyes, fractal patterns swirled as reality undulations. It was as though I could see the matrix of multiple realities as the serpentine scales of the sage world rushed about me. The fractal swirls were wrapping around each other and stretching out, much like a taffy machine works, wraps, and stretches taffy. Within this psychedelic fractal mix were multiple realities, countless universes and dimensions. It was as though I had been granted an exterior, albeit temporary, perspective on all of this. Somehow, my perspective was outside of the mix, able to observe how the various layers of multiple realities pass through, around, and between each other. And there was a sense of humor to it too, as though some giant alien figure was standing at the controls of the great cosmic taffy mixer, saying, "Yep. This is *IT*. Betcha wouldn't have guessed it, would ya?" with a dry sense of irony.

Letting the strange taffy mixer vision fade, I felt compelled to throat sing. The urge was strong. The tones wanted to come out. I felt inhibited at first, though, as I didn't want to impose my experience on others by vocalizing. I got over it and began to sing anyway.

It was amazing. I immediately understood techniques to manipulate overtones in a way I had never understood before. I was able to easily find the precise locations of the overtone notes as determined by the precise position of my tongue. I found that I could really produce melodies with these notes and it was akin to a scale, though not a normal one. I could hear Tuvan melodies. I visualized the roof of my mouth as like a keyboard or flute. I went through the scale again and again. I could have gone on for hours like that. It's something that I intend to work on. I can't overemphasize how impressed I was and how this experience has revolutionized my understanding of throat and overtone singing techniques. I can't wait to explore this more!

Rod wanted to go for another round, so I packed him up a bowl after we talked about my experience. This time, I gave Rod my rattle for him to use for himself. When we talked afterward he expressed how surprised he was by how his active rattling changed his experience. As I had told him, he found that he was able to both extend and structure his experience.

"And I think I know what you mean about that cosmic taffy stretcher," he said with a smile. "I thought I understood what you meant before, but I didn't. Now I think I know just what you mean!"

A good sage session, indeed!

Comments

*T*his particular session, building upon the "soundstructures in hyperspace" sessions of December the previous year, was a real revelation for me. While the cosmic taffy mixer was interesting and something truly fascinating to behold, the real value of the experience is what I learned about working overtones in a precise and exact way that I had never before experienced. The methods and techniques for dramatically manipulating my voice became so profoundly immediate and clear. My throat and overtone singing techniques were forever changed by this sage session, and I thank the sage directly for this gift.

Later that week, still at Burning Man, we held another sage session with the enhanced leaf. For my turn (always the last), I went directly into my overtone work and stayed there for probably 30 minutes or so, developing the new and exciting techniques I had learned.

After Burning Man 2006 I continued to work on my throat and overtone signing techniques, both with *Salvia divinorum* and without. The new vibratory territory was exciting to explore. A notable session with salvia and throat signing came in early January of 2007, as recounted below.

Pure Tones

I started off with frame drum and new rattle close at hand. I drummed four times, announcing the session. I was excited with the pre-psychedelic nervousness and took up the pipe.

The first couple hits were small, so the sage came on gentle and soft. I started drumming slowly. The sage passed through me and the vibrations took shape, my eyes half closed and the singing poured out of me, but it was as though the sage was pushing me into new ranges that were difficult for me, so I had to work the sounds very slowly, introducing only small modulations. It produced a hyper resonant chamber in my head with the sound of my voice echoing into my ears, almost as though it were the voice of another, singing with and through me. I had the impression that the sage was showing me different power patterns that swept out into metaphysical hyperspace – very shamanic.

I thought of how playing the drum this way helped me channel otherness more than my rattle, which is a more intimate and personal instrument of communication and focus. The drum set me in on the sage vibrations that carried power and locked me in with my voice, a circuit of cosmic vibration.

I packed another bowl and took bigger, deeper hits, searing the back of my throat (as a good sage hit tends to do). This was much more powerful than the first round. "I've been waiting for you," and I had an immediate recall of the throat signing session from December 2005 when I first sought to intentionally work with the soundstructures in hyperspace. The sage remembered, and it was waiting for me to return to this work. The image of my rattle came to mind, of sitting in the same chair, of drumming and singing. The source of the lessons. He's been waiting for me to come back for more, to inhabit my space and sing.

The voice/thought that spoke in my mind came with a physical presence of a Tuvan/Siberian throat singing shaman character that was ready to sing through my voice (Mark later described my signing as Inuit after a sage session at his house), but it was hard for me to do it – his register and technique is different from my own and he was pulling me into a different space. As I've felt before, it was pushing in my throat, reconfiguring me for better vibrations, clearer sound, more resonate. I felt unworthy as I couldn't quite make all the sounds as smoothly as he would have me, but he was teaching me, showing me. I felt empowered, like a shamanic spirit is there. It just flows out of the sound. It's no wonder that I've gotten such strong reactions from others when singing like this – something IS coming out. But it's also this otherness, this force that comes from beyond.

We bounced through different patterns and vibrations, layers upon layers, finally settling down into a smooth melody with rapid, but soft, drum pulses. Gradually he passed away and it was more me directing it all.

Lesson well received.

I rattled a little. Intimate. My personal space.

I thought of technique, ceremony.

Empowering.

Nicci's stone is coming. I'll sing for her when it arrives.

Comments

The experience of having another entity or persona sing through me was so distinct in this experience, and has been since then, that I wrote of it as an external force working through me. In the account, I describe this persona as a Tuvan or otherwise Siberian shaman singing through me. Naturally this perception was influenced by the fact that I was performing throat and overtone signing, which comes from Tuva, Tibet, Mongolia, and other Siberian cultures. However, the feeling of having a force that is *other than me* was quite distinct, and one can see that such experiences are relatively common, in one way or another, throughout my descriptions of my *Salvia divinorum* experiences.

Is there "really" some other force there? Does it matter?

This is my experience, and it is what it is. The fact is that I've reached new levels of abilities with throat and overtone singing techniques that I did not previously possess, and I strongly feel that I have the sage to thank for that. In the end, it doesn't really matter what the ontological and metaphysical truth of my experience is. The experience itself is the source of learning, growth, and inspiration. It is empowering, and that is enough.

Furthermore, I think that there is something to be said for emptying one's self out, letting go of our ego-structured sense of self, and becoming a conduit for whatever it is that we perceive and experience as coming from beyond ourselves. The transpersonal experience is profound and is an essential part of shamanic practice and many spiritual traditions.

Enduring transpersonal experiences can take some measure of fortitude, however. They can be disorienting, strange, and some might even find them frightening. That *Salvia divinorum* can produce such profound states of consciousness is good reason to carefully monitor what kind of access young people have to this and other entheogens. Such radical experiences are best left to people with a well-developed sense of self in order for such experiences to be fully integrated with one's normal sense of reality.

In traditional societies where entheogens are used as part of youth initiation ceremonies, the disorienting, transpersonal effects of entheogens are mitigated through narrative, ceremony, and symbolic structure. Initiates are given a mythological and symbolic framework in which to place their experiences, allowing them to integrate their visions into their sense of self and identity as defined within the context of a traditional society.

Unfortunately, Western cultures have long lost any kind of truly meaningful initiation ceremonies for young people. Perhaps the best we have is the adventurous teenager consuming psychedelic substances at a music festival, as was my own personal introduction to psychedelics. While this may be an archetypal reflection of American individualism, it is not necessarily the most healthy or beneficial use of psychedelics, and has contributed to the view that psychedelics are hedonistic drugs with no societal value.

Coming at these experiences as a mature adult with a spiritual background and education, I feel that I have benefited greatly by my entheogenic experiences with *Salvia divinorum*. As a culture, however, I highly encourage all of us to engage in meaningful discussion about how to make these experiences safely accessible to younger people in a way that is beneficial and growth inspiring, rather than simply "mind blowing." The "war on drugs" is a dismal failure and it is time to reassess our approach to entheogens and their place within our culture.

But I get ahead of myself and these issues will be taken up again in a concluding section of this work. I wanted to address some of these issues here, given that my account above featured a fairly dramatic example of transpersonal experience. While transpersonal experiences have been a part of my *Salvia divinorum* experiences from some of my earliest visits with the sage, this has now become more of the norm for me, especially when vocalizing and singing while in sage space.

Not long after the account given above, I had the opportunity to specifically sing for a friend from a direct request for spiritual intervention. From my work with Mescalero Apache medicine people and my initiation into their medicine traditions, when specifically asked for help, I am to give it if the person requesting help provides me with particular ritual objects. When this friend asked for a spiritual intervention, I asked her to send me the required gifts with the understanding that I would perform a ceremony for her. The following account comes from an email that I sent to this friend after I concluded the long distance ceremony between southern California and eastern Canada.

Songs for Nicci

I've just finished singing for you/your stone, and wanted to share how things went.

I smoked several rounds of sage and just let the songs come. The first song started off really low, playing my drum, letting the drone and rhythm build. I was in a kind of mushroom stone chamber. There were sounds of others there, but I didn't want them to distract me from the structure of the song and the environment it was creating. This was a powerful place and energy was channeling through here.

But then my voice change to where I wasn't making the low vibrations so that it was just my normal voice, but it wasn't my voice at all. I was still tone singing, but not in a way that I've ever done before. It was completely natural, however. My voice took on the sound of an old Native American man, and the song chanted out of me, just flowing, not my voice, not my voice.

Still overtones, but different. Not my voice!

I sang like that for a long time and eventually stopped. I can't make that sound again. I can't repeat that song that came out while doing this for you.

So, smoked more sage. High, resonant tones this time. It was just pure tone light, flowing out of my mouth and throat. Not even changing, just this pure crystalline sound. It vibrated my nasal passages and made me cough a little (strange). Kept going.

Eventually this changed to deep vibrations again. Deep structure. Lots of architecture and form.

More sage.

An utter wailing sound comes out. Just lamenting, wailing, anguishing.

Changes to higher tones.

More sage. Using my rattle this time instead of the drum. Very bizarre, but totally natural, moment where my right arm seems to be a part of someone else and in fact, there's this continuum of beings all shaking the rattle, and I forget who I am for just a moment, lost in the dream, and then pull back into myself. There are just so many here! Still singing though – low tones I think – I'm actually not sure. I eventually pull back into myself, focus on all the medicine around me.

I put your stone in pollen and put it away.

The end!

So that's what we got when I asked the sage to sing for you through me.

Comments

*T*his experience does an adequate job of speaking for itself. Here I have put into action the lessons and techniques learned in early sage sessions with the intention of performing a blessing ceremony for a friend in need many miles away. All the while, throughout this experience, my intention was to send blessings and healing vibrations to my friend in Canada, directing the flow of sage energy with my mind as I sang. My understanding of shamanic work is that it is the shaman's goal to get him or herself out of the way as much as possible and just be an open conduit for power and blessings, and this is just one example of such a state of being.

The last entry that I'm including here is one final example of signing while in the *Salvia divinorum* experience. The difference here is that I was not singing for myself or for another person, but for the sage itself. As this short account needs no commentary, we will finish with this brief story.

The Golden Temple

I am very happy to say that I now have my very own living, breathing, growing, *Salvia divinorum* plant.

I sat with her today, and smoked some enhanced leaf and sang to her. Behind closed eyes, while I sang, she invited me to this radiant golden temple, like a tall pyramid whose top I couldn't see, lost in the psychedelic sky above, with large steps, the width of the temple, leading down into the shimmering blue waters. The water lapped at the steps, forming into psychedelic fractal eddies that were interdimensional portals. The colors, the precision of the vision – so beautiful! I was enraptured by how the water played against the radiant golden steps.

All I could do was sing.

Final Thoughts

Looking back on these accounts of my *Salvia divinorum* experiences, it is easy to see a progression of themes. Many strange and unusual vistas were opened up along the way and there have been many profound experiences.

From the very beginning of my adventures into sage space, I have tried to approach *Salvia divinorum* as the powerful entheogen it is, treating it with care, humility, and a healthy respect for its sacred power. I strongly feel that my experiences have been shaped for the better by approaching *Salvia divinorum* as an entheogen and not merely a psychedelic novelty, and I encourage others to do so as well. To that end, the concluding chapter concerns the creation of *Salvia divinorum* rituals and suggestions for incorporating the sage experience into ceremonial practice.

However, before entering into a discussion of salvia ceremonialism, I would like to share some thoughts on *Salvia divinorum* and the mythic imagination. As my salvia experiences have been tremendously influential in my creative life, especially with music and writing, I would like to share some of those thoughts in the next chapter as examples of how salvia experiences can be processed and rendered in artistic and meaningful ways that can be shared with others.

Salvia and the Mythic Imagination

*M*y experiences with *Salvia divinorum* have had a direct impact on my exploration of spirituality through fictional writing and artistic expression. In 2002, shortly after the birth of my daughter, I began writing a series of novels that I titled *Tales of Aurduin*. Four novels in all, *Tales of Aurduin* is an intricate fantasy epic that combines a variety of inspirations from my studies and my life, and my entheogenic experiences have been deeply influential in my writing. Furthermore, the act of writing about my entheogenic experiences, both through journals and fiction, has helped me to process and make sense of them from a more neutral perspective.

Given the otherworldly nature of entheogens, fictional or creative explorations of what they reveal can be instructive in our own personal understandings of their significance for ourselves and our lives. Working with entheogens in fiction is really just one of many ways that the symbols, experiences, and content of entheogenic experiences can be explored through art and creative activity. Exploring the content and ideas of entheogenic experiences through creative acts can be very fruitful and rewarding for the artist. It allows for the artist to come to a new perspective on his or her experiences and also allows for a medium of communication with others about the content and significance of such experiences from more than a purely personal perspective. In other words, such practices can partake of the mythic imagination and help to highlight the more archetypal, universal, and transpersonal aspects of entheogenic experiences.

Writing, storytelling, myth making and narrative have long histories as hermeneutic mediums in the discourse on altered states of consciousness. Throughout history, people have gathered to share their personal narratives of dreams, vision, encounters, and personal revelations and spiritual experiences. Visions and entheogenic trances may be recounted in song, story, or even reenactment, but each involves narrative, the ordering of the experience into sequential events with characters, scenes, and symbolic and philosophical content that can be communicated from one person to another.

Historically, many narratives of altered states of awareness, the practices that engender them, and the kinds of experiences that can be expected from them, have been encoded into traditional stories and myths that have been passed down for generations. Rather than being accounts of personal experiences, such stories speak to the universal and transpersonal nature of altered states of consciousness. Encoded in the myths from many cultures are clear examples of shamanic trances, near death experiences, entheogenic states, and other forms of altered consciousness. Extending even beyond culture, such stories are often filled with archetypal symbols and universal meanings. Such symbols give structure and stability to the otherwise strange and otherworldly flux of altered states of awareness and also serve to instruct new initiates into the mysteries of altered states of consciousness and their significance for the initiates' culture.

Being often non-linear, disjointed, and characterized by ruptures, revelations, and sudden insights and discoveries, altered states of consciousness are both alien to linear narrative while perhaps simultaneously crying out for narrative structure, one of the primary means through which human minds make sense of their experience. Narrative, both expressed externally and repeated internally, allows us to make sense of our experiences.

Visions unfold in a multidimensional field in the entheogenic experience. Ideas, images, feelings, intuitions, meld and flow through one another. They can be chaotic, ordered, random, meaningful, and symbolic of our deeper selves, our dreams, our secret awareness. Like dreams, they move quickly and abruptly shift, or linger on strange and unusual details. Logic is suspended and symbolic or unconscious association supersedes rational order. Revelations and meaning break through in unexpected moments, coupled with deep sensations, cloaked in symbols or archetypal imagery. The mythic and transcendent breaks into our awareness and demands recognition. Characters, personas, and scenes all unfold to our inner eye. Energies coalesce into other places and other times. Yet all the while it unfolds within our conscious minds, playing out before our inner vision, like a dream, waiting to be made sense of.

Thus narrative, discourse, storytelling, and myth become a crucial medium for processing the symbolic and imaginal content of the entheogenic trance. This is perhaps especially so with *Salvia divinorum*, it being such a rapid and quickly moving experience filled with so much strangeness. It is narrative that allows the voyager to communicate the sense of journey that is so characteristic of the entheogenic experience. The entheogenic experience is always one of change and progression. Thoughts, feelings, insights, revelations, all flow from one to the other. Our minds struggle to order them coherently, to make a story of them, one that gives insight into the deeper meanings of what was revealed. The narrative allows us to relive and re-explore the journey, and helps us to recall the things that were learned and discovered along the way.

In short, the narrative is what allows us to communicate in detail both to ourselves and to others what the entheogenic experience is for us and what it means. Within the narrative there is the reality shaping and structuring force of language, of syntax, choice of words, and shared understandings of meaning. Embedded within the story, either literally or metaphorically, are the symbols that express the essence of the entheogenic experience.

In traditional societies, such narratives could become myths and pedagogical stories, intentionally created to pass on specific information.

For example, among the Chumash, the native people of the Santa Barbara region where I live, the powerful entheogen *datura* is personified in the grandmotherly character of *Momoy*, the old woman who washes her hands and gives initiates a powerful elixir – just be careful if she washes up to her shoulders, and beware if she takes a bath and gives you that water to drink! Or one could look to the mythical narratives of the Huichol and their annual peyote hunt. Indeed, many researchers with knowledge of entheogens are now re-examining traditional stories from around the world, finding possible clues and references to entheogens and entheogenic use. Such examples appear to abound throughout history and across the globe.

My experiences with *Salvia divinorum* have definitely inspired my own sense of the mythic imagination. In writing my novel series, *Tales of Aurduin,* I have incorporated and mythologized many of my own personal entheogenic encounters, dreams, and spiritual experiences and practices. In what follows, I have selected a few sections of my novels that are directly inspired by my experiences with *Salvia divinorum*. Each excerpt is followed by a brief discussion of the particular ways in which sage plays a role in the work. These passages are presented here as examples of my personal explorations into the mythic imagination.

The first example here comes from my first novel, *Orobai's Vision*. In this scene, Orobai is about to embark upon a quest to the four mountains of Aurduin. Before he leaves, his friend, Nataali, performs an empowerment ritual for Orobai by manipulating the energies of both his body and the environment around him.

Orobai's Vision, pages 201-202

The two friends sat down together in the green grass in the shade of the trees facing downhill towards the east as they drew their minds inward. Each concentrated on the flow of breath, in and out, in and out. Orobai sat in silence, but as Nataali sank deeper into the meditation, she began to vocalize the chants of the Xhutai-Ku, sacred syllables that drew upon the living power of the universe. The sisters used such chants and sounds to free the mind and body of all limitations and attachments. When done with the proper state of rarified meditation, one could dispel all illusions of separateness. In such a state, one could experience the direct Suchness of existence. It was an ancient and profound philosophy that the sisterhood had practiced and perfected for millennia.

Deep as he was in his own meditation, Orobai did not at first notice that Nataali stood before him now. Seeing her, he was not sure if there was one of her, or four, all standing in the four directions about him. It was a perplexing sensation, for he could not really focus on her and time had taken on a peculiar quality. Was he seeing Nataali in four places simultaneously or was he seeing her in four different times simultaneously? He did not know.

Nataali continued the chants she had begun in her meditation, but now she added rhythmic and stylized movement, carefully posturing and manipulating her hands, arms, legs, and body. She moved about Orobai in a graceful dance where there was no distinction between thought, body, music, and action. As she did so, Orobai's perception became fluid and clear. He could distinctly see every blade of grass, every leaf, and every crevice and crack in the bark of the ancient trees about him. Through everything moved an energy that was a living life force, a great organic flow of being. Every ripple of the grass in the wind, every sway of the branches of the trees, the glide of an insect or bird – all responded to this living flow. Even the clouds above and the waters below danced to the same subtle rhythm that was now being articulated through the aesthetics of Nataali's body. Orobai felt his own breathing and the rhythms of his body join in unison to the vast undulation of the world in his sensory field. It gave him the impression that Nataali was drawing the power through him and bringing him into deep harmony with it.

At first it felt as though he were being drained. He was so drained that he struggled to maintain his awareness as consciousness slipped down into darkness. It was emptiness. It was not a full emptiness, not the boundless, chaotic energy of the Abyss, but just empty, as though he had been sucked dry and remained as only a withered bag of flesh. But just as quickly as the sensation of this emptiness had come upon him, it changed. Now Orobai felt as though he were being filled up. The energy and power rushed in through his abdomen. From there it spread out to his limbs, climbing up his spine and spiraling to the very top of his head and to the tips of his finger and toes. It was as though he himself were part of some great lung that breathed the fullness of pure and rarified air. The wind blew through his body, inflating him with new life. He could almost hear it, he thought, and almost feel it as it spiraled out the whorls on his fingertips. From his lower abdomen and feet the great wind joined his body to the breath of the earth itself. From his head and shoulders the great wind joined him to the breath of the infinite sky above. And there was no longer his breath, or Nataali's breath, or the breath of anything else. There was only the One Breath, the great Xhutai-Ku, and he knew the Shaping of the Wind.

Slowly the four images of Nataali resolved back into one cohesive form before Orobai's eyes. Once more he could see the distinct shape and form of her body. Looking at her now, however, she seemed more alive than she had before. It was as though a great sleep had fallen from Orobai's eyes and he could now see the course and pulse of life through her. He could see the centers of energy in her body and how the physical limits of her being could not bind them, but rather the energy radiated outward in all directions. It was beautiful to look upon, seeing one so healthy in mind, body, heart, and spirit. It reminded Orobai of seeing T'inshar sick with the spider eating at his heart, but free from all disease. Here the life flowed like a strong river that filled the space granted it, and in it he saw the delicate interconnection and balance between all things.

It was almost enough to make Orobai weep. The sheer beauty was incomparable. And looking at himself he could see that he too looked much like Nataali. There was a new vitality in him and it filled all the space of his being. He saw that his own heart energy was bound to the heart energy of Nataali, and that they themselves were bound to the heart energy of the other beings around them. And this binding extended on infinitely to encompass all living beings. And not just conventionally living beings, but clouds, rocks, streams, mountains, oceans, the sky . . . there seemed to be no limit. It was just beauty. Orobai could think of no other words. Just beauty . . .

Nataali stood smiling at Orobai, extending her hand to help him up. "You have now felt the Shaping of the Wind, the Xhutai-Ku. You will find both your body and your perception altered for quite some time to come, for I completely emptied you before filling you back up. Gradually, this will wear away as your old energy patterns begin to reassert themselves. But what you have now will carry you far."

Comments

Though influenced by Yoga, Tai Chi, and other martial arts, the above passage also strongly reflects my experience of the flowing, energetic nature of the *Salvia divinorum* experience, and is also somewhat reminiscent of the sage sessions with my friend Mark as related earlier in this book. "The Shaping of the Wind" is a phrase that I felt described this aspect of the experience, and I often think of the feeling of the sage moving through me as a wind or breeze, as can be seen in my early sage journal entries.

In my own experience, I have found that sage energy can be structured and directed through the use of sound. In this passage, the "breeze" of the sage flow is directed Nataali's chanting, which gives structure to the energetic flow of the experience. Significantly, this was written before my own direct experience of working with sage and chanting and overtone singing.

There are other characteristics that are indicative of *Salvia divinorum* in this passage as well. Early on in this account, as the experience begins, Orobai encounters a brief moment of disorientation. He sees four images of Nataali, and has trouble distinguishing between his perception of time and of space. This is very common at the fast onrush of *Salvia divinorum*, especially when smoking the enhanced leaf. Using sound as a driver can help to establish stability. Deep vibratory rhythms in particular allow a deeper awareness and perception of the subtler structures of the sage experience. This is especially true when eyes are closed, opening to the inner sight where the sage visions truly unfold in all their fractal complexity.

With sonic vibration, there is often the sense that the rhythmic structures extend far beyond the body. This is the entry into sage space. Sound tunnels through multiple dimensions, psychedelically articulating itself as alien architecture, harmonies, patterns, complex organic flow. With personal awareness enjoined in this larger vibratory pattern, identity extends outward, blending with the larger psychedelic environment, flowing both inward and outward simultaneously and paradoxically. By going within, one flows outward into transpersonal appreciation of the larger, more encompassing flow of reality. Such paradoxical tension is very common in the entheogenic experience and can be experienced in any variety of ways. In fact, the simultaneous appreciation of disparate paradoxical truths is often a hallmark of entheogenic states of consciousness.

As the sage comes on, however, this overpowering flow, wrapped in paradox, can almost empty one. The flow, the "shaping of the wind," as I write about it here, can blow one away, temporarily sending one out upon the psychedelic waves. This early point of the experience can literally be physically disabling, and for practical reasons, *Salvia divinorum* should always be used where one is not in danger of falling over, especially at stronger doses.

Within a few minutes, the overpowering aspect of the sage experience is often replaced by a profound sense of empowerment. For me, this is one of the greatest gifts of *Salvia divinorum*. Especially when I approach the sage in a reverential and ceremonial way, I come away from the experience feeling so deeply empowered. This is greatly enhanced through my vibratory participation in the *salvia* experience. Throat singing, playing the didjeridu, drumming and rattling all help me to reach this state of empowerment. It is pure Spirit Flow and there is a deep sense of beauty, power, energy, and awareness to the experience. I come away from the experience profoundly grateful and I thank the sage with deep sincerity. All of these aspects of my *Salvia divinorum* experience are reflected in Orobai's sense of first emptying, and then filling with energy, reaching a new and profound state of energetic awareness and spiritual empowerment. In short, Orobai is receiving a spiritual recharge through the ritual actions of his friend, Nataali, who is here representative of the actions of the *Salvia divinorum* experience.

This particular passage is also influenced by the mystical nature of the psilocybin mushroom experience. When Orobai sees into his heart, and into Nataali's, and feels himself connected to the heart of all of creation, he is mystically united with the world, opening his being to all that is. He is able to perceive this connection through his awareness of the energies that bind everything together.

While *Salvia divinorum* has similar qualities to such psilocybin experiences, for me, psilocybin is more of a reflective heart medicine and is more conducive to such experiences than the sage.

This next excerpt is from the second book in my series, *The Fate of Miraanni*. Here, Orobai's young sister, Miraanni, has been brought by Nataali to the Temple of the Serpent King, where she is to meet with the mighty Mwataan, the Serpent King, in entheogenic trance. A priest of the temple, Ixshan, plays his didjeridu-like instrument while taking the elixir of the Mwataan with Miraanni, who has been lost in a catatonic state. The hope is that Miraanni will be able to find herself once more and begin to define herself with the help of the Serpent King.

The Fate of Miraanni, pages 147 - 151

Ix bolted the door so that none might enter the sacred chamber and disturb their proceedings. "Lay her here," Ix said to Nataali, gesturing to an altar-like platform in the center of the room. Nataali did as she was instructed as Ix placed a silken pillow under the child's head and proceeded to put some incense resin crystals on burning coals, filling the room with a sweet and pungent fragrance. "It's the Mwataan's favorite," he said, noticing that Nataali was watching him. "Surely you remember it."

"Yes," said Nataali, "I know. I remember." A cold chill went down her spine. How could she forget her own meeting with the Mwataan? How could anyone? She too had been bathed, dressed, and anointed with oils and taken to an incense-filled chamber much like this one. There she had lay prostrate before the mighty serpent. No. She would never forget. As the scent of the incense filled her nostrils her mind was filled with the memories of her own experience and she once again felt the anxiety and worry of what was about to take place for Miraanni.

Ix drew Nataali's attention to a comfortable chair that was placed just off to the side. "Please have a seat. There is nothing that you need worry about," he said, reading her thoughts upon her face. "Know that I will watch out for her. Everything will be fine."

Ix then pulled a small vial from his tunic that was filled with a clear liquid that looked no different from water. "I will take some too," he explained to his sister, "in order to monitor her experience. You may as well, if you like."

Nataali declined. She would rather watch from her own perspective, she explained.

"Very well," said Ix. "Then we shall begin."

Removing the top from the small vial, he gently took Miraanni's head in his free hand and tilted her back so that her mouth opened slightly. Carefully, he poured three drops into her mouth, causing her to swallow several times. He then set her head back down and then poured three drops into this own mouth as he looked up at the ceiling. Then, taking a seat next to the altar-bed, Ix reached over to an ashkaabwa, one of the long, hollow, resonating instruments of the Alngbwat, and began to play. The drone of the instrument instantly filled the chamber, which greatly amplified its deep undertone and rapidly vibrating harmonics. Using his tongue, mouth, diaphragm, and lips, Ix began to produce complex patterns that had a feeling of being simultaneously natural and otherworldly. It was almost as though the sound swallowed up the entire room and all of its contents. Nataali could feel the primal pulsing and gliding tones of the ashkaabwa throughout her body. She closed her eyes for a moment and saw an open and vibrating space before her in her mind that reacted to the instrument, rising, falling, rising again, like a vast sea that had been set in motion by the wings of an unseen being. The Mwataan was coming.

Nataali opened her eyes. Ix swayed back and forth slightly to his own rhythm as the ashkaabwa took over and played him more than he played it. Miraanni also moved to the sound of the instrument, the first time Nataali had seen her react to external stimuli in months. She moved only slightly at first, lifting herself slightly by arching her back, or twisting from side to side. As Ix's playing grew in intensity, so did Miraanni's movements. *It's coming on now*, thought Nataali to herself. *The elixir is taking effect. It consumes them both.*

Using her eyes of the Xhutai-Ku, Nataali could see the energy that was Miraanni's essential nature begin to coalesce. What was disordered became ordered and what was distant became near. Thinking of the analogy her mother had used, Nataali looked upon Miraanni as a star exploding in reverse, as though it were gathering all its substance back into itself and somehow reintegrating, reversing the inexorable flow of time.

Ix suddenly let out a great cry through the ashkaabwa that echoed about the stone chamber. He did so again, and then twice more. At the fourth cry Miraanni sat up upon the altar. She drew her legs underneath herself, sat upon her bent knees, and prostrated herself on the altar. Her arms were extended out before her, palms open, facing upwards. She breathed heavily as her torso bobbed up and down to the pulse of Ixshan's playing. Such a submissive posture could only mean one thing, Nataali knew. Miraanni was in the presence of the Mwataan, the Serpent King.

* * * *

The vastness of space and time lay open to her, devoid of barriers, limits, or boundaries. Yet this vastness was also devoid of signs, landmarks, or maps. It was simply a vast emptiness, an infinite horizon with no beginning, and no end. In this vastness there was no self, no other, no mind, no body, only pure consciousness, fathomless, uncreated, and undifferentiated. At times this vast ocean crested into a discernable form, like a wave upon the surface of the ocean that rises for only a moment, takes shape, and then inevitably falls back into the source, the place of origin. In this way dream-like images might parade by, both fantastic and mundane, all without sense or substance and devoid of context. There was nothing upon which to judge the significance of these phantasms. There was no ground, no self or identity, no perspective from which to interpret their meaning. And behind the forms was only the vast emptiness, a complete lack of meaning or definition. With no limits there was no meaning. There was no frame through which the content of consciousness could be limited or defined.

Three drops broke the surface of this endless ocean. The drops drew the ocean into themselves, gathering the void into form, coherence, identity. For the first time in what could have been an eternity, Miraanni felt her body. It was not necessarily physical, but it had form to it. It had substance and depth, though of a mental or psychic nature, not merely the crude stuff of the material side of nature, but consisting of the profound depths of the mind, of consciousness. She felt it distinctly, pulling back into itself, taking shape, closing itself off from the rest of creation. Limits. Borders. Boundaries. Definition. These were the things of selfhood. Here there were fingers, toes, limbs, eyes, mouth, nose, all the aspects of a physical body, and a mind to contemplate and experience this physicality. It sensed. It felt. It understood its experiences as belonging to itself and no other. It was *her* body. It was *her* mind. It was not some phantasm, some vision, some echoing pattern in space-time. It was she, and she knew it as such. She was a thinking and experiencing thing. For the first time in what could have been ages, Miraanni knew herself as a self-conscious being, though she did not know who she was.

Miraanni did not have time to contemplate her new psycho-physical form. The idea passed that it was not what she thought she remembered. The body was bigger, heavier, older, but these were all impressions that she could not put into definitive thought or meaning within her mind, so quickly did the process overtake her. She only knew that things were different, that what was taking place was far removed from anything that had come before, and that she had somehow regained a perception of herself as existing within the confines of a physical body with a self-identified mind. Some part of her had returned.

No sooner had this reintegration begun than Miraanni felt something pushing and coursing through her new dream body and self-image. It came from behind her and seemed to be driven on by some pulsing, droning, relentless sound. It felt cool and smooth, pushing at her and through her. It felt like pointed leaves, perhaps, or even scales. It was soft, even inviting, and unmistakably powerful.

The sensation quickly grew in intensity, rapidly rising to a point of consuming Miraanni's dream body. There was no longer something moving through her, but rather she had become the movement itself, or was somehow caught up within the movement so thoroughly that it defined her psycho-physicality in some mysterious way. Pushing, moving, writhing. She was consumed by it as wave after undulating wave moved through her being.

As the power flowed, it began to take shape. Infinitely long, limitless in power, it was a serpent. As though her dream body was the medium in which the great serpent swam, it propelled itself through her by means of its rhythmic undulations and serpentine pulses of muscle and scales, cold and smooth. As it passed through her it drew her body upwards, arching her back, seeming to pass directly through her torso and gut, through the very core of her being. It pulled her up, causing her to sway from side to side, as though she were between the coils of the mighty serpent as it surged forward.

At last it passed completely through her, causing her body to fall backwards slightly. As the snake coiled up into itself it rose up high into the darkness above it. Slowly its massive head came into view as the serpent locked its eyes directly on Miraanni as it rapidly flicked its tongue in the air.

Immediately upon receiving its gaze Miraanni was overcome by a sense of profound humility and supplication. It was a mix of reverence, fear, and awe, as the serpent swayed hypnotically in front of the mesmerized child. The feeling was overwhelming. Even if she had wanted, she could not have helped herself. Miraanni fell down upon her knees, head to the floor, arms extended outward with palms up, in complete supplication to the great being. It was an act of worship and an act of prayer. In that moment, Miraanni gave herself completely to the Mwataan, the Serpent King.

The great serpent embraced its newest worshipper, wrapping his endless body around the supplicant, almost caressing her delicate form. The serpent lowered its massive head, hovering directly over Miraanni, testing her skin with its long, cold tongue, flicking over her face, neck, and hands. The serpent then coiled up into itself, raising his head high in the blue-green firelight.

In unspoken words, the Mwataan spoke to Miraanni in a voice that penetrated to the deepest and most hidden parts of Miraanni's being.

"I've been waiting for you . . . " it said. "Look upon me."

Miraanni had no choice but to do as she was told. Slowly, she raised her torso and pulled her arms inwards, keeping her palms open and facing upwards. First her gaze met the base of the serpent. As she looked at it, the very scales on the serpent's outer surface seemed to melt and meld into one another in a constant, yet subtle, movement. She found it difficult to focus clearly on the serpent despite the overwhelming immediateness of its presence. Slowly and deliberately, Miraanni's lifted her eyes to meet the cold stare of the Mwataan. For a moment she looked the terrible serpent directly in his deep yellow eyes and noticed how the pupil was bordered by a deep green. As the serpent sharpened his focus and met Miraanni's gaze directly, she was compelled to look away, once more assuming a more submissive posture, unable, or unwilling, to look the beast in the eye.

"Do not be afraid," came the voice that was not a voice in a soft and seductive hiss. "Look at me. I have waited long to see you with my own eyes."

Miraanni did as she was told. She took in more this time, taking the opportunity to look about her. She saw that she was in a large room with high stone walls and vaulted ceilings that recessed into darkness high above the great serpent's head. The room was lit with an eerie greenish-blue light that came from several torches that were fixed to the walls at even distances from each other. There did not appear to be anyone else in the room, but she could distinctly hear a continual pulsing sound, which she now realized was the first definite aspect of the experience that she could remember. Looking out into the room, everything was alive, for the surfaces of all things flowed and moved like light reflecting off of the surface of moving or rippling water. Even the stones moved as they continuously flowed and melted into one another.

Comments

The above passage is a mixture of both literal and more metaphorical aspects of the *Salvia divinorum* experience. The scene opens with a ritual setting for the experience of the sage. As with all entheogens, ritualizing their use greatly enhances the spiritual quality of the experience. For ritual, attention to set and setting are paramount, as is preparation.

Here the catatonic child, Miraanni, is brought into a ritual chamber to meet with the Serpent King, the Mwataan. She is given drops of a psychedelic elixir on her tongue, which almost immediately launches her into a visionary state, as the sensation of the Serpent King moving through her pulls her up and then into a posture of submission. The experience itself is driven on by the didjeridu playing of the priest, Ixshan.

In many ways the experience of *Salvia divinorum* can be likened to the sensation of a profound, cosmic snake, moving through ones being, and you feel pushed and pulled as the "coils" wrap around and through you. Behind closed eyes, infinite regressions of scale or leaf-like patterns stretch out into the strange world of sage space. In many respects, the vein patterns on the actual *Salvia divinorum* leaves somewhat resemble these subtle psychedelic patterns manifested within the visionary state.

As the sage courses through, it pushes and pulls at your body. People may move, bend, sway, or even fall over, especially at higher doses. This sense of energetic power sweeping around and through one can create a sense of pure overwhelming awe as you are pulled into sage space. There is also a strong sense of otherness to this power that is almost alien. Yet within its otherness there is an intuition of its presence and greater awareness, as though one has entered a stream of consciousness that resides beneath the things of our everyday perceptions. This awareness is a dreamspace, where the dreams that reside behind our actions lie, playing themselves out continually beneath our conscious awareness. Here, one is pulled into the dream and it is other, but also knowing. And it is power.

In the above passage, this quality of the sage has been given symbolic and archetypal form in the character of the Mwataan, the Serpent King. Within the context of the story, the Mwataan is something of an oracle, and also an object of worship. For the priests, such as Ixshan, the Mwataan is primarily an experience and a state of mind.

As is no doubt clear, much of the passage can be taken as a literal description of a sage session. There are some important differences, however. Sage can be taken in a liquid or "elixir" form, but it would be held under the tongue for 15 minutes, and a larger amount than three drops, as is described in the story, would be required. Furthermore, liquid sage comes on more slowly than the rapid, seconds-long onset of smoked enhanced leaf, which is more the direct inspiration for this passage.

It is also important to emphasize that the experience of *Salvia divinorum* as a "cosmic serpent" is more of an impression and sensation than it is a literal object of awareness. It is a way of talking about the salvia experience, as is the "shaping of the wind," as described from the earlier passage. Here, this aspect of the sage is rendered as the Mwataan, and dramatized as a god-like being.

Miraanni's state of catatonia being cured by the Mwataan is also not meant as a literal representation of *Salvia divinorum* or other entheogens, but rather is a metaphor for both the healing and centering properties of the entheogenic experience. There is often the sense of finding oneself, of revealing deeper, inner truths about one's self and life that is revealed in the entheogen trance. This is where personal growth and understanding comes from through the use of entheogens. The entheogens can work to focus your inner eye and sharpen your awareness of yourself as a spiritual being, giving one a sense of understanding of personal meaning. Indeed, it can be like finding oneself after being lost and awakening to a new sense of being and renewed life. Particularly with *Salvia divinorum*, such an experience is often characterized by a sense of overwhelming power that inspires awe, thanks and humility.

This final excerpt comes from later in *The Fate of Miraanni*. Here, Miraanni comes to Ixshan, having shape-shifted into his own likeness, greeting him in his room and asking him questions about the nature of the Mwataan, religion, faith, and spiritual experience.

The Fate of Miraanni, pages 204-205

"You want to know if I am the Mwataan and if you, being like me, can also be the Mwataan." Ix's other nodded in agreement.

"Yes, and no" answered Ix. "I am no more the Mwataan than any of the other Chaxta-Rhul. You see," he said, "the Mwataan is somewhat paradoxical. It seems to exist without us, but is only actualized by one of the Chaxta-Rhul. Without us, it is merely a potential, at least in the personal and interactive sense. There is no Mwataan 'out there' to be seen or experienced in some objective and absolute sense. When we Chaxta-Rhul take the elixir, along with a supplicant, if present, and play the ashkaabwa, the Mwataan manifests. Without us, our minds, and the driving force of the ashkaabwa, there is no Mwataan. Yet curiously, he knows things that we do not, and can show us many things. Strange, isn't it? So yes, when you and I took the elixir and I played for you, I was, in a sense, the Mwataan. I saw what he saw, heard what he heard, and felt what he felt. It would be the same for any other of the Chaxta-Rhul. So you see, my answer to your question must be 'yes' and 'no.'"

The voice in Ix's mind came again, this time with an edge of confusion. *That is not what the Mwataan said.*

"No, of course not," said Ix. "I am merely telling you of my experience of the Mwataan. For me, and the other Chaxta-Rhul, the Mwataan is not an objective or absolutely existing thing. That is how we *experience* the Mwataan. And this, of course, is all we have. What the Mwataan may be in-and-of-itself is a completely different matter. To this question the Mwataan will provide his own answers, just as he did for you.

"Like many, you wondered if the Mwataan was God. You were given a good answer and should think on it. Know, however, that that is precisely how many people think of the Mwataan, and it is their choice to do so. Yet such a belief tells you little about the Mwataan. Thus the people look to us to help them understand this thing that they perceive as divine. These beliefs turn us Chaxta-Rhul into priests. That is what 'rhul' means – someone who officiates religious rites and ceremonies. The people worship the Mwataan. We do not. We conjure the Mwataan. That is why we are also 'chaxta,' or sorcerers. We have our own understandings of the Mwataan based on our own direct experiences. We are able to manifest the Mwataan for others through our secret techniques. If others want a religion, then they create it. We simply play our role as mediators between the Mwataan and those who would worship him."

So you knowingly deceive them? asked the voice, somewhat upset, yet curious.

"If that is what you want to call it, then so be it," said Ix. "I think of it as letting them think for themselves, or refraining from imposing our own particular understanding on the people. We have not created a dogma for people or a system of belief. If such exists, they created it themselves for their own purposes. We have found these beliefs to be an effective social tool and therefore have not sought to suppress or change them. It may be deceptive, but it is ultimately practical. Every culture, and even every person, must decide for him or herself what to accept and believe. We do not tell the people what to believe. We only facilitate their direct experience with what they perceive to be the ultimate. The meaning that they assign to it is their own individual creation, though it is undoubtedly influenced by their culture and life-situation. You may choose to call this manipulation or deception. I would call it freedom. Whether it is good or bad is another matter. These may not be the answers that you seek, but it is what I have to offer."

Comments

While clearly not a passage directly relating a *Salvia divinorum* or entheogenic experience, this passage does express some philosophical reflections that may be inspired by such an experience, and in some ways harkens back to my personal journals of my salvia experiences.

The passage speaks largely for itself, so there is no need to review the content in detail. The primary message is that in the end, how one appreciates and chooses to interpret entheogenic experiences is ultimately a matter of personal choice. Deeply personal, radically subjective, and often paradoxical, the meaning of one's experience must be an individual choice. This can be mediated and influenced by culture, community, personal history, religious belief, and countless other factors, but there is no single interpretation for the entheogenic experience. Each person will have to decide for him or herself what the experience is and what it means.

For myself, I enjoy the *Salvia divinorum* experience as a fascinating object of study and as a source for inspiration and spiritual sustenance. I appreciate its power and cherish the inner vistas it opens up before me. I give my experiences my own interpretations, and in the end, that's all I have. Within these experiences are lessons to be learned, insights to be gained, and novelty to be explored. Wonder and amazement, awe and power, energy and flow. In the end, it is what it is, and for ourselves, it is what we make of it, how we approach it, and how we use it that matters most.

To that end, the final chapter of this book that follows will focus on the ritual and ceremonial use of *Salvia divinorum*. This is meant more as the beginning of a discussion of such use than a final thought, and will hopefully inspire others to carry the discussion so that we can collectively find new ways to work with the entheogenic experience.

Ritual and Sage

*S*alvia divinorum is a powerful entheogen and can easily launch one into profound states of awareness with strange alien landscapes, otherworldly architecture, and mystical and shamanic states of consciousness. No special preparation is needed in order to arrive at such experiences, especially when using the enhanced leaf form of *Salvia divinorum*.

However, ritual and the structured, controlled use of *Salvia divinorum* can greatly enhance the salvia experience, as it can for any entheogen, and furthermore, *Salvia divinorum* can enhance any ceremony, when used in a careful and intentional manner.

Unlike some other entheogens, *Salvia divinorum* does not lend itself to overtly social situations. The experience is radically personal and introspective, and in fact, the outside world and others can be a distraction from the sage experience. In other words, salvia is not a "party drug" in any sense. It turns one's attention inward so rapidly and powerfully that interacting with others can be a near impossibility, especially at higher doses, and the person under the influence of salvia might not even have any awareness of the "outside" world. At somewhat lower, but still strong doses, one may retain awareness of the outside world, but the object of one's attention is the subjective inner state of awareness that is opened up by the sage.

There is also often a lack of physical coordination and dexterity that accompanies the use of *Salvia divinorum*, which is another factor against its use as a "party drug." With a big hit of enhanced leaf, for example, even putting the pipe down can be a challenge as the rush of sage comes over one.

What this all leads to is the fact that *Salvia divinorum* is far more properly suited for sessions of private reflection, meditation, introspection, and inner journeying. When used alone, it is easy to make a private space and time to enjoy these qualities of the salvia experience. When used with others, it is important to create an environment that recognizes, respects, and enhances this very personal nature of the salvia experience.

In *Mushroom Wisdom* I discussed the art of ritual and wrote of some of my own personal practices for ritualizing use of psilocybin mushrooms. Much of the advice that I gave there applies equally well to *Salvia divinorum*. Attention to set and setting, establishing one's intention and focus, use of symbols, attention to sound and silence – all of these are very important factors to keep in mind when creating and participating in ceremony.

The primary purpose of ritualizing the use of entheogens is to set the intentions of those using the entheogens and provide a context to approach the entheogen experience as an inherently sacred and spiritually meaningful event. It also provides a grounding structure for the experience in that it can give participants a sense of beginning, middle, and end to the entheogenic experience. Having a larger structure of ritual can help to ground one and give a sense of stability and a safe and supportive context in which to navigate the often confusing and disorienting states of consciousness opened up by entheogens.

Given the fast acting nature of *Salvia divinorum*, especially in smoked form, salvia ceremonies are inherently somewhat different from other entheogen rituals and ceremonies. Most entheogens have a much longer duration with a much longer build up, peak, and decline than *Salvia divinorum*. Such longer-acting entheogens might require several hours for a ritual or even an entire day or night. Salvia, on the other hand, lasts for only a few minutes when smoked in enhanced form. The most powerful effects last only 5 minutes or so, though the entire experience can be drawn out and lengthened by the use of sound as a driving force to the entheogenic experience. Generally, most salvia users will feel that their experience is "over" within 10 – 15 minutes, though mild after effects may linger for another 15 – 20 minutes. A very strong dose of enhanced leaf might last for 20 – 30 minutes before the user feels that he or she has fully "returned."

Given the intensely private nature and relatively brief duration of the salvia experience, it is crucial for these factors to be taken into consideration when ritualizing the use of the sage. The setting is also extremely important. It should be private and secure where participants are not inhibited by the thought that someone might walk in and disturb the proceedings. The setting should be a space where people feel that they can let themselves go into the salvia experience without fear of interruption where they are surrounded by respectful and supportive people. The ritual space should also be relatively dark and quiet with few distractions that might interrupt participants' perceptions of their inner worlds and subjective experience.

Ritual use of salvia can be done either alone or with others. Most of my salvia experiences have been in private, completely on my own. I can ritualize these experiences as much as I like, or choose not to ritualize them. I generally approach the sage with at least a minimal amount of ritualization and ceremonial preparation. While one can easily pick up a pipe of sage and just jump into the experience, I personally find that taking at least a few moments to center oneself, set one's intention, and perform a few ritual gestures or say a few prayers tends to give the experience greater focus. Simply put, the more you put into it, the more you tend to get out of it.

The same basic considerations should be taken into account when working with salvia alone as when experiencing it with others. A private, secure space that is dark, quiet, and comfortable where one will not be disturbed or interrupted is crucial for having a rewarding experience.

There are of course other factors to take into consideration when conducting salvia ceremonies with multiple participants. The level of formality of the ritual depends on the personal tastes and inspirations of those creating and participating in such ceremonies, and as with human culture in general, there are infinite numbers of ways that creative and spiritually minded individuals could create and enact salvia ceremonies. I would like to share how I have conducted salvia ceremonies with multiple participants, and I have some basic advice, but really it is up to one's inspiration, culture, and tradition to dictate the details of any ceremony.

For group sessions, a ritual leader is important. This can either be formally recognized and established, or as is often the case, the group may naturally look to one or two participants as the leader of the ceremony based on personal relationships, personality, charisma, or personal knowledge of the *Salvia divinorum* experience. Personally, when I conduct salvia ceremonies, I take on what I would describe as a "priestly" role, in that I will officiate the ceremony. I find that others tend to appreciate having someone in this role and thus I recommend that all group ceremonies have someone either formally or informally recognized as having the primary priest or priestess role, or however one might like to identify this role, within the ceremony.

Setting the mood and atmosphere among the group is one of the primary roles of the priest or priestess leading the ceremony.

Participants should know that everyone participating will have the same opportunity, space, and time to visit with the sage and that each participant will be afforded the same respect and support as the others. The priest or priestess should also be welcoming to all participants, gracious, and inviting, while also exhibiting a sense of authority and compassion towards all. While important among friends, this is perhaps even more important for newcomers, especially those who may be unfamiliar with the sage experience.

For salvia ceremonies where the sacrament is enhanced salvia leaf, my recommendation is that everyone take turns visiting with the sage. If the sacrament of choice is chewed or liquid sage, then everyone can participate together. As most contemporary Western consumption of salvia is with smoked leaf that has been potentiated with salvinorin A extract, we will focus on the turn taking technique of ceremonial practice here.

In small group gatherings, a circle of participants is a natural and spontaneous formation for the ritual. Some kind of altar or shared symbolic space might be set up for the central focus of the group. I recommend keeping the group small – perhaps five to eight participants. More than that and it could be difficult to maintain everyone's focus and attention on the ritual, and it could mean excessive waiting to partake of the sacrament by those who are at the end of the session.

The ritual priest or priestess can set the tone of the session by giving a little speech or introduction to the purpose of the session. Especially if there are newcomers to the group then it should be clearly established that silence, support, and respect for others and their experiences are important for the ritual. It might be important to make clear whether people are invited to come and go from the ceremonial space and what expectations are in place for such activity. The overall concern should be to maintain the sanctity and security of each individual's experience. For example, some talking, getting up and moving around, making noise, or walking through the ceremonial space can be highly disruptive to someone's salvia experience and should be avoided whenever possible, especially in more formal sage ceremonies.

The ritual leader can also take the lead in saying a prayer or benediction for the ceremony, and invite others to do so as well. Often participants might want to express what they hope to gain from the session or might even want to speak directly to the sage itself. However, there should be no pressure for anyone to speak at any time as the private and personal nature of the salvia experience should be respected at all times.

The priest or priestess can also perform a blessing for the opening of the ceremony according to his or her tradition or inspiration. This may involve blessing the participants, the ritual space, the altar, or the sage, or all of the above. However one chooses to perform such acts is fine and there are no rules here, only suggestions. The general thought to follow is that the more preparation and attention to ceremonial factors, the more centered and serious the minds of the participants will be, and the potential for a spiritually and personally meaningful experience is increased and augmented.

Attention to ritual detail and formality does not mean that the ceremony has to be all seriousness, however. Humor, chaos, and unpredictability have extremely important roles in ceremonial practice and spiritual experience. In fact, the tension that exists between jocular levity and ceremonial seriousness can help to highlight the often-paradoxical nature of the entheogen experience. Ritual can therefore be both extremely serious and light and humorous simultaneously. There is no need to banish humor, joking, and play from ceremony, and when embraced, these can greatly enhance the communal feeling of the ceremony or ritual.

Humor and levity also help to create comfort and familiarity among participants and let people know that it's OK to embrace the absurd – and sometimes entheogenic experiences can be absurd. This is perhaps especially true of *Salvia divinorum*, which often has the feel of something of a trickster, almost being impish at times. It is not all that uncommon, for example, for people experiencing *Salvia divinorum* to spontaneously burst into laughter for no apparent reason.

Once the mood, set, and setting have been established and any preliminary prayers, benedictions, and statements of intent have been made, then the sharing of the sage sacrament can commence.

Participants will often look to the ritual priest or priestess for guidance and instruction. I feel that my role as a sage ceremony leader is to make sure that everyone is given the same opportunity to fully go into his or her private experience of the sage in a safe and supportive environment. As the ceremonial leader, I take on the role of the administrator of the sacrament, meaning that I will take responsibility for the sage pipe. I will begin by making sure that the pipe is cleared from previous sessions and then pack a bowl of sage for the first participant. If the participant is unfamiliar with salvia, I will give instructions on holding the smoke in and what to expect. Often newcomers to sage will not smoke enough at first to get a true salvia experience, so I might encourage them to smoke more or finish off the bowl if they have not done so.

As the sage comes on, people often become slightly disoriented and physically uncoordinated. As their minds are turning inward, their awareness of the outside world becomes limited. I will watch carefully for this and will be sure to take the pipe from the participant as they will often not know what to do with it or might not even be able to effectively set the pipe down.

Prior to the participant taking a hit of sage, I will ask if he or she would like any sonic stimulation for the journey such as rattling or didjeridu playing. Many find such sonic driving to be a stabilizing factor in the experience. As the one making the sounds, I will watch the participant very carefully to do my best to match my sonic stimulation with how the sage is expressing itself to him or her. There are some obvious signs when people are strongly affected by sage such as eyes being forced closed, odd swaying of the body, slumping over, and body hair standing on end and rapid perspiration. Participants can of course be invited to perform their own sonic driving as well and they should feel free to drum, chant, rattle, or do whatever they find useful and meaningful for themselves.

Such monitoring and sonic driving can be enhanced by the priest or priestess consuming small amounts of salvia throughout the course of the ceremony. When I begin a session and clear out the bowl from previous sessions, I will smoke whatever remainder is left from before. This will often be enough to slightly put me into sage space. Then when I take the pipe back from the other participants, I will again clear out the bowl, making sure everything was smoked. Often there is a small amount left to burn, and this will help to maintain my slightly enhanced state of awareness throughout the ceremony, but not enough to enter me fully into the intimately subjective awareness of sage space.

Having the ritual leader consume small amounts of the entheogen for the duration of the ceremony helps the leader more accurately and intimately monitor the proceedings, and the state of mind of the other participants. However, the ritual leader should not take a fully psychedelic dose until it is specifically his or her turn, as such a dose will render the leader briefly incapacitated from his or her leadership role. For myself, I will generally go last in a sage ceremony after everyone else has had a turn for precisely this reason.

When I conduct salvia ceremonies I give each person however long he or she needs to pass through the sage experience. Given its highly personal and subjective nature, and the personal attention the ritual leader might give to the sonic driving of an individual's experience, I find it best to give every person his or her turn to visit with the sage without competition or interference from other ceremonial participants. In fact, participants might feel cheated of a deeply intimate and personal experience if they are distracted or interrupted by others during their turn. Respect for all involved is crucial here.

In my experience, it will become clear when a participant feels that he or she has emerged from the sage experience. As the sage comes on, people visibly turn inwards. Their eyes close, their heads droop down, their bodies become lax or they sway slightly as the sage pushes and pulls at them. As the sage experiences is passing away, they will tend open their eyes, look up and make eye contact with others. It is important not to act on the assumption that they are actually done right away, however, as many will open their eyes and look around just to "check in" that things are still as they were in the "outside" world, and then might journey back into the sage experience. Thus the ritual leader should wait until it is quite clear that the participant is finished before moving on.

When it is their turn, participants can also be encouraged to rattle, sing, chant, or do whatever they like to help drive their experience along. Also, some participants might like to request that particular other participants do the sonic driving for them and the ritual leader should respect this and should not be attached to being *the* sonic driver for the ceremony. Entheogenic ceremonies should always be open to sharing and allow the maximum amount of freedom for individuals to express themselves within the pre-established boundaries of the ritual.

Many individuals will want to discuss their experiences, yet others may want to keep their experience private, and there should be no pressure placed on those who do not want to share to do so. If there is a large number of participants, sharing might be best to leave until the conclusion of the ritual. Otherwise, such sharing can drag out the ceremony and make those near the end wait a long time for their turn with the sacrament.

Ritual leaders and participants need to be prepared for the fact that some participants might have a difficult experience or might have dredged up issues that they will feel they need to discuss in detail, or perhaps even in private with a trusted confidant. As with all things in ceremony, it is important for participants to be aware of such possibilities and should be supportive, compassionate, and respectful of all other participants.

Sharing of experiences should be approached as an opportunity to express oneself and one's experience, but shouldn't be a competition. Some people may have deeply profound spiritual experiences, and others may come away with little from the experience. It isn't a competition, however. This is one of the reasons that sharing might be best to leave to the end, so that no one feels that they have to have an equally profound experience as anyone else. Again, it is about respecting the uniquely individual and personal nature of the *Salvia divinorum* experience. Despite some fairly universal characteristics, the actual content of any sage experience will be highly personal and subjective.

After everyone has had a turn with the sacrament and has had an opportunity to share their experience, the ceremony can either be brought to a conclusion or those who are willing might want to go for another round. I like to finish by thanking the sage. Often this is a natural and spontaneous act on my part. I come out of the sage experience so empowered and grateful that I can't help myself. I'll thank the sage over and over again and invite others to do so as well.

Some participants might want to talk further about their experiences after the formal (or informal) conclusion to the ceremony, so ritual leaders need to be prepared for this. My advice is that the ritual leader should be intimately familiar with salvia so that he or she can easily relate to and understand the experiences of others. All entheogens can open one up to difficult and challenging experiences and the ritual leader must be emotionally, psychologically, and spiritually prepared for such events. The leader should therefore make a commitment to educating him or herself and be willing to take on the responsibility of counseling and helping other participants, if needed. In short, the role of a ritual leader, and entheogenic rituals in general, should be taken seriously and treated with respect, humility, and caution. The structure of ritual helps to mitigate against undesirable experiences, but they can happen. The role of ceremonial leader should therefore not be taken up casually and one must be committed to the responsibility that it brings.

Salvia divinorum need not be the primary focus of the ritual activity, however, as is the case with the ceremonial suggestions given above. Salvia could just as easily be used for enhancement and enrichment of other kinds of ceremonies such as meditations, healings, blessing ceremonies, or whenever a moment of spiritual power or consciousness alteration could work to deepen the participants' experience of the given ceremonial process.

This is probably especially the case with milder doses of sage, such as using natural salvia leaf. Natural leaf, as opposed to enhanced or potentiated leaf, has a much gentler effect and is not the same dramatic launch into sage space that smoking the enhanced leaf is. Smoking a few of the natural leaves can send one into a mildly psychedelic, dream-like state that is unmistakably salvian in nature, but one can still easily maintain awareness of the immediate surroundings as well as maintain full physical and mental control.

These mild states of sage awareness can add a sense of mystery, power, and spiritual energy and intent to any ceremonial act. Prayers, when said in a mild sage state, feel powerful, full of intent and consciousness, for example. Ritual actions, such as moving a feather or stone or other sacred object takes on deep significance and meaning.

In these moments of power and altered awareness, our actions, thoughts, and words take on special intent and purpose. The significance of the ritual becomes deeper, more meaningful, more profound.

There can also be the sense of invoking the powers through the use of sage, or of welcoming the spirits to the ceremony or special occasion. It doesn't need to be much sage to feel the presence of the unmistakable essence that is the *Salvia divinorum* experience. In calling in the power and awareness that is the sage, the energies can be brought into harmony and the veil between worlds can be lifted, if only for a moment. But once the veil is drawn, one knows that that spirit, that presence, that energy is there, and it will share its magical awareness and shape our ritual and our actions according to that deeper connection with the earth, the spirits, and the universe.

Conclusion

It is my sincere hope that those who have read these pages have now come away with a deep appreciation and understanding the strange and wondrous herb that is *Salvia divinorum*. While certainly not exhaustive of the possibilities of the *Salvia divinorum* experience, if I have done my job, then readers of these pages should have a fairly good idea of what *Salvia divinorum* is, how it affects consciousness, and how one may strive to work with this unique entheogenic teacher in a way that recognizes its special character and qualities. It is also my hope that readers have been inspired to approach *Salvia divinorum* in a respectful and reverential way, honoring the plant and the powerful experiences it opens up within the consciousness and spirit of those who choose to visit with it.

May all your journeys be blessed and may you walk the path of spirit in wisdom, humility, and compassion for all beings, and may all your voyages into sage space be blessed.

Journey well!

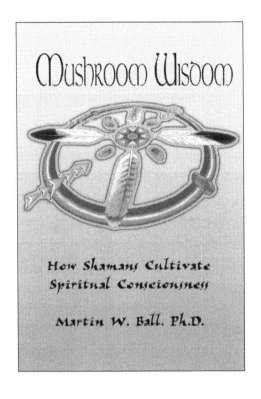

Mushroom Wisdom: How
Shamans Cultivate Spiritual
Consciousness
By Martin W. Ball, Ph.D.
Ronin Publishing, 2006

This book explores shamanic techniques and methods for cultivating deep introspective and mystical states of consciousness. Presented from a practical and philosophical perspective for spiritual practitioners of all kinds, this work is invaluable for any who would like a deeper understanding of the spiritual nature of psilocybin mushrooms and their use in ritual and spiritual practice.

Available at www.martinball.net and bookstores everywhere.

www.myspace.com/mushroomwisdom

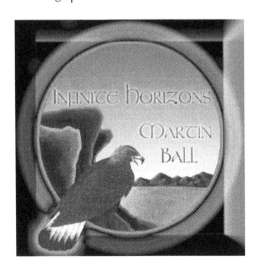

Infinite Horizons
Embracing the archaic revival, the world fusion music of this CD brings together acoustic percussion, didjeridu, throat and overtone signing, chanting, flutes, and more with electronic beats and contemporary sophistication. The official audio companion to *Mushroom Wisdom*.

Available at iTunes, Cdbaby.com, and www.martinball.net

Tales of Aurduin, volumes I-IV

by Martin W Ball

Orobai's Vision

The Fate of Miraanni

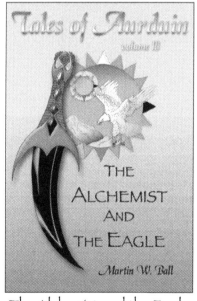

The Alchemist and the Eagle

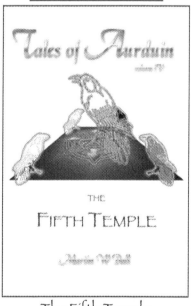

The Fifth Temple

Tales of Aurduin – a postmodern shamanic fable for a new ecological age
Available at www.martinball.net, www.lulu.com/martinball, www.aurduin.net
and www.myspace.com/orobai.

Martin W. Ball holds a Ph.D. in Religious Studies with an emphasis on Native American traditions and shamanism. *Sage Spirit* is his second book on entheogenic spirituality, and his book *Mushroom Wisdom* is available at bookstores everywhere. More of Dr. Ball's music, art, and writings are available at www.martinball.net. Dr. Ball lives in the Santa Ynez valley in California with his wife and children.

Divinorum
by Martin Ball

Companion Audio CD to *Sage Spirit.*

All original music by Martin Ball, featuring an ecstatic mix of electronic instrumentation and throat and overtone singing, didjeridu, and more. Inspired by Burning Man and *Salvia divinorum.*

Available at
www.martinball.net

The official myspace page for *Sage Spirit* and *Divinorum* is
www.myspace.com/salviasoundsystem

March 2014

ALSO BY DAVID J. HAND

Statistics: A Very Short Introduction

Information Generation: How Data Rule Our World

THE
IMPROBABILITY
PRINCIPLE

THE
IMPROBABILITY
PRINCIPLE

Why Coincidences, Miracles,

and Rare Events Happen Every Day

DAVID J. HAND

Scientific American / Farrar, Straus and Giroux
New York

Scientific American / Farrar, Straus and Giroux
18 West 18th Street, New York 10011

An excerpt from *The Improbability Principle* originally appeared, in slightly different form, in *Scientific American*.

Library of Congress Cataloging-in-Publication Data
Hand, D. J. (David J.), 1950–
  The improbability principle : why coincidences, miracles, and rare events happen every day / David J. Hand.
     pages   cm
  Includes bibliographical references and index.
  ISBN 978-0-374-17534-4 (hardback) — ISBN 978-0-374-71139-9 (ebook)
  1. Probabilities.   I. Title.

QA273 .H3545 2014
519.2—dc23

                                                         2013034007

Designed by Jonathan D. Lippincott

Scientific American / Farrar, Straus and Giroux books may be purchased for educational, business, or promotional use. For information on bulk purchases, please contact the Macmillan Corporate and Premium Sales Department at 1-800-221-7945, extension 5442, or write to specialmarkets@macmillan.com.

www.fsgbooks.com • books.scientificamerican.com
www.twitter.com/fsgbooks • www.facebook.com/fsgbooks

1   3   5   7   9   10   8   6   4   2

For Shelley

The really unusual day would be one where nothing unusual happens.
—Persi Diaconis[1]

Contents

Preface

This book is about extraordinarily improbable events. It's about why incredibly unlikely things happen. But more: it's about why they just keep on happening, time after time after time.

At first glance, this seems like a contradiction. How can events be incredibly unlikely and yet keep on happening? Unlikely surely means rare.

The fact that it isn't a contradiction is suggested by many real-life examples: people winning lotteries multiple times, lightning repeatedly striking the same unfortunate man, extreme financial crashes occurring again and again, and so on. But it certainly needs explaining.

The universe has laws which describe the way it works. Newton's laws of motion tell us how dropped objects fall and why the moon orbits the earth. They explain why a car seat presses into your back when you accelerate, and why the ground hits you so hard when you trip and fall. Other laws of nature show us how stars are born and how stars die, where humanity comes from, and perhaps where it's going.

The same applies to exceedingly unlikely events. The Improbability Principle is my name for a set of laws of chance which, together, tell us that we should expect the unexpected, and why.

The laws composing the principle arise at several levels. Some refer to fundamental aspects of the way the universe is constructed—as fundamental as the basic, abstract truth that two plus two equals four. Others hinge on deep properties of what we mean by probability. And yet others arise at the level of human psychology: the brain is not a simple recording device. In the right circumstances, any one of the laws is sufficient to lead to an instance of the principle, but it's when they come together and work in unison that the force of the principle becomes really striking. And the inconceivably unlikely happens.

Books like this one are built on research, conversations, and discussions with many people over many years—far too many to acknowledge properly. But some were especially helpful in seeing the ideas through the final stages to becoming a book. My friends and colleagues Mike Crowe, Kate Land, Niall Adams, Nick Heard, and Christoforos Anagnostopoulos kindly gave me comments on various drafts. My agent, Peter Tallack, and my editor, Amanda Moon, played critical roles in the journey from rough draft to finished product. Coincidentally (or perhaps not, since coincidences are one manifestation of the Improbability Principle), while the book was still at the conceptual stage, David Harding, founder of Winton Capital Management, approached me about a role in his company. The deep inferential challenges I encountered there encouraged me to think more deeply about rare events. And finally, I am most grateful to my wife, Shelley, for tolerating, yet again, my spiritual absences as the book gradually took shape, as well as for making invaluable comments on its content.

THE
IMPROBABILITY
PRINCIPLE

1

TIIE MYSTERY

Fortune brings in some boats that are not steer'd.
—William Shakespeare

Simply Unbelievable

In the summer of 1972, the actor Anthony Hopkins was signed to play a leading role in a film based on George Feifer's novel *The Girl from Petrovka*, so he traveled to London to buy a copy of the book. Unfortunately, none of the main London bookstores had a copy. Then, on his way home, waiting for an underground train at Leicester Square tube station, he saw a discarded book lying on the seat next to him. It was a copy of *The Girl from Petrovka*.

As if that was not coincidence enough, more was to follow. Later, when he had a chance to meet the author, Hopkins told him about this strange occurrence. Feifer was interested. He said that in November 1971 he had lent a friend a copy of the book—a uniquely annotated copy in which he had made notes on turning the British English into American English ("labour" to "labor," and so on) for the publication of an American version—but his friend had lost the copy in Bayswater, London. A quick check of the annotations in the copy Hopkins had found showed that it was the very same copy that Feifer's friend had mislaid.[1]

You have to ask: What's the chance of that happening? One in a million? One in a billion? Either way, it begins to stretch the bounds of credibility. It hints at an explanation in terms of forces and influences of which we are unaware, bringing the book back in a circle to Hopkins and then to Feifer.

Here's another striking incident, this time from the book *Synchronicity*, by the psychoanalyst Carl Jung. He writes: "The writer Wilhelm von Scholz . . . tells the story of a mother who took a photograph of her small son in the Black Forest. She left the film to be developed in Strassburg. But, owing to the outbreak of war, she was unable to fetch it and gave it up for lost. In 1916 she bought a film in Frankfurt in order to take a photograph of her daughter, who had been born in the meantime. When the film was developed, it was found to be doubly exposed: the picture underneath was the photograph she had taken of her son in 1914! The old film had not been developed and had somehow got into circulation again among the new films."[2]

Most of us will have experienced coincidences rather like these—if not quite so extraordinary. They might be more akin to thinking of someone just before she phones you. Strangely enough, while I was writing part of this book, I had precisely this sort of experience. A colleague at work asked me if I could recommend some publications on a specific aspect of statistical methodology (the so-called "multivariate t-distribution"). The next day, I did a little research and managed to identify a book on exactly that topic by two statisticians, Samuel Kotz and Saralees Nadarajah. I had started to type an e-mail to my colleague, giving him the details of this book, when I was interrupted by a phone call from Canada. During the conversation, the caller happened to mention that Samuel Kotz had just died.

And so it goes on. On September 28, 2005, *The Telegraph* described how a golfer, Joan Cresswell, scored a hole in one with a fifty-yard shot at the thirteenth hole at the Barrow Golf Club in Cumbria in the UK. Surprising, you may think, but not outlandishly so—after all, holes in one do happen. But what if I tell you that, immediately afterward, a fellow golfer, the novice Margaret Williams, *also* scored a hole in one?[3]

There's no getting away from it: sometimes events occur which seem so improbable, so unexpected, and so unlikely, they hint that there's something about the universe we don't understand. They make us wonder if the familiar laws of nature and causality, through which we run our everyday lives, occasionally break down. They certainly make us doubt that they can be explained by the accidental confluence of events, by the random throwing together of people and things. They almost suggest that something is exerting an invisible influence.

Often such occurrences merely startle us, and give us stories to tell. On my first trip to New Zealand, I settled down in a café, and noticed that the notepaper being used by one of the two strangers at the neighboring table was from my own university back in the UK. But at other times, these uncanny events can significantly alter lives—for the better, as with a New Jersey woman who won the lottery twice, or for the worse, as with Major Summerford, who was struck by lightning several times.

Humans are curious animals, so we naturally seek the underlying cause of strange coincidences. What was it that led two strangers from the same university to travel to the far side of the world and end up sitting at neighboring tables in the same café at exactly the same time? What was it that led the woman to pick those two winning sets of lottery numbers? What was it that brought huge electrostatic forces to hit Major Summerford time and time again? And what steered Anthony Hopkins and *The Girl from Petrovka* through space, and through time, to the same seat in the same underground station at the same moment?

Beyond that, of course, how can we *take advantage* of the causes underlying such coincidences? How can we manipulate them to our benefit?

So far all my examples have been very small-scale—at the

personal level. But there are countless more-profound examples. Some seem to imply that not only the human race, but the very galaxies themselves wouldn't exist if those very unlikely events hadn't occurred. Some relate to how sequences of tiny random changes in our genetic constitution could end up producing something as complicated as a human being. Others relate to the distance of the earth from the sun, the existence of Jupiter, and even the values of the fundamental constants of physics. Again the question arises as to whether blind chance is a realistic explanation for these apparently staggeringly unlikely events, or whether there are in fact other influences and forces directing the course of events behind the scenes.

The answers to all these questions hinge on what I call the *Improbability Principle*. This asserts that *extremely improbable events are commonplace*. It's a consequence of a collection of more fundamental laws, which all tie together to lead inevitably and inexorably to the occurrence of such extraordinarily unlikely events. These laws, this principle, tell us that the universe is in fact constructed so that these coincidences are unavoidable: the extraordinarily unlikely *must* happen; events of vanishingly small probability *will* occur. The Improbability Principle resolves the apparent contradiction between the sheer unlikeliness of such events, and the fact that they nevertheless keep on happening.

We'll begin by looking at prescientific explanations. These often go far back into the mists of time. Although many people still hold to them, they predate the Baconian revolution: that is the idea that the way to understand the natural world is to collect data, conduct experiments, take observations, and use these as test beds through which to evaluate proposed explanations for what's going on. Prescientific notions predate the rigorous evaluation of the effectiveness of explanations through scientific methods. But explanations which have not been or cannot be tested can have no real force: they are simply anecdotes, or stories, with the same status as a child's bedtime tale about Santa Claus or the tooth fairy. They serve the purpose of reassuring or placating those who are unwilling or unable to make the effort to dig deeper, but they don't lead to understanding.

Understanding comes from deeper investigation. In this deeper investigation, thinkers—researchers, philosophers, scientists—have sought to devise "laws" that describe the way nature works. These laws are shorthand summaries encapsulating in simple form *what observation shows* about how the universe behaves. They are abstractions. For example, the progress of an object falling from a tall building is described by Newton's Second Law of Motion, which says that the acceleration of a body is proportional to the force acting on it. Natural laws seek to get to the heart of phenomena, stripping away the superfluous, crystallizing the essence. The laws are developed by matching predictions with observations, that is, with data. If a law says that increasing the temperature of an enclosed volume of gas will increase its pressure, is this what actually happens, is this what the data show? If a law says that increasing the voltage will increase the current, is this what we actually see?

We've been extraordinarily successful in understanding nature by applying this process of matching data to explanation. The modern world, the cumulation of the awesome achievements of humanity's science and technology, is a testament to the power of such descriptions.

Of course, some people seem to think that understanding a phenomenon takes away its mystery. This is true in the sense that understanding means removing obscurity, obfuscation, ambiguity, and confusion. But a grasp of the cause of the colors of the rainbow doesn't detract from its wonder. What such a grasp brings is a more profound appreciation, and indeed awe, of the beauty underlying the phenomenon being studied. It shows us how all the pieces come together to give us the amazing world we live in.

Borel's Law: Sufficiently Unlikely Events Are Impossible

Émile Borel was an eminent French mathematician, born in 1871. He was a pioneer of some of the more mathematical aspects of probability (of so-called *measure theory*), and several mathematical objects and concepts are named after him—such as Borel measure, Borel sets, the Borel-Cantelli lemma, and the Heine-Borel theorem. In 1943 he wrote a nonmathematical introduction to probability called Les *probabilités et la vie*, translated as *Probabilities and Life*. As well as illustrating some of the properties and applications of probability, in this book he introduced what he called *the single law of chance*, nowadays often simply called Borel's law. This law says, *"Events with a sufficiently small probability never occur."*[4]

Clearly, the Improbability Principle looks as if it is at odds with Borel's law. The Improbability Principle says that events with a very small probability keep on happening, while Borel's law says they never happen. What is going on?

Now, your first reaction on reading Borel's law may well have been the same as mine when I first came across it: Surely it's nonsense? After all, you might think (as I did) that events with very small probability certainly occur, *just not very often*. That's the whole point about probability, and about small probabilities in particular. But when I read further into Borel's book, I saw that he meant something rather more subtle.

He illustrated what he intended by referring to the classic example of the monkeys who, randomly hitting the keys of a typewriter, happen by chance to produce the complete works of Shakespeare.[5] In Borel's words: "Such is the sort of event which, though its impossibility may not be rationally demonstrable, is, however, so unlikely that no sensible person will hesitate to declare it actually impossible. If someone affirmed having observed such an event we would be sure that he is deceiving us or has himself been the victim of fraud."[6]

So Borel is relating "very small probabilities" to human scales, and that's what he means: in *human* terms the probability is so small that it would be irrational to expect ever to see it happen; it should be regarded as impossible. And, indeed, after stating his "single law of chance" (which, you'll recall, was that *events with a sufficiently small probability never occur*) he added the comment, "or, at least, we must act, in all circumstances, as if they were *impossible*" [his italics].[7]

He gave a further illustration later in his book: "For every Parisian who circulates for one day, the probability of being killed in the course of the day in a traffic accident is about one-millionth. If, in order to avoid this slight risk, a man renounced all external activity and cloistered himself in his house, or imposed such confinement on his wife or his son, he would be considered mad."[8]

Other thinkers had said similar things. For example, in the 1760s Jean d'Alembert had questioned whether it is possible to observe a very long run of occurrences of an event in a sequence in which occurrence and nonoccurrence are equally probable. A century before Borel, in 1843, in his book *Exposition de la théorie des chances et des probabilités*, Antoine-Augustin Cournot had discussed the actual, as opposed to theoretical, probability of a perfect cone balancing on its vertex.[9] The phrase "practical certainty" has been associated with Cournot, being contrasted with "physical certainty." Indeed, the idea that "It is a practical certainty that an event with very small probability will not happen" is sometimes called Cournot's principle. Later, in the 1930s, the philosopher Karl Popper wrote, in his book *The Logic of Scientific Discovery*, "the rule that extreme improbabilities have to be neglected . . . agrees with the demand for *scientific objectivity*."[10]

Given the other illustrious thinkers who have described similar concepts, we might ask why it's Borel's name that's generally attached to the idea. The answer probably lies in Stigler's law of eponymy. This law says that "no scientific law is named after its original discoverer" (and then has the corollary, "including this one").

There's an analogy between Borel's law and the points, lines, and planes we learn about when we study geometry in school. We learn that these geometric objects are mathematical abstractions, and that they don't exist in the real world. They are merely convenient simplifications—which we can then think about and mentally manipulate, and hence draw conclusions about the real-world objects we're representing with them. Similarly, it's a mathematical ideal that, although incredibly small probabilities are not actually zero, they may be treated as if they were zero because, in *real practical human* terms, events with sufficiently small probability never occur. That's Borel's law.

Here's Borel again: "It must be well understood that the single law of chance carries with it a certainty of another nature than mathematical certainty, but that certainty is comparable to one which leads us to accept the existence of an historical character, or of a city situated at the antipodes, of Louis XIV or of Melbourne; it is comparable even to the certainty which we attribute to the existence of the external world."[11]

Borel goes on to give a scale showing what might be meant by a probability being "sufficiently small" that an event would never occur. Here are (slightly paraphrased) versions of the definitions he gives of the points on his scale. In each case, I've tried to convey the sizes of the numbers involved by giving some examples.

Probabilities which are negligible on the human scale are smaller than about one in a million. The probability of being dealt a royal flush in poker is about 1 in 650,000, almost twice a one-in-a-million chance. There are just over thirty million seconds in a year, so, in terms of Borel's scale, if you and I each randomly pick a second in which to do something, the chance that we will do it at the same time is negligible on the human scale.

Probabilities which are negligible on the terrestrial scale are smaller than about 1 in 10^{15}. (If you're unfamiliar with this notation, see my explanation in Appendix A.) The earth's surface area is about 5.5×10^{15} square feet. So if you and I were each to randomly choose a square foot to stand on (ignoring niceties such as the fact that many of those square feet would be in the ocean), our chance of picking the same square feet would be pretty well negligible on the terrestrial scale. The probability of one player in a game of bridge getting a complete suit is roughly 1 in 4×10^{10}, vastly more likely than an event which is negligible on the terrestrial scale.

Probabilities which are negligible on the cosmic scale are smaller than about 1 in 10^{50}. Earth is composed of some 10^{50} atoms, so if you and I independently pick single atoms from the entire Earth, the chance we would pick the same one is negligible on the cosmic scale. To put that into perspective, in turn, there are "only" something like 10^{23} stars in the universe altogether.

Probabilities which are negligible on the supercosmic scale are smaller than about 1 in $10^{1,000,000,000}$. Since the number of subatomic baryon particles in the universe is estimated to be around 10^{80}, it's difficult to devise any examples which put such small probabilities into context!

Borel's scale of the "negligibly small" tells us when we should regard events as so unlikely that for practical purposes we can treat them as impossible. But the Improbability Principle tells us that, in contrast, highly unlikely events, even those as unlikely as the ones Borel characterizes, keep on happening. That is, not only are they not impossible, but we see such events again and again. Surely both of these cannot be right: either they're so unlikely that we'll never see them happen, *or* they're so likely that we'll see them again and again.

By peeling back the meaning of improbability, we'll see that this apparent contradiction can be resolved. We can think of the different strands of the Improbability Principle as layers, like those of an onion, so that as each layer is peeled back the explanation becomes clearer. The different strands of the principle—the *law of truly large numbers*, the *law of near enough*, the *law of selection*, and other strands—each shed their own light on how both Borel's Law and the Improbability Principle can be right simultaneously.

Some of the strands of the principle are very profound. The law of truly large numbers, for example, plays a critical role in determining whether apparent clusters of sickness are caused by a pollutant or are merely due to chance. But others are less so. You might like to see if you can come up with an explanation for the following event which, at face value, would seem so improbable that we wouldn't expect to see it; so improbable that we should regard it as impossible. The observation is described in *U.S. News & World Report* of December 19, 2011.[12] It refers to the late Kim Jong-Il, former leader of North Korea, and says, "In 1994, the very first time he played golf, Kim Jong-Il dominated the 7,700-yard Pyongyang Golf Course. He shot an unimaginable 38-under par, recording no worse than a birdie at the country's lone golf course. His round included 11 holes-in-one, and the feat was verified by 17 bodyguards who were present."

You might want to recall Borel's hypothetical reaction to monkeys producing the complete works of Shakespeare when randomly hitting the keys of a typewriter. As I said, some strands of the Improbability Principle are straightforward. But others are very profound indeed, and this book explores them.

2

A CAPRICIOUS UNIVERSE

Teacher: "You know the Earth isn't flat, don't you."
Pupil: "It is where I live."
—Will Hay and Billy Hay in *The Fourth Form at
St Michael's*, Part 2[1]

Why Me, Why Here?

Imagine the following scene: One comfortable summer evening
you're sitting out on your lawn, a glass of chilled white wine by
your side. You're idly tossing a small ball from hand to hand. On
a whim, you throw it high into the air. It shoots skyward, gradually slows under the pull of gravity, stops at the apex of its trajec-
tory, and then begins to fall, gathering pace, moving faster and
faster. Until it lands . . . plop! right in your wineglass.

This was certainly unlucky. It was also highly improbable. Of
all the spots on the lawn where the ball could have landed, it just
happened to choose the few square inches framed by the rim of
your glass.

You know very well that if you had *tried* to throw the ball
high into the air intending it to land in your glass, you certainly
wouldn't have succeeded. So there's clearly something mysterious
going on here. It's as if some agent had taken control of the path

of the ball and steered it to its destination—perhaps a mischievous imp that had decided to change the laws of nature to amuse itself at your expense.

You may well have had similarly improbable experiences yourself. They might not have been quite so unfortunate as the ball landing in the wineglass, but perhaps they were strange enough to make you sit up and take notice—to make you think, how could that happen? Such events indicate a dissonance between how we expect the universe to behave and how it actually behaves.

In general, the notion that the universe behaves capriciously is an uncomfortable one. We want to know why things happen, to establish the causal connections, and to understand the rules that lie behind what we observe. The basic human drive for safety and security induces a fundamental unease with the notion that events might happen just by chance. After all, if it turned out that there are no causes, then there'd be no way to manipulate or control outcomes. Illnesses, accidents, and failures couldn't be avoided. We'd live in a constant state of fear, awaiting the unpredictable disaster just around the corner.

On the other hand, someone who could predict such events, or better still, control them, would be immensely powerful. They'd be able to dodge bullets, avoid car crashes, pick winning horses and profitable stocks, and move wineglasses before plummeting balls land.

Early—prescientific—attempts to explain such mysteries adopted what, following the ball-in-the-glass example, I might call "the imp explanation." This is the notion that there's some mysterious force or being behind what happens, often acting with malicious intent. A vast number of different explanations along these lines have been invented. They include superstitions, prophecies, gods and miracles, parapsychological explanations, Jung's "synchronicity," and many, many others. I'll begin by looking at superstitions.

Superstitions

Our instinctive drive to understand the causes behind events leads us to look for patterns. We search for sequences. We note that when event A happens, it's often followed by event B. For example, we notice that people who step out into the road without looking are frequently hit by cars, and that dark clouds overhead are often followed by rain. Many of these observed patterns make physical sense, and are extremely useful guides through life's vagaries. They don't tell us what will happen with absolute certainty, but they do tell us what is likely to happen next.

Many of the patterns we detect have a causal basis. If they didn't, we would have become extinct long ago. We would never have realized that the movement in the long grass meant there was a lurking tiger, or that the thunderous din coming from farther downstream meant we were drifting toward a waterfall.

Investigating patterns often yields evidence that explains them, showing that we did attribute the causes correctly. Early epidemiological work detected a connection between smoking and lung cancer, and later biological investigation showed there was indeed a causal relationship. And when observation suggested there were links between obesity and heart disease, subsequent experimental work showed that there were such links.

But not all the patterns we observe represent real physical relationships. Sometimes the patterns we see are simply the consequence of chance. I might realize that twice recently I've fallen down soon after seeing a black cat cross my path, but I'll also recognize that it's unlikely to represent any real causal relationship. The fact that every play I've seen this year has been excellent whenever I've driven to the theater, but disappointing when I've taken public transport, doesn't mean that this pattern will hold in the future. The trick is being able to distinguish between those patterns that do represent a real underlying cause-and-effect relationship and those that don't. Indeed, we could characterize the whole of science, in the broadest sense, as an ongoing attempt to do just that.

Patterns we spot but that are mere accidents, without any underlying cause, have often formed the basis of superstition: a belief that there is a causal relationship where there is none, such as the belief that I'm more likely to throw a double six if I kiss the dice before I toss them on the craps table, or that carrying a furled umbrella means it's less likely to rain. (You need to bear in mind that I live in London).

The evolutionary usefulness of the ability to recognize patterns and then infer the causal relationships they represent is demonstrated by the fact that precisely the same development of "superstitions" occurs in animals. The psychologist B. F. Skinner put hungry pigeons in a cage with a device that dispensed food at regular intervals regardless of what activity the bird was involved in at the time. He observed that the birds seemed to learn to associate the delivery of food with whatever they were doing when it appeared, because they'd repeat those actions, presumably in the hope of getting more food. Skinner wrote:

> The experiment might be said to demonstrate a sort of superstition. The bird behaves as if there were a causal relation between its behavior and the presentation of food, although such a relation is lacking. There are many analogies in human behavior. Rituals for changing one's luck at cards are good examples. A few accidental connections between a ritual and favorable consequences suffice to set up and maintain the behavior in spite of many unreinforced instances. The bowler who has released a ball down the alley but continues to behave as if he were controlling it by twisting and turning his arm and shoulder is another case in point. These behaviors have, of course, no real effect upon one's luck or upon a ball half way down an alley, just as in the present case the food would appear as often

if the pigeon did nothing—or, more strictly speaking, did something else.[2]

The "cargo cult" is an example of observed patterns that have no basis in an underlying cause. The phrase originally described practices developed by the native inhabitants of islands in the South West Pacific after the Second World War. They'd observed first the Japanese and then the Allied soldiers building airstrips, marching, directing landing aircraft, and wearing certain styles of dress. Associated with these curious behaviors was the arrival of giant flying machines carrying vast quantities of exotic material goods—canned food, clothes, vehicles, guns, radios, Coca-Cola, and so on—called "cargo" by the newcomers. When the war ended and the visitors left, the natives reasoned that if they carried out the same sort of activities, the planes would return. So they built airstrips out of straw and coconuts, and control towers out of bamboo and rope, and dressed themselves to resemble the military personnel they'd encountered during the war. They sat wearing carved wooden headsets, and duplicated the waved landing signals from their "runways." They'd observed a pattern—the curious behavior of the visitors followed by the arrival of rich rewards—and deduced that there was a connection, an underlying causal link. But the inferred relationship was not actually a causal one.

Even if one event follows another surprisingly often, it doesn't necessarily mean that the first causes the second. Statisticians have a sound-bite for this: *correlation does not imply causation*. Increasing sales of sunscreen are often associated with increasing sales of ice cream, but it's unlikely that one leads to the other. It's more likely that they have a common cause—more hot summer days. Similarly, if you study me you might spot that I carry an umbrella whenever my roof is wet in the morning. But it's not my wet roof that causes me to carry an umbrella. There's a Latin phrase that philosophers and logicians use to describe this fallacy: *post hoc ergo propter hoc*, meaning "after this, therefore because of this." A progression in time is necessary for a causal relationship, but it's not enough.

Superstitions are especially prevalent in gambling and sports, two domains in which chance plays a central role. If you've ever visited a casino, you may well have seen a gambler who believes that if he shakes the dice a certain way they'll show the numbers he wants. But, he believes, he has to shake them in a very special way—and if he doesn't get it *precisely* right the dice won't show his numbers. This conveniently explains why he doesn't always win: it's not that he's mistaken in his belief, but merely that he didn't follow the procedure exactly. He thinks.

Or take baseball pitcher Turk Wendell, who would draw three crosses in the dirt before pitching. Or Manchester United soccer player Phil Jones, who puts his left sock on first when the team is playing at home, and puts his right sock on first when they're away. Tiger Woods wears a red shirt for the final round of a tournament, though this seems to be because of his mother's beliefs rather than his own.

The "hot hand" belief is a common superstition that arises in sports and games involving chance. It's the belief that players who have a sequence of successful shots will be more likely to continue to have success—that such players are "in the zone." Now you'd expect this to be true at some level. We all have "off days" (perhaps we were feeling under the weather) so we might also be expected to have "on days." If we're having an on day then we're simply more likely to score. But the hot hand belief is more subtle than this: it says that the probability of continuing to score is increased by a series of successes. And it says that this is true even if the plays are random, such as throws of a die. It's all complicated by the fact that if we look *back* at how players have done in the past, we're bound to find spells when they've performed better than average, and also spells when they've done worse. That's what "average" means: sometimes better, sometimes worse. But the hot hand belief is that if a player is in a hot streak, the chance that that player will *continue* to score is higher than his or her personal average; and that this is true even if the game is purely random. It says that the mere fact of success in the past alters the probability of success in the future.

There's a very strong belief in this phenomenon—even to the extent that it influences play. In basketball, teammates will often pass the ball to players believed to be in a hot hand streak, believing that their sequence of successful shots makes them more likely to score next time. This complicates matters. It means that the belief in the hot hand phenomenon changes how the players are behaving, and that very change might alter the chance of scoring. It will certainly give the player who receives the ball more opportunity to score, even if it doesn't alter the chance of scoring at each attempt. And if those increased opportunities to score translate into more points, it could well reinforce the impression of a hot hand streak.

Of course, superstitions can vary from culture to culture. In China it's bad luck to sweep or dust on New Year's Day; in Japan a black cat crossing your path is a sign of good luck, while in the United States it's bad luck; in European countries the number 13 is considered unlucky, whereas in Japan, China, and Korea the number 4 is considered unlucky. There are also superstitions that are common across many cultures. Seeing a single magpie is unlucky, but seeing two together is lucky; opening an umbrella indoors is unlucky; breaking a mirror is unlucky; walking under a ladder will bring bad luck. That last example might well be an illustration of how such superstitions can form from observed patterns of events: having a paint pot dropped on you from a ladder could make you think it's unlucky to walk underneath.[3]

Once established, superstitions tend to strengthen themselves. This is because, outside of formal scientific experiments, we're not very good at testing hypotheses to see if they're true. We tend to note only evidence and events supporting our theories, and ignore any pointing in the other direction. This is called *confirmation bias*. For example, I might take the fact that I saw a black cat and then tripped over a paving stone as evidence that seeing the cat was unlucky, ignoring the other occasions I'd seen a black cat and not tripped.

Although confirmation bias has become the subject of intensive study by psychologists and behavioral economists only recently, it's been known about for centuries. In his *Novum Organum* (*The New Organon*), Francis Bacon, who was a pioneer in laying down the principles of science, said:

> The human understanding when it has once adopted an opinion . . . draws all things else to support and agree with it. And though there be a greater number and weight of instances to be found on the other side, yet these it either neglects and despises, or else by some distinction sets aside and rejects . . . men, having a delight in such vanities, mark the events where they are fulfilled, but where they fail, though this happen much oftener, neglect and pass them by.[4]

Prophecies

Prophecies are attempts to foretell the future. They're based on the assumption that the universe is proceeding along a preordained path, and their aim is to remove doubt about the direction of that path. They also often convey hints of the divine or supernatural. Oracles typically serve as channels for prophecies or other predictions, although sometimes they are also sources of advice.

Many prophecies are based on explicit signs: patterns of tea leaves at the bottom of a cup, the fall of yarrow stalks for the I Ching, the specific cards that a seer turns over during a tarot reading, the appearance of a comet, strange cloud formations, the configuration of the stars when you were born, the birth of a deformed animal, and so on.

But even if the signs are there for everyone to see, prophecies aren't based on carefully evaluating the predictions arising from a body of evidence. This makes prophecies quite different from scientific predictions. Medical researchers, for instance, know that diabetics are likely to suffer from retinal neuropathy because of the accumulated evidence derived from studying patients over time. Weather forecasters know how accurate their predictions are because they've developed statistical measures called *scoring rules* to evaluate them. Our ability to predict when an eclipse will occur derives from the large amounts of data describing the motions of the sun, earth, and moon that have been collected. In contrast to all of these, there've been very few formal evaluations of how often the pattern of tea leaves in a cup allows a fortune teller to correctly predict an event. (I've seen none, but want to be fair, and it's possible I missed some.)

Although the aim of a prophecy is to remove uncertainty about the future, uncertainty in the form of randomness is frequently the mechanism used to generate prophecies. The random way in which tea leaves and yarrow stalks fall illustrates this. It's as if the randomness serves as a doorway to the powers divulging the "information." Théophile Gautier had a nice way of describing it. He said, "Chance is perhaps the pseudonym of God when he didn't want to sign [his own name]." The tea-leaves and yarrow-stalks examples also show that often a special type of knowledge is required to interpret the supernatural messages. Indeed, mystics, priests, clairvoyants, prophets, and oracles maintain their positions in societies in part thanks to their unique intermediary role as the only people able to understand the messages passed down from above. When the German priests of Tacitus's time made choices by randomly choosing bark strips inscribed with runes, and the Jews made important decisions by drawing lots, the random procedures apparently gave an opportunity for the will of the superior being to manifest itself. The Bible says, "The lot is cast into the lap, but its every decision is from the Lord." (Proverbs 16:33)

Prophecies are often couched in cryptic terms, making them ambiguous and permitting multiple interpretations of their meaning. This can make them difficult to refute. It's tough to argue with a prophet who can always say "Ah yes, but that was exactly what I meant," whatever the outcome. Sometimes a single "prediction" may even have two opposite interpretations.

This is nicely illustrated by the story of Croesus, King of Lydia from 560 to 546 BC, who is said to have consulted the oracle at Delphi to help him decide whether to attack Persia. The oracle told him that if he crossed the river a great empire would be destroyed. Croesus took this as a favorable message and duly attacked—only to have his own empire destroyed by the Persians.

The predictions of Michel de Nostredame, or Nostradamus, are examples of the ambiguity in prophecies. This sixteenth-century French apothecary, healer, and occultist published his many prophecies in a series of almanacs, calendars, and quatrains. Nostradamus's prophecies focus on epidemics, earthquakes, wars, floods, and so on, but as far as I'm aware none give unambiguous details of particular events before they occurred. Moreover, his predictions were for events far in the future—once again a good tactic, since you won't be proven wrong while you're still living. Especially revealing is the fact that the many fans of Nostradamus don't agree on exactly what outcomes he predicted: a clear win for ambiguity!

An abundance of predictions is also always a good strategy for would-be prophets, since by chance they should expect to get some right—and they can then stress those and conveniently forget the ones that were wrong.

Based on these properties of prophecies, if you were writing a manual on how to be a successful soothsayer, three fundamental principles would make a great start:

(i) use signs no one else can understand;
(ii) make all your predictions ambiguous;
(iii) make as many different predictions as you possibly can.

It's noteworthy that the opposites of the first two of these principles essentially define fundamental aspects of the scientific method:

(i) describe your measurement process clearly, so that others know exactly what you have done;
(ii) give clear descriptions of what your scientific hypothesis implies, so you can see when it's giving incorrect predictions.

Making a very large number of predictions, the third principle for soothsayers, is known as the "Jeane Dixon effect," after the clairvoyant Jeane Dixon, who wrote a successful syndicated astrology column in the mid-twentieth century. She was made famous by the 1965 publication of Ruth Montgomery's biography of her: *A Gift of Prophecy.* It says something about people's eagerness to believe in prophets and prophecies that this book sold millions of copies. Even world leaders of the time took note of her predictions: Richard Nixon prepared for terrorist attacks (which didn't happen) on the basis of them, and she personally advised Nancy and Ronald Reagan. And in fact she was not the only psychic to advise the Reagans. Donald Regan, President Reagan's chief of staff, says in his biography *For the Record: From Wall Street to Washington*, "Virtually every major move and decision the Reagans made during my time as White House Chief of Staff was cleared in advance with a woman in San Francisco who drew up horoscopes to make certain that the planets were in a favorable alignment for the enterprise."

Subject to reservations about ambiguity, Jeane Dixon did make *some* predictions that turned out to be correct—such as the one published in a 1956 issue of *Parade Magazine* that a Democrat would win the 1960 U.S. presidential election and then be assassinated or die in office. This sounds very impressive, but this success should be balanced against her even more dramatic predictions that someone from the Soviet Union would be the first to walk on the moon and that World War III would begin in 1958.

To give credibility to any kind of prediction, we really ought to require that a convincing explanation of the rationale behind it can be provided. This is true even if the prediction turns out to be right. After all, it's one thing for me to say "I correctly predicted that my toss of the dice would show two sixes," and quite another for me to say "I correctly predicted that the dice would show two sixes, because I know that all of the faces of the dice have sixes on them." I'm sure you'd be much more confident in my predictive ability if I told you that the dice were like this. (Included in my own large collection of dice, I have several that do in fact have sixes on all faces. I call them my beginner's dice: for people who want to practice throwing double sixes.)

As a general principle, if you can explain how you arrive at your predictions, assuming people agree that it's a reasonable explanation, they're more likely to believe in your predictive powers. For example, I might predict that older people are less likely to default on loan repayments. If I support my assertion by saying that it's because older people, on average, have more secure financial circumstances, you might agree it makes sense and thus be more inclined to believe my assertion. In fact it *is* true that age is a predictor of default risk—though whether this predictive power is actually because of having more secure financial circumstances is another matter.

There's another twist to some prophecies—these are so-called "self-fulfilling prophecies," where the very fact of predicting that something will happen causes it to happen. The term was coined by the eminent sociologist Robert K. Merton, who gave the example of an anxious student who, groundlessly convinced that he is destined to fail, spends more time worrying than studying and then, as a predictable consequence, ends up failing. Demonstrating that the idea was an important one, Merton also described national leaders who "become persuaded that war between them is inevitable. Actuated by this conviction, they become successively more alienated from one another, apprehensively countering each 'offensive' move of the other with a 'defensive' move of their own. Stockpiles of armaments, raw materials, and armed men and women grow ever larger, and in due course the anticipation of war helps create the actuality."[5]

Mass suicides of doomsday cult members provide yet another, all-too-real example of a self-fulfilling prophecy. Sometimes, convinced that the world is about to end, they kill themselves, so that, for them at least, the prophecy does come true. A bizarre twist on this occurred in Indonesia in September 1999: three cult leaders were beaten to death by disillusioned followers who had sold all their belongings in preparation for the predicted end of the world on 9/9/99: for the cult leaders, at least, the prediction did come true.[6]

Self-fulfilling prophecies are not all negative. Another is the opposite of Robert Merton's anxious student example: a teacher, believing that a student is exceptionally able, expects her to do well and so gives her more challenging work. And as a consequence of being stretched, the student does indeed do well.

Sometimes prophecies are based on the dreams of the seer, which of course no one else can witness. We all dream, and we know that dreams can seem very real indeed, but they've always been mysterious. Even nowadays psychologists are not completely clear what their function is. In the past they've been regarded as supernatural communications, often taking the form of visions of what will come, and some people still hold to this belief. You may well have had "precognitive" dreams yourself: dreaming of meeting an old friend you then see the next day, or dreaming of an aircraft crashing, only for this to happen soon afterward. Both Caligula and Abraham Lincoln dreamed they'd die, and they were indeed both later assassinated.

As with other modes of prophecy, dreams are typically not unambiguous and skill is needed to interpret them—or perhaps I should say, to make up interpretations for them. Priests and psychoanalysts have often taken on that task.

Gods and Miracles

I've mentioned gods in the context of superstitions and as the source of the information contained in prophecies. As purported superior beings who oversee, guide, and manipulate human affairs, they are by definition not limited by the constraints of nature: they're *super*-natural. At first glance, this sounds like a great way of explaining chance events. But a little thought shows that it is in fact a *useless* explanation; it's just too powerful, since it can explain everything. No event, no matter how bizarre, would fail to fall under its spell. Whatever happened, we would just say: "The gods made it so." If you saw me get out of bed, fly into the air, and become twenty duplicates of myself, you'd expect to have to do some tough explaining—but it's readily accounted for by the gods explanation: "They made it happen." It's clear that, to be useful, an explanation has to have some limitations, so that we can say, "That's surprising—I wonder if this explanation is right." Otherwise we're all wasting our time.

Over history, in many cultures we've seen a gradual shift from beliefs in pantheons of gods to beliefs in a single all-powerful God. This shift has entailed another, from a system in which gods could compete with each other (think of the problems Loki caused the other Norse gods) to one in which there was no competition. From a human perspective, the possibility of indeterminate, chance, and contingent events was lost with the rise of monotheism. It meant all events were predetermined. When there were many gods, people could attribute inexplicable events to one god disrupting the plans of another. But when there's only one God, who sees and controls everything, there seems to be no scope for chance and for luck. If we believe there's a single intelligence directing the universe, we ascribe events to chance only because we don't know their cause. Chance is then a matter of ignorance of fundamental cause rather than a fundamental cause in itself. This shift leads us to the notion of a deterministic universe, which is following the steps of a master plan, as set up by the one God.

Sometimes, however, the cause-and-effect chain appears to be broken. When this happens, some claim that a miracle has occurred. A miracle is an inexplicable event (normally a welcome one) attributed to a god: a supernatural event. Miracles are similar to transgressions of natural laws attributed to other causes, such as the occult or paranormal, with the key difference being their divine nature, and they're generally regarded as pretty rare events. After all, if they happened all the time, we'd see them as part of the normal background phenomena of the universe, and not worth talking about.

Progress in science leads to natural explanations for many things that were previously taken to be miracles. Take eclipses again. To someone who had no understanding of the natural forces underlying them, eclipses would be miraculous indeed: the world suddenly plunged into darkness in the middle of the day, for no apparent reason. But science long ago clarified the physics behind eclipses, as well as that behind more specific and well-known miracles, such as Moses's parting of the Red Sea. This was described by St. Thomas Aquinas in his *Summa contra Gentiles* as an example of the highest degree of miracle. But there are various natural explanations. Computer simulations have shown how a strong east wind blowing overnight could have pushed water back to reveal a land bridge, and an underwater earthquake causing a tsunami in which the waters first retreat, like the 2004 Indian Ocean earthquake, is another possibility.

The great philosopher David Hume had something relevant to say about miracles. He wrote that "no testimony is sufficient to establish a miracle, unless the testimony be of such a kind, that its falsehood would be more miraculous, than the fact which it endeavours to establish."[7] In other words, the evidence for a miracle is convincing only if alternative explanations are less probable—and these alternative explanations include fraud, mistakes, and so on. Hume went on to say:

"When any one tells me, that he saw a dead man restored to life, I immediately consider with myself, whether it be more probable, that this person should either deceive or be deceived, or that the fact, which he relates, should really have happened. I weigh the one miracle against the other; and according to the superiority, which I discover, I pronounce my decision, and always reject the greater miracle."

Hume balanced alternative explanations against an apparent miracle, choosing the explanation that seemed less surprising ("its falsehood would be more miraculous"). But even if we don't have an alternative explanation now, the strategy of "I cannot explain it, so it must be a miracle" is a shaky one—as anyone who has watched a skilled magician at work will agree. Magicians aside, many people would be hard-pressed to explain how televisions work, what goes on inside a nuclear power plant, why electricity doesn't leak from electric sockets, or why heavy aircraft don't fall from the sky, but they'd almost certainly agree that their inability to explain these phenomena doesn't mean they're miracles. We would probably think there are perfectly natural explanations that we just don't understand! The science fiction writer Arthur C.

Clarke expressed this rather nicely when he said, "Any sufficiently advanced technology is indistinguishable from magic."

The word "miracle" is also used in everyday conversation in another less formal sense. We speak of "miracle diet pills," "a miraculous escape," a "miraculous cure," and so on. Here we don't actually mean we think a miracle has occurred, merely that something highly improbable but within the bounds of reality has happened.

Parapsychology and the Paranormal

In contrast to those who believe in miracles, with a supernatural origin, people who believe in telepathy, precognition, psychokinesis, extrasensory perception (ESP), parapsychology, and psychic phenomena generally think that these have a basis in natural laws, even if the laws are not yet understood. Hence the approach to investigating such beliefs tends to be scientific, with experiments being conducted to detect and measure the phenomena. As we've seen, there's no point conducting experiments in the context of miracles, since, with a wave of a supernatural hand, a god could produce any result he or she wished. Unfortunately, the scientific consensus is that there's no convincing evidence in favor of paranormal abilities—a U.S. National Academy of Sciences report concluded, for instance, that there was "no scientific justification from research conducted over a period of 130 years for the existence of parapsychological phenomena."[8] One hundred thirty years! A testament to the power of hope over experience if ever there was one.

Many types of experiments have been used in psychic research, but only those that produce quantitative results are really susceptible to scientific evaluation. The experiments often take the form of asking volunteers to try to influence the fall of tossed coins or dice, or to attempt to alter the distribution of numbers generated from naturally random events such as radioactive decay, using only the power of their mind.

One of the main difficulties for psychic researchers is that the effects they're seeking are very small, if they exist at all. If the effects were large—if someone could influence tossed coins to come up heads almost every time, for example—their powers would be obvious. Instead the researchers find themselves trying to see if someone can make the tossed coin come up heads a little more than half the time—just enough so that chance can't account for it.

This means that the researchers have to use statistical methods to detect the effects, and also that the experiments are susceptible to other tiny influences. For example, imagine that you're investigating whether people can influence the outcome of a coin toss simply by concentrating on the outcome they want. We assume the coin is a fair one, so, if our volunteers can't influence the toss, the coin has equal probabilities of coming up heads or tails. This means that if they have no paranormal ability, then in any given number of tosses, we'd expect to see about equal proportions of heads and tails—not exactly equal, but large departures from equality would be rare.

Some straightforward probability calculations show that if we toss the fair coin 100 times, and a volunteer can't influence the outcome, the chance of getting 60 or more heads is 0.028. Or, to put it another way, if we repeated the exercise of 100 coin tosses many times, we'd expect just 2.8 percent of those repetitions to have 60 or more heads. Since this is such a small probability, if we tossed the coin 100 times and got 60 or more heads, we might wonder if our volunteer did indeed have some psychokinetic ability.

But now suppose a slight fault in the design of the experiment meant that the probability of the coin coming up heads on each toss was not 0.50, but was 0.52. This is just a tiny difference. Maybe the coin was slightly bent, for example. Now, if the coin has a probability of 0.52 of coming up heads on each toss, it's not difficult to show that the chance of getting 60 or more heads in 100 tosses is 0.066, or 6.6 percent. That's more than twice 2.8 percent. So the slight difference in probabilities on each toss, 0.52 instead of 0.50, has more than *doubled* the chance of observing an outcome which could make us suspect that our volunteer might have some psychokinetic ability.

Dice expert John Scarne challenged the famous parapsychologist J. B. Rhine's psychokinesis experiments, carried out at Duke University in the 1930s and '40s, on the basis that Rhine's dice were not "fair." In Rhine's experiments, volunteers were instructed to use the power of their minds to cause mechanically thrown dice to fall with particular faces showing. Rhine described the dice as of the "common commercial variety," but Scarne pointed out that these "store dice" were very different from the precisely made "perfect dice" used in casinos. Federal law requires casino dice to be engineered to an accuracy of ⅕,₀₀₀th of an inch, somewhat different from the dice used to play Monopoly. Scarne said, "Throws made with such [store] dice are bound to show deviations from what chance says can be expected—deviations which are not constant but which shift [as the dice become worn]. To use admittedly imperfect dice and then conclude that the deviations found must be due to a mysterious psychic PK factor which, if it is ever proved to exist, will upset the whole scientific applecart, is in my opinion scientific applesauce."[9]

A dice maker agreed with Scarne: "Once in a blue moon you might find a single store die that classes as a *perfect*, but the chance of finding two of them in a box of 60 and the chance that they would both be sold to the same purchaser as a pair is so small you can forget about it. It never happened." That last sentence brings us back to Borel's law—the idea that sufficiently unlikely events are impossible.

By clever experimental design, we could overcome some of these difficulties. In the case of the coin tosses, for example, we could repeat the experiment another 100 times, with the same coin, but now with our volunteer concentrating on producing tails rather than heads. If he managed to produce an unusually large number of tails, it couldn't be explained by the distorted coin, which had a tendency to produce more heads. However, there's no guarantee that we could control for every subtle distortion and bias. Toss a coin often enough and perhaps the edges begin to wear. Maybe our volunteer is a magician tricking us in some way (not unknown in such research, as we shall see). Perhaps the way we toss the coin leads to a tendency for it to rotate a fixed number of times. And so on. The disrupting influence might be small, but we've already seen that even tiny changes can have a substantial impact on the results.

Holger Bösch, Fiona Steinkamp, and Emil Boller reviewed 380 studies of attempts to psychically influence randomly generated sequences of 0's and 1's to favor one or the other.[10] Consistently with earlier analyses, they found slightly more results matching the value the volunteer was aiming for. Although the difference in proportions of 0's and 1's was only slight, the probability of obtaining such a difference purely by chance was very small. So it looked as if the effect was real: something was leading to an outcome favoring the volunteer's target. The question was whether the difference was caused by the participants' psychic powers, or by something else—analogous to the bent coin.

One possibility Bösch and his colleagues suggested was that it could be due to something called *publication bias*. This is the very real phenomenon that editors of scientific journals are more likely to publish experiments that report positive results than those that report negative results. In random-number-generator experiments of the kind outlined above, a positive result is one that shows a difference in the proportions of 0's and 1's in the direction the volunteer was aiming for, while a negative result is one where no such difference was found. Publication bias isn't due to dishonesty or malevolence on the part of journal editors, but is subconscious, probably arising from the fact that it's much more exciting to show that something, instead of nothing, has happened.

The fact that publication bias might explain the results doesn't *prove* that genuine psychic powers didn't play a role. But it is another way to account for the results. And then the onus is on those proposing the more unorthodox explanation to show why publication bias cannot account for the results—remember David Hume's comment that he accepted an explanation only if the alternative seemed less likely.

If all that isn't enough for you, then consider this, from Scarne again: "I would like to ask Dr. Rhine a few questions. He admits that, as in his ESP tests, when a subject's score is not above chance expectation or when it drops to that level, he eliminates that person on the ground that it is not worth experimenting with subjects who have no psychophysical abilities or who have lost interest . . ."[11] He's suggesting that Rhine dropped people whose results didn't match the theory, and kept only those whose did. If Rhine really did that, what do you think he would have concluded from his experiments? I can easily make it look as if I can always throw a six using this strategy: I just ignore the dice that didn't come up six. This bias and publication bias are each special cases of a more general phenomenon termed *selection bias*, in which the results shown are in fact merely a specially chosen subset of the complete set of results.

Bent coins, worn dice, selection bias—the history of research on parapsychology and psychic phenomena is littered with examples where small and typically subconscious distortions have crept in, casting doubt on the conclusions. It's also littered with cases of deception.

The Italian medium Eusapia Palladino, who conducted séances around the end of the nineteenth and the beginning of the twentieth century, appeared to be able to levitate both tables and her own body, play musical instruments without touching them, and communicate with the dead. Arthur Conan Doyle, creator of

Sherlock Holmes, was convinced by her "abilities." But close investigation by scientists revealed her to be a fake: she levitated small objects by tying them to long hairs, surreptitiously used her feet to manipulate objects in the darkness of the séance room, and so on. It may be relevant that she had married a conjuror when she was young.

More recently, Uri Geller became famous when millions of people watched him, on TV, bend spoons and restart stopped watches using what he claimed were psychic powers. But when investigators such as the magician James Randi showed that fairly basic tricks could be used to replicate his feats, Geller switched from calling himself a psychic to referring to himself as an "entertainer."

The triviality of all of these apparent abilities and manifestations will not have escaped your notice. Levitating tables, bending spoons, starting stopped watches! You might have thought that anyone with those powers could have used them for purposes more beneficial to humanity, so this very triviality must surely, in itself, arouse suspicion. Furthermore, people with psychokinetic abilities would surely be tempted to put their powers to personal gain in places like casinos—but the financial success of such establishments shows that the dice continue to fall with their expected frequencies.

It's not unknown in scientific investigations of psychic phenomena for the scientist carrying out the research to be committing fraud. The investigator Walter J. Levy, who succeeded Rhine at the Duke University parapsychology laboratory, as well as Rhine's assistant James D. MacFarland, were both accused of manipulating data.[12]

It can be tricky to detect deception in experiments. Scientists in general don't assume that nature is setting out to deceive them and so are unpracticed at recognizing when they're being tricked. Magicians, on the other hand, are experts at it, making them the perfect people to investigate claims of psychic ability. One of J. B.

Rhine's participants, Hubert Pearce, Jr., guessed correctly around 32 percent of the time in hundreds of card-guessing experiments, compared with a chance expectation of 20 percent. Except, that is, when a magician watched him guess the cards, at which point his performance fell to chance levels. This sort of impact has led some parapsychological investigators to suggest that psychic powers are influenced by the attitudes of those carrying out the experiments, and are thus less likely to manifest themselves if observed with a critical eye: if you don't believe, it won't happen. We might charitably characterize this explanation as grasping at straws.

Nonetheless, there do appear to be differences between believers and nonbelievers. Neuroscientists Peter Brugger and Kirsten Taylor found that believers in ESP and related phenomena judged coincidences in random sequences to be more meaningful than did nonbelievers.[13] They also behave differently. For example, if volunteers are asked to produce random sequences of digits, believers have a stronger tendency to avoid consecutive repeated values: real sequences of random digits quite often have identical pairs, triples, and so on, one after the other.

James Randi, who replicated Geller's supposedly psychic acts, is famous for exposing psychic frauds: a magician himself, he knows the tricks of the trade. He established the James Randi Educational Foundation (JREF) to investigate claims of the paranormal.[14] Here's a passage from the foundation's website:

> At JREF, we offer a one-million-dollar prize to anyone who can show, under proper observing conditions, evidence of any paranormal, supernatural, or occult power or event. The JREF does not involve itself in the testing procedure, other than helping to design the protocol and approving the conditions under which a test will take place. All tests are designed with the participation and approval of the applicant. In most cases, the applicant will be asked to

perform a relatively simple preliminary test of the claim, which if successful, will be followed by the formal test. Preliminary tests are usually conducted by associates of the JREF at the site where the applicant lives. Upon success in the preliminary testing process, the "applicant" becomes a "claimant."

To date, no one has passed the preliminary tests.

Synchronicity, Morphic Resonance, and More

Superstitions, prophecies, gods, miracles, psychic phenomena, and paranormal powers are just some of the explanations that have been put forward for improbable events like the ball dropping into your wineglass. There have been many other proposed explanations. The psychoanalyst Carl Jung felt that coincidences occurred more frequently than he could explain by chance, and this led him to develop a theory of "synchronicity," which he characterized as a "hypothetical factor equal in rank to causality as a principle of explanation." He argued that cause/effect relationships necessarily involved force or energy. Since ESP is unaffected by distance, which would attenuate physical force or cause energy transmission to take time, psychic phenomena therefore couldn't be explained in cause/effect terms.[15] As he wrote: "it cannot be a question of cause and effect, but of a falling together in time, a kind of simultaneity." As this idea fell outside the realm of familiar physics, he felt it required a new name, and chose the word "synchronicity." He continued: "I am therefore using the general concept of synchronicity in the special sense of a coincidence in time of two or more causally unrelated events which have the same or a similar meaning, in contrast to 'synchronism,' which simply means the simultaneous occurrence of two events."[16]

But Jung was a psychoanalyst, not a statistician. He wasn't

interested in quantifying phenomena, and certainly not in quantifying something as slippery as chance. Moreover, his examples of synchronicity and his justifications for it have more than a tinge of subjectivity about them. Here is an example. Jung says:

> The wife of one of my patients, a man in his fifties, once told me in conversation that, at the deaths of her mother and her grandmother, a number of birds gathered outside the windows of the death-chamber. I had heard similar stories from other people. When her husband's treatment was nearing its end, his neurosis having been cleared up, he developed some apparently quite innocuous symptoms which seemed to me, however, to be those of heart-disease. I sent him along to a specialist, who after examining him told me in writing that he could find no cause for anxiety. On the way back from this consultation (with the medical report in his pocket) my patient collapsed in the street. As he was brought home dying, his wife was already in a great state of anxiety because, soon after her husband had gone to the doctor, a whole flock of birds alighted on their house. She naturally remembered the similar incidents that had happened at the death of her own relatives, and feared the worst.[17]

But let's step back a bit. Perhaps the birds gathered outside the windows because the "death-chamber" was warm, and birds tend to congregate in warm places. Moreover, we have no way of assessing how often such swarms of birds settled on roofs, and on that roof in particular.

Jung then went on to make the whole story even more outlandish: "the death and the flock of birds seem to be incommensurable with one another. If one considers, however, that in the Babylonian Hades the souls wore a 'feather dress,' and that in ancient Egypt the *ba*, or soul, was thought of as a bird, it is not too far-fetched to suppose that there may be some archetypal symbolism at work." Not too far-fetched? Perhaps—but it's easy to suppose that you could find similar approximately matching characteristics for any type of sign or omen you care to imagine, from some ancient religion.

Given the intriguing nature of coincidences, perhaps it's not surprising that Jung felt the need to invent an explanation beyond the laws of physics. Many others have felt the same urge. The Austrian biologist Paul Kammerer came up with something he called *the law of seriality*, and described it in a book, *Das Gesetz der Serie*.[18] Kammerer collected and collated hundreds of apparent coincidences, classifying them into various types. Then he developed a theory, based on three principles, that he claimed explained these coincidences. The first principle he called *persistence*, representing something analogous to physical inertia. It increases the longer things go on, and when a system fragments, the pieces retain its stamp. If and when two parts encounter each other in the future, it seems to an outside observer that an unexplained coincidence occurs. The second principle, *imitation*, described how systems achieved equilibrium or sympathetic resonance. And the third principle, *attraction*, described the tendency for like to converge with like.

There are some similarities between Kammerer's ideas and those of the biologist Rupert Sheldrake, who has more recently developed a theory he calls *morphic resonance*.[19] According to Sheldrake, if an event happens in one place it's more likely that similar events will happen in other places, for (he claims) there exists a natural field, a *morphic field*, which organizes events and structures. Examples he gives include birds in different locations learning at the same time how to peck open the silver tops of milk bottles, even though they were geographically dispersed and couldn't have learned by mimicking each other, and rats in the UK learning how to run a maze with greater ease once rats in America had mastered the same trick.

Ideas such as synchronicity, seriality, and morphic resonance are inventions designed to explain surprising phenomena. They are attempts to overcome apparent ignorance in our understanding of cause and effect. This perspective, that we lack some core idea or critical information, is also what underlies pre-twentieth-century ideas of science.

A Clockwork Universe

Between the seventeenth century and the start of the twentieth, scientists made immense strides in understanding how nature works. They established all sorts of laws describing planets flying through space, the flow of electrical charges and currents, the expansion and contraction of gases, the colors of the rainbow, and a host of other physical phenomena. From this understanding came not only the power to predict, but also the development of new technologies which allowed us to manipulate nature.

These scientific laws were deterministic laws, mathematical equations in fact, that told us how natural objects would behave. If we knew the state of a physical system to start with, then Newton's laws, the gas laws, Maxwell's equations, and so on, told us how it would evolve over time, and what would happen to the system later on. There was nothing in the universe that was uncertain or unpredictable, at least in principle, according to science. And the huge success of the technologies built on those ideas showed they were largely correct.

The great mathematician Pierre Simon Laplace described the basic assumption underlying that view of nature's laws. He wrote: "An intelligence which, at a given instant, would know all the forces by which Nature is animated, and the respective situation of all the elements of which it is composed, if furthermore it were vast enough to submit all these data to analysis, would in the same formula encompass the motions of the largest bodies of the universe, and those of the most minute atom: nothing for it would be uncertain, and the future as well as the past would be present to its eyes."[20]

This view of nature is sometimes called the *clockwork universe*, since it describes a universe ticking along a well-defined path. Anything you couldn't predict—lightning, for example—was not unpredictable in principle. You were unable to predict it merely because of your ignorance, either about the conditions surrounding it or about how the process developed. And this ignorance would be gradually eroded as science advanced.

But then small gaps began to appear in this view. And gradually over the twentieth century these gaps grew into chasms. It seemed as if the universe was not deterministic after all, but that randomness and chance lay at its very foundations.

Randomness, chance, and probability also underlie coincidences such as the extraordinarily unlikely events I described in chapter 1. Although they look remarkable and entirely unpredictable, in fact these events are to be expected. No mysteries are required to explain them—no superstitions, no miracles, no gods, no supernatural interventions or psychic powers, no synchronicity, seriality, morphic resonance, or any of the host of other imaginary imps. All that's needed are the basic laws of probability.

In the next chapter we look at these basic laws, which form the foundations for the Improbability Principle.

3

WHAT IS CHANCE?

All life is chance.   —Dale Carnegie

In 1986 Bill Shaw survived a train crash in Lockington in East Yorkshire, England, that killed nine people. Although train crashes attract a lot of media attention, fortunately they're quite rare: in 2001 there were about 0.1 fatalities per billion passenger miles in the UK, meaning that rail travel is an exceptionally safe mode of transport. Since train crashes are so rare, the chance of a husband and wife *both* being involved in different train crashes must be incredibly small. And yet this is just what happened to the Shaws: fifteen years after her husband, at Great Heck near Selby, Bill's wife Ginny also survived a deadly train crash. This one killed ten people. Both accidents were caused by vehicles on the tracks. "I couldn't believe what she was telling me," said Bill, thinking back to when he was woken by the 7:00 a.m. phone call from his wife. "It looks like someone wanted her to experience what we had been through . . . Uncannily, then it turned out to have been caused by a van straddling the lines. This is exactly the same situation in which Ginny found herself. It's got to be a freak coincidence, it's just totally unbelievable . . . It seems for some very odd reason the family have all been in the wrong place at the wrong time."

Anyone experiencing such an unfortunate coincidence as the Shaws did would naturally seek an explanation, some linking factor. Is there something about this coincidence, or coincidences in general, that helps us understand why it happened?

There are various definitions of the word "coincidence." The statisticians Persi Diaconis and Fred Mosteller defined a coincidence as "a surprising concurrence of events, perceived as meaningfully related, with no apparent causal connection."[1] My *Concise Oxford Dictionary* defines it as "a remarkable concurrence of events or circumstances without apparent causal connection." The *Wikipedia* definition is more elaborate: "a collection of two or more events or conditions, closely related by time, space, form, or other associations which appear unlikely to bear a relationship as either cause to effect or effects of a shared cause, within the observer or observers' understanding of what cause can produce what effects."

The first definition includes the fact that there must be an element of surprise. Even if, just as I reach the end of a chapter in the book I'm reading, it starts to rain, I'm not going to sit up and say, "Wow, what a coincidence." And there must be more than one event involved: while a single unusual event is one thing, two or more occurring close together is something else. If the leg of my chair breaks just as a peal of thunder rings out, I might wonder if it was simply chance. Many people noted the coincidence in 2013 when, only hours after Pope Benedict XVI announced that he would be resigning, St. Peter's Basilica in Rome was struck by lightning.

The definition also says that the events must be seen as meaningfully related, despite having no obvious causal connection. Two entirely disconnected events, even surprising ones, which had no apparent link at all would not arouse comment. You'd probably not see as related the fact that a roulette ball fell on number 7 at 9:00 p.m. in a casino, and you broke the heel of your shoe as you stepped out of a taxi on the way home from work three days later. Why should they be? An infinite number of events happen all around us all the time—life is just a series of events—so for a coincidence, something has to single out these particular events and link them in a meaningful way. The link could just be one of time—my chair leg and the peal of thunder—but it mustn't be an obvious causal one: if you stamped your foot at the casino when the 7 came up, and broke your heel, you'd hardly regard it as a coincidence; simple causality explains it. On September 11, 2001, the National Reconnaissance Office was planning a simulation in which a malfunctioning private jet would crash into the agency's headquarters in Chantilly, Virginia, about four miles from Washington's Dulles International Airport. At 8:10 a.m. on that day, about an hour before the simulation was scheduled to start, American Airlines Flight 77 took off from Dulles. An hour and a half later its hijackers flew it into the Pentagon. The reality and the simulation just look too similar for there to be no meaningful relationship, and yet there is no causal connection between them.[2]

We've already seen that countless explanations have been advanced for surprising co-occurrences of events. Many of these cite powers and causes outside the familiar natural world; in a word, they're *super*natural. The Improbability Principle provides an alternative explanation, one based on science rather than the supernatural. It all hinges on what we mean by "probable."

What Does It All Mean?

The concept of probability has had a long, troublesome, even controversial history. As recently as 1954, Leonard Jimmie Savage, one of the founders of a leading school of statistics, said: "As to what probability is . . . there has seldom been such complete disagreement and breakdown of communication since the Tower of Babel."[3] Fortunately there has been some improvement since then, and scientists and statisticians now recognize that there are different kinds of probability, although since everyone still uses that word, there remains plenty of room for confusion. Technical discussions often put adjectival qualifiers in front of the term ("aleatory probability," "subjective probability," "logical probability," and so on) to identify more precisely how they are using it. I'll say something about these different kinds later.

The long history of the word "probability," as well as its importance and the confusion that still surrounds it, are reflected by the fact that there are many other words for very closely related concepts. These include *odds, uncertainty, randomness, chance, luck, fortune, fate, fluke, risk, hazard, likelihood, unpredictability, propensity,* and *surprise,* among others. There are also other concepts that touch on similar ideas, such as *doubt, credibility, confidence, plausibility,* and *possibility,* and also *ignorance* and *chaos.*

The word "probable" derives from the same Latin root as "approve," "provable," and "approbation" (from the word *probare,* meaning test or prove), and early uses have these sorts of meanings. This explains how Edward Gibbon, in his *Decline and Fall of the Roman Empire,* could say, "According to Rufinus, an immediate supply of provisions was stipulated by the treaty, and Theodoret affirms that the obligation was faithfully discharged by the Persians. *Such a fact is probable, but undoubtedly false.*"[4] This example also shows how the meaning of the word has changed since Gibbon's time: nowadays "probable" would mean likely, and so quite the opposite of "undoubtedly false."

The 1662 book *La logique, ou l'art de penser*[5] (often called just *Logic* or *Port-Royal Logic,* after the Jansenist convent of Port-Royal) by Antoine Arnauld and Pierre Nicole included a criticism of the principle of "probabilism." This referred to how issues should be decided by appealing to authorities. The book also included one of the first usages of the word "probability" in a more modern sense. In this single book, we can see the transition from medieval notions of truth derived from authority to scientific notions of truth derived from evidence.

I might define the probability of an event as "the extent to which that event is likely to happen." Or, alternatively, as "the strength of belief that the event is likely to happen." These capture notions of uncertainty, and convey the meaning that a highly probable event is likely to happen and an improbable event is unlikely to happen. And since they contain the words "extent" and "strength," they suggest that probability can be measured, or at least expressed in numerical terms. But these definitions are rather deceptive because they don't actually tell us anything: I could have added "likely" to my list of informal synonyms for "probable," so that these definitions would be circular. Somehow we need to dig deeper.

Whenever we express something in numerical terms, we have some freedom about how we do it (I could give my height in inches, or in centimeters). To remove any such ambiguity in probability, scientists define it as taking values lying in the range 0 to 1. The value 0 corresponds to impossible events: nothing can be less likely than impossible, so probability values smaller than 0 cannot occur. Likewise, the value 1 corresponds to certain events: nothing is more probable than certainty, so probability values greater than 1 cannot occur. Now, certain events are all very well, but they're not really that interesting: all you can do is prepare for them! The same for impossible events: all you can do is prepare for the world where the event will not happen. It's events with an element of *uncertainty* which are much more interesting (at least for our purposes in this book): they might happen, they might not, and we can't be sure. Events which might or might not happen have a numerical probability value somewhere *between* 0 and 1. The smaller this number is, the less probable the event. The nearer to 1 the numerical probability is, the more likely the event is to happen. In this book we're concerned with highly improbable events, those with a probability value very near 0, but not quite 0. Such highly improbable events hover at the boundary of the impossible and the possible. They're the *really* interesting ones.

Another way of expressing the numerical values of probabilities is using "odds." This is a term that is widely used in gambling, sports, and finance. Odds are merely a different way of presenting probabilities. There are, in fact, several ways of defining odds. The simplest way is as a *ratio* of probabilities. The odds that I will miss my train are the probability that I *will* miss my train divided by the probability that I *won't* miss it. The odds that you will hit a home run are the probability that you *will* divided by the probability that you *won't*. If an event is impossible (probability 0), then the odds favoring it are also 0. If an event is certain (probability 1), then the odds favoring it are infinite (since it's 1 divided by 0). If you can express something in terms of odds, you can express it in terms of probabilities. Scientists tend to use probabilities rather than odds, although odds are common in some medical contexts.

"Chance" is another word that people often use in place of "probability." Technically the "chance" of an event means the same as the "probability" of that event, but chance is often used as a less formal alternative, and is seldom associated with a numerical value. We talk of the chance of it raining, and so on.

"Luck" is probability overlaid with notions of good or bad outcomes. We speak of being unlucky if an adverse event we think improbable happens: being involved in a car crash; being caught in the one rain shower in an otherwise dry day; being struck by lightning. We wouldn't say that someone was unlucky if they were hit by a car when dashing across a twelve-lane highway in full flow. But we might well say so if they were hit by a car in a sleepy village. We speak of being lucky if an event we perceive as improbable happens and brings us good fortune. And "fortune" itself is another closely related word. Someone might have the good fortune to win a prize, or be unfortunate enough to be in the wrong place at the wrong time. All of this is closely tied in with "fate." This has overtones of being manipulated by powers beyond our control. We are back to some of the notions described in chapter 2.

"Risk," like luck, mixes up the chance that an event will happen with the value or utility of the outcome. But risk is restricted to adverse outcomes. Examples are the risk of being hit by a car, or the risk of getting food poisoning. We don't generally talk of the risk of passing an exam or the risk of winning the lottery.

Randomness is another closely related concept. Confusingly, it has slightly different but overlapping meanings in different fields. In statistics, a sequence of numbers is random if it's not possible to predict successive values. In algorithmic information theory, on the other hand, a sequence of numbers is random if it cannot be described in a shorter way. For example, a sequence consisting entirely of the same value, 33333333333333333333, would be highly nonrandom because it's easy to describe very briefly (twenty 3's), whereas a sequence like 37686332408651378654 is not easy to summarize.

I should also mention *chaos* here because of its connection to randomness. We can predict a sequence of numbers generated by a chaotic system if we have complete knowledge about the starting value and how it evolves over time. Unfortunately, however, we never have *complete* knowledge about the starting value—accurate to an infinite number of decimal places. Edward Lorenz, one of the founders of chaos theory, summarized this very elegantly: "Chaos: when the present determines the future, but the approximate present does not approximately determine the future."[6] Unfortunately, we always have only approximate knowledge about the present. I'll return to this at the end of the chapter.

Perhaps it's not chance (!) that we have so many words describing probability and its related concepts. The uncertain and unpredictable are central to the mystery of human existence and to our attempts to understand the universe. They're closely tied in with notions of predestination and free will: by definition a chance outcome can't be predetermined. Randomness and predictability are mutually exclusive: if you have one, you don't have the other. And, as with other fundamental concepts which are central to human understanding, probability and its related concepts are often anthropomorphized. We speak of "lady luck," "dame fortune," and of "tempting fate."

Where Does Chance Come From?

We've already seen how certain paraphernalia—such as tea leaves and yarrow stalks—have been used to produce chance outcomes for purposes of prophecy and fortune telling. Artifacts have also been used for generating chance outcomes in games. Modern examples include dice, roulette wheels, and lottery machines. Lottery machines can be quite elaborate and come in various forms, such as spinning drums containing numbered balls which emerge one at a time, or vertical cylinders with balls blown into the air by fans, to emerge one by one from a hole at the top. Typically the drums or cylinders are transparent to add to the excitement and anticipation. The history of randomizing devices—whether for divination or for gambling—goes back thousands of years.

One of the earliest known randomizing devices was the *astragalus* or *talus*—the knuckle bone or heel bone of a running animal. Illustrations on ancient Egyptian tombs make it very clear that these were employed in games of chance, as forms of dice. However, there are very few early records of tabulations of the frequencies with which the different faces came up. This is critical, since such a tabulation is the key to quantifying probability—to putting numbers on the chance that one or other face will show. There is an isolated medieval poem, *De Vetula* (dated between 1220 and 1250), which gives a tabulation for three dice, but it wasn't until the 1600s that the ideas became more widespread. Galileo examined the falls of triples of dice in about 1620, and then, in the middle of the seventeenth century, understanding suddenly blossomed.

While chance events can't be predicted, the idea that they might have some sort of higher level of regularity requires a remarkable leap of intellect. It's a major conceptual advance to recognize that, while it's *completely unknown* which of heads or tails will come up on any individual toss of a coin, about 500 out of 1,000 tosses will nonetheless show heads. It's on a par with the intellectual leap which led to the concept of gravity as a universal force acting between objects.

The size of the giant intellectual advance is demonstrated by the difficulty many people have, even nowadays, in understanding some of the properties of chance events. For example, knowing that the tossed (fair!) coin is expected to come up heads about half the time, and observing a preponderance of heads among the first ten tosses, many people expect to see this counterbalanced by a preponderance of tails in later tosses. But that's not what happens. This misunderstanding is so widespread it has a name: *the gambler's fallacy*.

What actually happens is that because later tosses are also expected to have about equal numbers of heads and tails, the initial preponderance gradually becomes less pronounced, so that the overall proportion of heads gets closer to a half. For example, if the first ten tosses happened to have eight heads, a proportion of 0.8, the next ten should not be expected to have just two, to balance things out. Rather, the next ten should be expected to have about five heads, just like any set of ten tosses. It might be more than five, it might be less than five, but the most common outcome would be somewhere near five, and the more extreme the deviation the less likely it would be. In these twenty tosses, we should expect to have about $8 + 5 = 13$ heads. Thirteen out of twenty is 0.65, which is nearer to the expected proportion of 0.5 than was the 0.8 observed in the initial ten tosses. The initial preponderance of heads is not *compensated for* by an extra number of tails in the next ten tosses, but is *diluted away* as the total number of coin tosses increases.

If you think this is counterintuitive, and find the gambler's fallacy appealing, you're in good company. Probability is renowned for its counterintuitive nature, more than any other area of mathematics. Even the most eminent mathematicians have been tripped up by it. For us here, however, what's important is the step from the unpredictability of individual events to the predictability of aggregates of events. Bookmakers may not be able to tell you which horse will win. But on average, over time, they get more right than wrong. (Which is why they say you never see a bookmaker riding a bicycle.)

It's likely that the notion of trying to quantify chance was literally inconceivable much before the seventeenth century because chance occurrences were seen as intrinsically unpredictable. If a cubic die could fall showing any of its six faces, you couldn't tell which would show, and that was the end of the story. This notion is reinforced by the fact that early randomization devices such as tali or Roman dice may not have been very consistent: different dice would have had slightly different probabilities of showing a 6, for example.[7]

It's notable that the idea that chance could be quantified arose at the same time as the view that the universe was intrinsically deterministic. This all happened when men such as Isaac Newton, Robert Hooke, Robert Boyle, Gottfried Leibniz, and Christiaan Huygens laid the foundations of science. Earlier, I described their view as that of a clockwork universe, something which was ticking through its preordained path, following well-defined physical laws of cause and effect. The trouble is that the existence of randomness on the one hand, and a deterministic view of the universe on the other, appear to be incompatible, the first being the antithesis of the second. Or perhaps it's better to describe them as complementary, with progress in deterministic science gradually eroding the uncertainty arising from ignorance. From this perspective, perhaps it's not surprising that advances in understanding one should be matched by advances in understanding the other. Moreover, the mind-set associated with teasing apart physical laws would have encouraged a similarly quantitative approach to understanding chance events. And once the attempt to understand natural physical laws was no longer regarded as blasphemous, it would also no longer be blasphemous to see through chance events to predict likely outcomes, even if they were regarded as representing the hand of a divinity.

The period just after the middle of the seventeenth century represents a turning point in the understanding of probability. It was around this time that the earliest books on the subject appeared, often motivated by gambling. *De Ratiociniis in Ludo Aleae (On Reasoning in Games of Chance)* by Christiaan Huygens was published in 1657. And *Liber de Ludo Aleae (The Book on Games of Chance)* by Girolamo Cardano was published in 1663 (but was written around 1563 or earlier). In addition to their work on probability, Huygens is well-known for his contributions to astronomy and physics (he's sometimes called "the Dutch Newton"), and Cardano was responsible for important advances in algebra, hydrodynamics, mechanics, and geology, illustrating that the development of deterministic theories and the understanding of chance advanced hand in hand. In 1671, the Dutch statesman and mathematician Johan De Witt published *Waardije van Lyf-renten naer Proportie van Los-renten (The Worth of Life Annuities Compared to Redemption Bonds)*, which described how to calculate the value of an annuity. This is the payment of a lump sum in exchange for which the purchaser receives a regular income until death. The calculation hinges on the probability of death in each year.

An important episode in the history of the understanding of chance, known as *the problem of points*, relates to how the stakes of a game should be divided when the game is terminated prematurely. It was finally solved during an exchange of letters between Pierre de Fermat and Blaise Pascal in 1654, but there are Italian documents describing the problem dating from as far back as 1380,[8] and it crops up again in 1494, in a book written by Luca Pacioli;[9] in the 1500s (Girolamo Cardano, again); and in 1558 (Giovanni Peverone).[10] The correspondence between Fermat and

Pascal was stimulated by the Chevalier de Méré, a courtier to Louis XIV and an educated man (though popular accounts often dismiss him simply as "a gambler"), who outlined the problem to Pascal. In the game, the number of points each player has won when the game is prematurely stopped is known, as is the total number of points needed to win the game outright. The question is then, what's the probability that each of the players would have won the game? If we can determine this we can divide the total stake in proportion to this probability, so that a fair settlement is reached even though the game is unfinished. If each player has an equal probability of winning each point, we can work out the probability that each player would have acquired enough extra points to win the game before the other did, if it had continued. This is their probability of winning.

If you're prepared to assume that basic outcomes have equal probability (for example, that a coin has an equal probability of showing heads and tails, or that each of the six faces of a die has a probability of one-sixth of showing), then it's not difficult to calculate more elaborate probabilities (for example, that three coins will all show a head, or that two dice will each show a 6). But calculating probabilities in other cases, where you might not be willing to assume equiprobable elementary outcomes, or indeed even work out what the "elementary outcomes" are, is much more difficult. For example, how would you apply the notion of equiprobable outcomes to the chance that you would slip and fall as you left your house tomorrow? The Port-Royal *Logic* contains some of the first descriptions of the numerical measurement of probability in such less-straightforward situations.

A mighty tree began to grow from the seeds of understanding of chance and probability which germinated in the seventeenth century. Jacob Bernoulli's *Ars Conjectandi* (*The Art of Conjecturing*) was published in 1713, Abraham de Moivre published *The Doctrine of Chances* in 1718, and the world never looked back.

But games of chance were not the only driver. The great

mathematician Leibniz proposed applying numerical probabilities to legal problems, also in the seventeenth century. This seems perfectly reasonable: after all, court decisions hinge on phrases such as "beyond reasonable doubt" and "the balance of probabilities." Unfortunately, the legal world illustrates that the revolution in understanding probability which began in the seventeenth century has not yet fully played out. Even today, formal methods of probability calculation are being adopted only slowly by the courts of law. The attitude in the not-too-distant past is conveyed by the comment made by the eminent British lawyer Sir David Napley in a discussion between statisticians and lawyers: "large parts of the things that have been said here have been absolute gobbledegook to me. I could not make head nor tail of most of it. Bear in mind, too, that the average lawyer cannot even work out figures with a computer. We are dealing in a field which we simply do not understand."[11] I don't know about you, but that hardly fills me with confidence! (Incidentally, my understanding is that U.S. courts are more advanced in this respect than are UK courts.)

We've seen how considerations of the role of chance in gambling and in the law helped thinkers to formalize the concepts of probability, but there were also many other influences.

Blaise Pascal, whom I mentioned earlier, is also famous for *Pascal's wager*, concerning the existence of God. He argued in his *Pensées*, published posthumously in 1670, that because eternal happiness is of infinite value, the rational choice is to pursue a religious life. This follows because, even if there's only a very small probability that leading a religious life will yield eternal happiness, a tiny probability multiplied by an infinite outcome is infinite. He wrote: "If there is a God, He is infinitely incomprehensible, since, having neither parts nor limits, He has no affinity to us. We are then incapable of knowing either what He is or if He is . . . you must wager. It's not optional. You are embarked. Which will you choose then? . . . Let us weigh the gain and the loss in wagering that God is. Let us estimate these two chances. If you gain, you gain all; if you lose, you lose nothing. Wager, then, without hesitation that He is." Pascal's wager has been discussed by philosophers ever since. The strategy for combining the probabilities and the consequences of different outcomes by multiplying them together is what now underlies modern *decision theory*, a mathematical approach to making optimal choices.

Yet another stimulus for understanding chance and probability came from the urgent need to understand the commercial world around us. Increasing global trade in the seventeenth, eighteenth, and nineteenth centuries forced nations and private companies to devise ways of coping with shipwrecks and other unforeseen disasters. Insurance could cover such incidents, but only if there was some way of quantifying how likely such unfortunate events were. One way of doing this is to look back at a large number of previous voyages and see what proportion ended in disaster. Understanding that there's some kind of consistency underlying such events, like the consistency of the proportion of heads in a large number of coin tosses, means we can estimate what proportion of all the ships' voyages made over the next year will end safely at their destination. Such ideas laid the foundations for actuarial calculations. Although notions of insurance and annuities had been developed prior to a formal understanding of the mathematics of chance—they go as far back as the Romans—the setting of rates was previously more of an art than a science.

Two centuries after the initial blossoming of understanding, Adolphe Quetelet, a Belgian statistician who inspired the founding of what became the British Royal Statistical Society, laid the foundations for modern social statistics by applying actuarial notions to a wider range of human activities. The same basic principles as above apply: while it's impossible to predict how any one individual will behave, look at enough people and patterns begin to emerge.

Figure 3.1 comes from the data on page 80 of Quetelet's book

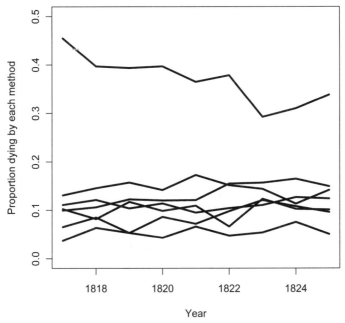

Figure 3.1. Methods of suicide, by year, for the Seine region of France.[12]

A Treatise on Man, and the Development of His Faculties, originally published in French in 1835, and in English translation in 1842. It shows, for all the suicides each year from 1817 to 1825 in the Seine Department of France, the proportion that occurred by various methods (or, as Quetelet put it, "modes of destruction")—in his terms, "submersion, fire-arms, asphyxia, voluntary falls, strangulation, cutting instruments, poisoning." The top line, for example, is for "submersion."

Now, potential suicides do not think, "Ah, the number of submersions is down this year, so I think I'll drown myself." Rather, each person's decision is independent of the others. And yet the lines in the figure are remarkably constant. The proportion of suicides by poison fluctuates between about 4 percent and 8 percent. It doesn't leap from 4 percent to 40 percent. So although we can't say what method any given person will choose, we can say roughly what the probability is that they'll choose any particular method.

From its original role in ancient games of chance through its applications in law, commerce, and elsewhere, our understanding of probability has grown. But be warned! Chance is a slippery concept. It can wriggle and twist even when we think we have a sound grasp of it. Now, let's examine some of these twists and turns.

Probability Does Not Exist

If we're going to use the ideas of probability to shed light on the world, then we need to be pretty clear about what we're talking about. Unfortunately, as I pointed out earlier, there are different kinds of probability. I gave a couple of informal definitions: "the extent to which an event is likely to happen" and "the strength of belief that an event is likely to happen." Although these are clearly rather different, the curious fact is that they can be represented by the same mathematics. I'll say more about that later, but to give you an idea, recall that probabilities are numbers lying in the range from 0 to 1, with 0 meaning impossible and 1 meaning certain. This holds for both of the informal definitions. A deeper example of the common mathematics is that if we have two events which cannot occur together, like a die showing a 2 or a 3 on a particular toss, then the probability that one or the other of these events will occur is just the sum of the two probabilities of the separate events (in this case $\frac{1}{6} + \frac{1}{6} = \frac{1}{3}$). This is called the *rule of addition* for probabilities, and it's true whichever of the two definitions above we adopt.

The mathematics used to represent the definitions can be written down very concisely, and scientists and statisticians can then use it for calculations: to work out the probability that two events will occur together, or that one will occur if another occurs, and so on. By far the most widely used way of summarizing the mathematics is the one described by the Russian mathematician Andrei Kolmogorov in his classic *Foundations of the Theory of Probability*, originally published in German in 1933. In fact, it's been shown that if we are to be *coherent* (so that, for example, we can't end up with probabilities greater than 1), then we *must* use mathematics like Kolmogorov's. In practical terms for us, what this means is that the consequences that constitute the Improbability Principle follow regardless of our philosophical perspective on what probability means.

I won't go into the details of Kolmogorov's so-called *axiomatization* of probability, but in the next section I'll look at some of the most basic and important rules which follow from it. First, let's go beyond the informal definitions of probability I gave above: they're not the only ways of thinking about what probability actually *means*. Different definitions each capture some aspect of the essence of probability, but none of them seems to capture it in its entirety. This is analogous to needing multiple views of an object to understand it properly. I need to look at *both* sides of a 1971 silver dollar to know that it has an image of Eisenhower on one side and the insignia of the Apollo 11 moon landing on the other. At a more exalted level, physicists simultaneously hold particle and wave interpretations of photons in order to explain the behavior of these objects under different circumstances.

The three most widely used interpretations of probability are the *frequentist, subjective*, and *classical* interpretations—though there are others, some of which I describe at the end of this section. The various interpretations have a tangled history, which I won't attempt to disentangle here, except to say that the distinctions between them have gradually been clarified over time: the differences were not always immediately apparent. Indeed, that there *were* differences often required considerable thought.

The frequentist interpretation of probability is based on the tendency of physical systems to produce roughly constant relative frequencies when situations are repeated. This is something we've already encountered—the tendency for a coin to come up heads about half the time it's tossed, or the 4 (or any other) face to show on a die about one-sixth of the time. The formal frequentist definition of the probability of an event is the proportion of times that the event would happen in an infinitely long series of repetitions (or "trials") of the same situation. So, according to this definition, the probability that the coin will come up heads is the proportion of times it comes up heads in an infinite series of tosses.

Now you'll immediately see some practical difficulties with this definition. Infinitely long series of repetitions? Apart from the fact that the coin would wear to a sliver and then to nothing after a long enough finite time (think of all those worn stone floors in cathedrals), we'd never actually reach the end of such a series. And repetitions of the same situation? No two situations are *exactly* the same. As the Greek philosopher Heraclitus said: "You can't step in the same river twice."

But if we think of the frequentist definition of probability as an ideal, much like the points and lines of school geometry I mentioned in chapter 1, then it makes sense: we can't produce an infinite series, but we can produce as long a series as we wish. This means that we can determine the probability as accurately as we like by taking a long enough (albeit finite) series. True, we can't guarantee to measure the probability with complete accuracy, since our series is necessarily only finite, but it's also true that we can't measure anything else *perfectly*. I can measure the length of my desk to within one centimeter, or one millimeter, or one millionth of a millimeter (though that would take some effort), but not to an infinite number of decimal places. So perhaps the fact that we don't know the probability of my coin coming up heads with complete accuracy isn't really a problem.

One thing that is clear is that the frequentist interpretation is a property of the external world—of the coin and die in these examples. It's like the length or mass of an object. Subjective probability is very different. Instead of representing an aspect of the external world, subjective probability is the confidence an individual has that an event will occur. When flipping a coin, you might believe it equally likely it will come up heads or tails—your probability of a head would be one-half. If you subsequently learned more about this particular coin or the person tossing it (that, for example, it was tossed by a magician who carries a double-headed coin), you might want to adjust your degree of belief, *your* probability. Instead of being a property of the external world, the subjective view has it that probability is an internal property of your mind. Each person will have their own subjective probability for each event. It's for this reason that Bruno de Finetti began his seminal *Theory of Probability* with the statement "Probability does not exist."[13] He meant it wasn't a property of the external world, but was rather a property of how we think about the world.

You might think it would be difficult to measure a subjective probability, but various schemes have been devised for doing so. For example, you can ask people to bet on an outcome. If they thought the coin was fair, so that their subjective probability for the coin coming up heads was one-half, they'd be prepared to bet equally on either outcome. But if they thought it was double-headed, they'd put much more money on heads.

The words "aleatory" and "epistemological" are also used to describe the frequentist and subjective interpretations of probability, respectively. "Aleatory" literally means "depending on the throw of a die" and "epistemological" means based on knowledge: the belief that events will occur. The fact that we're really dealing with two rather distinct kinds of ideas here is very apparent in statements like, "The probability that the next president will be a woman is 0.9." There is no notion of repeated trials here, some proportion of which result in a woman being elected, but merely of degree of certainty or confidence.

The epistemological interpretation of probability as a "degree of belief" is also interesting because it essentially treats chance as a measure of ignorance. So epistemological probability fits in well with the heavily monotheistic religious context in which the foundations of probability were laid in the mid-seventeenth century, where a chance event was regarded merely as one for which we didn't understand how God caused it to happen. However, as we'll see, modern thought has it that uncertainty arises in a way more fundamental than mere ignorance of unknown true causes.

Since these two notions are fundamentally different, you might think they shouldn't both use the word "probability." The philosopher Ian Hacking has pointed out that a similar issue arises with weight and mass. Only recently in human history have we understood them to be different, so that now we describe them using distinct terms. Thinking along these lines, the great mathematicians Siméon-Denis Poisson and Antoine-Augustin Cournot suggested that we should use the French words *"chance"* for epistemological probability and *"probabilité"* for aleatory probability, but it's not something which has taken off in English.

The third main interpretation of probability is the *classical* interpretation. Classical probability is based on notions of symmetry. If you had a *perfect* cubic die, with six faces, then there'd be no reason to expect any one face to appear more often than any other. Since some face must come up, it's natural to think of the probability as distributed equally across the six faces, so that each face has a probability of one-sixth of coming up. This interpretation is very convenient for games of chance, based on symmetrical randomization tools such as dice and coins. I mentioned Girolamo Cardano's book on gambling above.[14] Here's his fundamental principle of gambling, illustrating this classical notion of probability: "The most fundamental principle of all in gambling is simply equal conditions . . . of money, of situation . . . and of the die itself. To the extent to which you depart from that equity, if it is in your opponent's favor, you are a fool, and if in your own, you are unjust." Even if dice are not geometrically perfect cubes, they're pretty good approximations, but it's less clear how we might apply classical probability to situations in normal life which lack such obvious symmetries. How, for example, could we apply it to the probability of someone dying from cancer?

The frequentist, subjective, and classical interpretations of probability are the most widely used, but there are others. *Logical* probability is an extension of logic in which straightforward yes/no answers are replaced by numerical degrees of support. Whereas in ordinary logic we can make statements like "A implies B," logical probability extends this to give the degree to which A implies B. This form of probability has gone under other names, including *credibility*, *rational degree of belief*, and *degree of confirmation*. The eminent economist John Maynard Keynes was a proponent of logical probability, describing it in his book *A Treatise on Probability*.

Yet another explanation of probability is the *propensity interpretation*. This is based on the disposition that objects have to behave in certain ways. I might regard my coin as having a certain physical disposition to come up heads (and the measure of this tendency is one-half for a fair coin). You can think of this kind of probability as analogous to fragility: the fragility of a plate is its disposition to break when dropped.

This brief tour over some of the mountains of the meaning of probability doesn't exhaust the entire range. It's an elusive concept, and countless philosophers and others have spent significant chunks of their lives trying to narrow it down. But one of its most remarkable features is that (at least) the three most widespread interpretations—frequentist, subjective, and classical probability—can all be described by the same mathematics.

The Rules of Chance

The Improbability Principle is built using the bricks of probability theory. In this section I'll describe the building blocks that are especially important for the principle. For a more detailed description, you can look in Appendix B, where I illustrate how to actually calculate various probabilities.

I've talked about the probability that a coin will come up heads, that a die will show a 6, that the next president will be a woman, and so on. But these are single events. Once you've worked out the probability of a single event, there's not much more to say about it. It's when you have multiple events that it gets interesting. Coincidences are an example. They involve two or more events which both occur. So the first important thing we need to work out is the probability that two events both occur: like the probability of the pope resigning *and* St. Peter's being struck by lightning. Once we can work out that probability, it's easy to work out the likelihood that three or more events occur: it's just the probability of the first two *and* the third.

The most straightforward situation is when the probability that one event will occur is unaffected by whether or not the other occurs. The probability that my alarm clock fails to go off is the same whether or not you win the lottery: you're not more (or less) likely to win if my alarm fails than if it doesn't. In such cases the events are said to be *independent*, and it's easy to work out the probability that they both occur: it's just the probability of one times the probability of the other. If the first occurs one in ten times and the second one in a million, then whether or not my alarm fails, you still have only a one-in-a-million chance of winning the lottery, so that the chance that my alarm will fail *and* you'll win the lottery is one in ten million.

It's rather more complicated when the events are *dependent*— when the chance one event will occur depends on whether the other one has occurred. It's much more likely that I'll miss my train when my alarm fails than when it doesn't. In this case we can't find the probability that both events will happen simply by multiplying the separate probabilities together. Instead we have to multiply the probability that one occurs by the probability that the other one does *if you know the first has*. The probability that my alarm will fail *and* I'll miss my train is the probability of my alarm failing times the probability I'll miss my train when my alarm has failed (which could well be 1!).

The probability of one event occurring when you know that another has occurred is called the *conditional probability* of the first given the second. Conditional probability is a very important aspect of the Improbability Principle because something might be very unlikely in general, but much more likely under other circumstances. The probability that my best friend will have an accident in New York is very small indeed, since he lives in London, rarely visiting New York. But obviously if he were to move to New York it would be substantially greater.

If being able to work out the probability that *both* of two events will happen is one leg of the Improbability Principle, another is being able to work out the probability that *at least one* of them will happen. An example is the probability that I'll be late for work on Monday, or Tuesday, or both. If the events cannot possibly occur together (called *exclusive* or *incompatible* events), then it's easy to work out the probability that at least one will occur: it's just the sum of their separate probabilities (because the probability of both happening together is 0). The probability that tomorrow I'll arrive at work before 7:00 a.m. or after 8:00 a.m. or both is just the probability I'll arrive before 7:00 a.m. plus the probability that I'll arrive after 8:00 a.m., because it's not possible to do both.

But if both *can* occur together, it's a little more complicated. Suppose I'm late 60 percent of the time on Mondays and 70 percent of the time on Tuesdays (that pesky alarm clock!). Just adding these together would suggest my probability of being late on one or the other or both days was $0.6 + 0.7 = 1.3$. But this is meaningless. A probability of 1 means certainty, and you can't be more certain than certain! The problem with this is made clear if we look at all the possible outcomes.

There are four: late on both days, late on Monday but not Tuesday, late on Tuesday but not Monday, and not late on both days. The probability of being late on Monday includes two of these: it includes the probability of being late both days *and* the probability of being late on Monday but not Tuesday. Likewise, the probability of being late on Tuesday includes two: the probability of being late both days *and* the probability of being late on Tuesday but not Monday.

If we simply add together the probability of being late on Monday and the probability of being late on Tuesday, we're double-counting the probability of being late both days. To correct for this, we need to subtract one of these double-counts. For example, provided the events are independent (that is, if being late on one day does not affect my probability of being late on the other) then, as we saw above, the probability of being late on both days is just the product of the two separate probabilities: $0.7 \times 0.6 = 0.42$. If we subtract that from 1.3 we get 0.88. Much more sensible!

As well as the basic rules we've just looked at, the Improbability Principle also makes use of some more advanced ideas. So, before leaving this section, I want to outline a couple of these.

One more advanced but still fundamental law is the *law of large numbers*. This says that the average of a sequence of numbers randomly drawn from a given set of values is likely to get closer and closer to the average of that set. For example, consider the set of six values {1, 2, 3, 4, 5, 6}. These have an average of $(1 + 2 + 3 + 4 + 5 + 6)/6 = 3.5$. Now suppose we randomly pick numbers from the set, replacing each after we've drawn it, so that we can pick each more than once. (So my picks might begin 3, 6, 2, 2, 4, 1, 5, 3, for example, continuing until I decide to stop.) Then the law of large numbers says that the more picks we take, the closer the average is likely to be to 3.5. By the time we've made a great many picks, the average is very unlikely to be far from 3.5.

You can easily test this for yourself. Throwing an ordinary die is a convenient way of repeatedly randomly drawing values from the set {1, 2, 3, 4, 5, 6}. So all you have to do is repeatedly throw a die and calculate the average of the throws as you go along.

To save you the effort, I've done it for you. But rather than throw a die 500 times, I cheated and used a computer to randomly generate 500 picks from the set {1, 2, 3, 4, 5, 6}. Figure 3.2 shows what happened. The plot on the following page shows the different values from 1 to 6 obtained at each throw of my virtual die, just for the first 20 throws. The horizontal axis shows the throw number, from 1 to 20. The vertical axis shows, for each of the throws, whether a 1, 2, 3, 4, 5, or 6 came up. So, for example, the first throw produced a 5, and the second throw produced a 3. The second graph shows the average as the number of throws gets larger and larger.

We see that, at the start, when I've made only a few throws (the left-hand side of the second graph), the average of the values leaps around all over the place as I make a new throw and use it to update the average. But gradually, as I make more and more throws, the average settles down and begins to converge. And by the time I've made 500 throws (the right-hand side of the second graph), the average is very close to 3.5.

You might recognize that we've met the law of large numbers (or, as it's also sometimes informally called, the law of averages) already. Recall the gambler's fallacy. This was the mistaken belief that an initial imbalance in the proportion of coin tosses that come up heads would be counterbalanced by an excess in the other direction as we made more and more throws. What actually happens is that the imbalance is diluted, so that over time, the proportion of heads gets closer and closer to one-half. One-half is just the average of 0 and 1. This is simply the law of large numbers.

It's not hard to see why the law of large numbers works. Imagine tossing a fair coin. Toss it once, and the proportion of heads must be either 0 or 1. Toss it twice, and the proportion could be

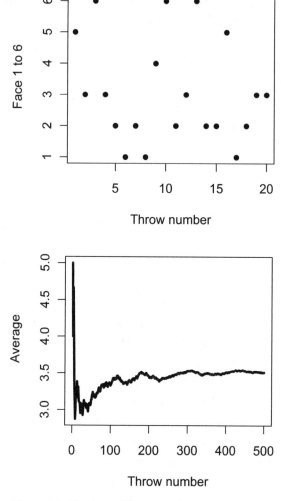

Figure 3.2. The law of large numbers. How averages converge to a limiting value as the sample size increases.

0 (neither toss showing heads), or 1 (both tosses showing heads), or 1/2 (one coin showing heads and one showing tails). That last outcome, a proportion of one-half, can occur in two ways (the first toss heads, and the second tails; the first toss tails and the second heads), whereas the other two outcomes (both heads, or both tails)

can each occur in only one way. Now toss it three times. There are more possible outcomes now, but the extreme proportions (all heads, all tails) can occur in only one way each, whereas the others (one-third heads, or two-thirds heads) can each occur in three ways.

Now let's jump to one hundred tosses. One hundred coin tosses can show 100 heads in only one way, but they can show 99 heads and 1 tail in one hundred ways (perhaps the first toss was a head, or the second, or the third, or . . .). And some arithmetic shows that one hundred coin tosses can produce 98 heads and 2 tails in 4,950 ways, 97 heads and 3 tails in 161,700 ways, and so on, up to one hundred coin tosses being able to produce 50 heads and 50 tails in about 10^{29} ways. As this illustrates, it's much more likely that we'll see roughly equal numbers of heads and tails than very different numbers. That is, it's overwhelmingly likely that the proportion of heads will be near to $1/2$, which is the average of 0 and 1.

Another more advanced idea that underpins the Improbability Principle is known as the *central limit theorem*. Again imagine choosing values at random from the set of values {1, 2, 3, 4, 5, 6}, replacing them after each choice. Again I could do this by repeatedly throwing a die. I'll draw five values in this way, and then calculate their average—just like we did for the law of large numbers. But now, instead of simply drawing more and more values, I'll repeat the whole exercise of drawing five and calculating their average. The averages from these two sets of draws of five are likely to be different. In fact, if I repeated the exercise many times, each time drawing five values and calculating their average, I'd get a whole distribution of averages.

Now, there's nothing magic about the number five in that example. Instead of five, I could have done it with samples of size ten or twenty or a hundred. For each sample size, the distribution of the averages would take a specific shape. The central limit theorem tells us what shape we will get as we use larger and larger sample sizes. It says that as the sample size increases, so the shape of the distribution of the averages will get closer and closer to a particular shape called the *normal distribution* (also called the *Gaussian distribution*, after Carl Friedrich Gauss). This has a characteristic shape that looks like a bell.

I've illustrated the effect in Figure 3.3. For simplicity's sake, I've compared only the distribution obtained if I draw samples of size one (the "average" of a sample of size one is simply equal to that one value) with the distribution I get if I draw samples of size five. The gray histograms show the distribution of the averages of my samples. The superimposed black lines are the normal distributions that best fit the distributions obtained from our random numbers. The histogram on the left is almost flat. This is no surprise, because when my samples each have size one, each sample average is one of 1, 2, 3, 4, 5, or 6, and each of these values is equally likely—each has probability one-sixth. In contrast, the distribution of the averages of samples of size five shown in the right-hand panel is much more similar to the characteristic bell shape of the normal distribution.

The normal distribution is very important in statistics. The Victorian polymath Francis Galton, who made seminal advances

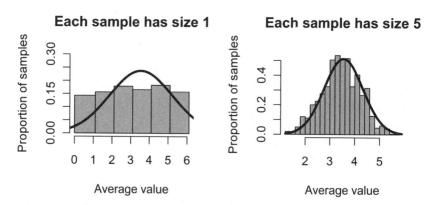

Figure 3.3. The central limit theorem. As we increase the sample size, so the distribution of sample averages gets closer and closer to the shape of a normal distribution.

in statistics and many other areas at the end of the nineteenth century, had this to say about it (he called it the "law of frequency of error"): "I know of scarcely anything so apt to impress the imagination as the wonderful form of cosmic order expressed by the 'Law of Frequency of Error.' The law would have been personified by the Greeks and deified, if they had known of it. It reigns with serenity and in complete self-effacement amidst the wildest confusion. The huger the mob, and the greater the apparent anarchy, the more perfect is its sway. It is the supreme law of Unreason. Whenever a large sample of chaotic elements are taken in hand and marshalled in the order of their magnitude, an unsuspected and most beautiful form of regularity proves to have been latent all along."[13] The beauty and power of the normal distribution, and its universal role in transforming the intrinsic unpredictability of individual random events to highly predictable aggregates, shines through in Galton's words.

The normal distribution is a good approximation to many natural distributions. This is because we can often think of measurements as the result of summing together or averaging many parts, like the averages I just calculated. For example, your height is the sum of the lengths of your vertebrae, femur, skull, and so on. But a little caution is appropriate. You shouldn't expect to find *exact* normal distributions in nature: the normal distribution is another of those mathematical abstractions, again like the points, lines, and planes we learned about in school geometry. This fact, that the normal distribution is an idealization, led the educationalist Theodore Micceri to title one of his papers "The Unicorn, the Normal Curve, and Other Improbable Creatures."[14]

Even in my little simulation above, the right-hand panel is not exactly a normal distribution. For example, the true mathematical normal distribution has "tails" which go to plus and minus infinity: there's no limit to the size of values it can take. In contrast, in my example based on averaging five values chosen from the set {1, 2, 3, 4, 5, 6}, the largest average I could possibly get would have been 6 (when all five chosen values were 6) and the smallest would have been 1 (when all five were 1). And the same occurs in nature. We don't get people who are a hundred feet tall, or people with negative height. The normal distribution is a useful mathematical abstraction, but we shouldn't forget that it's not a perfect model for what occurs in nature. As we shall see, the fact that the normal distribution is merely an approximation to naturally occurring distributions is very important for the Improbability Principle.

Beyond the Clockwork Universe

The clockwork universe I described in chapter 2 is completely deterministic: given the initial conditions, the universe followed the laws of mechanics, running along its inevitable path like a train constrained to run forever on its tracks. But as understanding of nature advanced, so gaps began to appear in that picture, casting doubt on its accuracy. Those gaps became most apparent around the beginning of the twentieth century—though, as with all scientific ideas, it's possible to trace their roots further back in time.

The first gap arises as a consequence of two facts: that some systems are intrinsically *unstable*, and that we can never measure anything with *perfect accuracy*. Let's look at instability first.

If I roll a marble down the side of a bathtub, no matter where it starts from it will end up at the drain (I'm assuming the bath is well-designed, so that it slopes down everywhere, and water runs out properly). If I set a child's swing in motion, it will eventually come to a stop, hanging vertically beneath its frame. On the other hand, if I try to balance a pencil on its point, it will fall, and the direction in which it falls, and where it eventually comes to rest, will depend critically on tiny differences in its starting position. If I try to position a marble on top of a ball, any slight perturbation of its position will set the marble rolling down the ball, and where it ends up depends on the direction of that initial tiny perturbation.

An example of such instability is the path of the cue ball re bounding from the cushions of a pool table and ricocheting off other balls. The path the ball follows as it bounces around is very sensitive to its exact starting direction and velocity. Since cue balls are spheres, a very slight alteration in the direction of one ball's approach toward another would mean that they'd collide at different points on their surfaces, and so bounce off at different angles. These differences in angle amplify at each collision so that after a series of collisions, the small initial difference becomes so large that it is impossible to tell anything about the position or direction of the cue ball. I'll look at some numbers associated with this in chapter 7, where we'll see that infinitesimally small differences in initial conditions can very rapidly multiply to have a huge macroscopic effect.

This idea—that slight differences in initial conditions can, with certain kinds of systems, rapidly amplify to produce huge consequences—is an old one. A hundred years ago Henri Poincaré wrote: "A very small cause, which escapes us, determines a considerable effect which we cannot ignore . . . even if it were the case that the natural laws had no longer any secret for us, we could still only know the initial situation *approximately* . . . it may happen that small differences in the initial conditions produce very great ones in the final phenomena. A small error in the former will produce an enormous error in the latter. Prediction becomes impossible."[15]

James Clerk Maxwell made a similar comment at the end of the nineteenth century: "There are certain classes of phenomena . . . in which a small error in the data only introduces a small error in the result . . . The course of events in these cases is stable. There are other classes of phenomena which are more complicated, and in which cases of instability may occur, the number of such cases increasing, in an extremely rapid manner, as the number of variables increases."[16] Systems like this are intrinsically unstable, so it becomes increasingly difficult to predict their state as time progresses.

These quotations imply that tiny errors of measurement in the initial values can grow to yield enormous uncertainty about a system's state later on. So, you might think, the way to avoid the problem is to measure things accurately in the first place. But I've already noted that *perfectly* accurate measurement is impossible. While I might be able to measure the starting position and velocity of my cue ball to one decimal place, or two, it won't be possible to measure it to a hundred decimal places, or a thousand (or choose any number beyond the accuracy of the measuring instrument). This means that, at least for certain kinds of systems, the ultimate explosion in our uncertainty about the state of the system is inevitable.

The idea that a very slight change to the initial conditions can rapidly result in our being completely unable to say what state a system is in has been called *the butterfly effect*. The term was coined by mathematician and meteorologist Edward Lorenz. It's based on the colorful image that something as inconsequential as the flap of a butterfly's wing in the Amazon jungle could multiply, in the same way as did the uncertainties in the path of our cue ball, until a hurricane is caused on the other side of the world.

Lorenz came up with the name when he was running computer simulations of weather systems and discovered that a very slight alteration to a number in his simulation resulted in a completely different weather pattern. The butterfly effect is real, not a metaphor, but it would be stretching the notion of "causality" to describe the flap of the wing as *causing* the hurricane. The chain of events connecting the flap to the storm contains a huge number of intermediate events.

The formal study of these kinds of phenomena is called *chaos theory*. A chaotic system appears to move between its states completely at random—and yet it's not random in the sense that its next state is unpredictable, because an explicit deterministic equation can be given to link successive states. It's just that the starting point can never be exactly known, and slight differences in that starting point can lead to vast differences further down the line.

Another gap in the deterministic clockwork view of the universe arose from puzzling and apparently contradictory observations relating to electrons and other particles, also around the beginning of the twentieth century. These observations culminated in the view that uncertainty lies right at the heart of physical observations. This view contradicted the familiar notion that there is a "true" value which we could measure, if only we had a sufficiently accurate measuring device. One example of this is radioactive decay, and the time at which a subatomic particle will split into other particles. Our inability to predict the time of the decay isn't due to our ignorance of the initial conditions or of the properties of the particle, but is simply because the event *is* actually unpredictable. All you can ever do is give the *probability* that a particle will decay at any particular time.

This intrinsic uncertainty also manifests itself in the famous "Heisenberg uncertainty principle": for certain pairs of attributes of objects, we can't know with complete accuracy both elements of the pair. One example of such a pair is the position and momentum of a particle. The more accurately we know the position of the particle, the less accurately will we know its momentum, and vice versa. The important point here is that this limitation is not due to the inadequacies of our measuring instrument, but is a fundamental property of nature. (And it's not because measuring something necessarily perturbs it, though that can also be true.)

To study inherently unpredictable subatomic events, scientists began to describe particles such as electrons by probability distributions or probability "clouds," which give the probabilities that the particles would be found to possess particular values of their attributes (like position, velocity, and so on) when these were measured. Implicit in this description is the idea that the values of the attributes don't actually exist until they are measured.

Not everyone found this fundamentally probabilistic view of nature easy to accept. Writing to Max Born in 1944, Einstein said, "You believe in the God who plays dice, and I in complete law and order in a world that objectively exists . . . Even the great initial success of the quantum theory does not make me believe in the fundamental dice-game."[17] But Einstein was representative of a small minority. The consensus now is that nature is indeed fundamentally driven by chance—that uncertainty lies at its very core.

The shift from the clockwork universe to the probabilistic universe began a century ago and is now virtually complete. We live in a universe dominated by chance and uncertainty. But as we've seen, chance has its own laws. Those laws are the foundations of probability. In the next few chapters, we'll see how the Improbability Principle is built on those foundations.

4

THE LAW OF
INEVITABILITY

The sum of the coincidences equals certainty.   —Aristotle

The Certainty of Events

While any one of the strands of the Improbability Principle might precipitate events that appear to be highly improbable, it's when they combine that the principle really shows its full force. Over the next few chapters, I'll examine these strands one at a time. We begin with one of the most important strands: the *law of inevitability*. This is a simple and often overlooked observation, and one that in a real sense underlies everything else: it's the simple fact that *something must happen*.

If we throw a standard cubic die, we know that a number from 1 to 6 will come up. If we toss a coin, we know that it will come up heads or tails. To be completely accurate, I should extend these two examples: we know that the die will show one of the six faces *or* that some other outcome will occur (e.g., it will bounce off the table onto the floor, where we cannot find it); we know that the coin will come up heads, tails, or end up balanced on its edge, or be swallowed by a passing bird, or be lost through a gap in the floorboards, and so on (though I have to say, in all my own experience with coin tossing it has always come up heads or tails). In each case, if we were able to compile a list of all possible outcomes, we would know that some outcome on the list must occur. When we hit a golf ball onto the green we know that it will come to rest on *some* blade of grass, or (if we are very lucky or skilled) it will go straight into the hole, or it will bounce over a fence into someone's garden, and so on. It's certain that *something* will happen.

And that's really all there is to the law of inevitability: *if you make a complete list of all possible outcomes, then one of them must occur.* However, while we know that one outcome on a complete list of possible outcomes must happen, *we don't know which one it will be.* Before throwing the die, we can't say which face will show; before tossing the coin we can't say which of heads or tails (or other very low-probability outcome) will come up; and before hitting the golf ball, we can't say which blade of grass it will land on.

In fact, in the golfing example, were we to pick a specific blade of grass beforehand, we could confidently say it was very unlikely that the ball would end up on top of that blade. We'd be prepared to bet money on it not landing on any particular blade, knowing that the chance of having to pay out would be very small indeed.

So we have a huge list of possible outcomes for where the ball might land—on each of the individual blades of grass, straight in a hole, or in the beak of a passing albatross, and so on, each of which has a very small chance of occurring, but one of which must occur. Perry Vlahos, spokesman for the Astronomical Society of Victoria, Australia, gave a nice illustration of this idea, like my golf ball example but on a larger scale. Talking about NASA's UARS satellite which was about to crash back to Earth, he said: "It's a little difficult to ascertain where it will come down because there are so many variables involved, but it will definitely come down in some part of the world." Well, he was certainly right about the last part: it's the law of inevitability.

Lotteries

We're all familiar with the law of inevitability in one situation, though we may not know it. This is the lottery.

My *New Oxford Dictionary of English* defines a lottery as "a means of raising money by selling numbered tickets and giving prizes to the holders of numbers drawn at random." The idea is a very old one. The same principle has long been used for selecting jury pools and choosing representatives for governing councils. King Carlos III of Spain set up a lottery in 1763 to finance the Spanish side of the Napoleonic Wars. But lotteries are often a source of tension between those running them and those who find them ethically objectionable. Indeed, since the chance of winning the jackpot is tiny (*that particular* blade of grass?), some have described lotteries as ways of extracting money from the poor—from those who can least afford it.

In modern lotteries each ticket shows a small choice of numbers from a larger set. So, for example, in the UK National Lottery, a ticket consists of 6 numbers drawn from the integers (an integer is a whole number) 1 to 49, the Finnish Lotto Jokeri uses 7 from 39, the Pennsylvania Cash 5 game has you pick 5 from 43, the Florida New Fantasy 5 uses 5 from 36, and so on. Sometimes, for convenience, such types of lottery are called r/s lotteries, meaning that for each ticket you have to choose r numbers from a set of s numbers (as in 6 from 49). The probability of any one ticket matching the r numbers randomly drawn by the lottery operator depends on the values of r and s. The larger are r and s, the smaller the chance that any particular ticket will win—because there are more ways to choose r different numbers from s numbers when these are bigger. If you buy one UK National Lottery ticket, the chance of winning (a share of) the jackpot is 1 in 13,983,816 (which I'll approximate by calling it 1 in 14 million). As the UK National Lottery advertising used to put it: *It could be you!* (and as it didn't add: *but the chance that it will be you is almost infinitesimally small*).[1]

Some lotteries complicate matters by requiring the ticket buyer to choose *two* sets of numbers. For example, to buy a ticket for the Euromillions lottery you have to choose 5 numbers from the first 50 integers and also 2 numbers from the first 11. So it's a 5/50 + 2/11 lottery. The American Powerball lottery requires you to choose 5 from 59 integers and 1 from 35—a 5/59 + 1/35 lottery (though these numbers have changed over its history). The probability that a single randomly chosen ticket will win the Powerball lottery is 1 in 175,223,510.

Now, if you bought a Powerball ticket—that is, you chose a set of 5 different numbers from 1 to 59 and a single number from 1 to 35—and your choice of numbers came up, you'd probably describe yourself as very lucky indeed. You might have chosen your numbers using some rationale—based on birth dates, for example—and then you might be inclined toward one of the explanations outlined in chapter 2. Or you might simply have chosen the numbers using the quick-pick facility (most lotteries have such a way of randomly generating numbers for you), in which case you'd probably say that it was simply a coincidence that the set of numbers you bought happened to come up.

On the other hand, if 175,223,510 people each bought differently numbered tickets, then we could guarantee that *someone* would win. There are only 175,223,510 different sets of numbers that can be chosen, so our players would have all the possibilities covered.

And that leads to a way you can guarantee winning the lottery—if you are rich enough. Simply buy all possible combinations of numbers. One of them must be the jackpot-winning ticket. Clearly it takes some organizational skill and a lot of money to buy all the millions of different possible numbers, but it could be done. And, in fact, it has been done.

In the 1990s, the Virginia State Lottery required choosing 6 numbers from 1 to 44, giving a probability of 1 in 7,059,052 that any one ticket would be the jackpot winner. That's a much better chance than the Powerball, and it meant you would have to spend only about $7 million to guarantee that you had the winning ticket, simply because you had all of them.

On February 15, 1992, because nobody had won in previous weeks, the jackpot in Virginia had swelled to a mammoth $27 million, a record for that lottery. Further smaller prizes, won if you matched some but not all of the numbers, added up to an extra $900,000, so that the overall potential winnings were over $27 million. Now you can do the math yourself: for an outlay of $7 million you stood to win over $27 million—though there was a catch, which we'll come to in a moment.

Thinking along these lines, in February 1992 a group calling itself The International Lotto Fund put together a consortium of 2,500 small investors, mostly Australian, but with others from the United States, Europe, and New Zealand, raising the requisite $7 million needed to buy every combination of lottery numbers.

Perhaps the toughest part of the exercise was the logistics: organizing the purchase of 7 million distinct tickets in one week. The International Lotto Fund had a team of some twenty people running around Virginia, buying tickets from 125 different grocery and convenience stores in eight chains. So tough was this task, in fact, that the consortium ended up with only 5 million tickets. This had the potential for disaster. You can imagine the nail-biting: instead of a sure thing, they had only a 5 in 7 chance of winning the jackpot, and a chance of *not* winning it greater than 1 in 4.

But there was another, more serious risk to the consortium's plan, and one that would apply even if their plan had gone smoothly and they had succeeded in buying all 7 million tickets: perhaps someone else would *also* buy a ticket with the winning numbers. If just one other person did, then the consortium would receive only half of the jackpot. In fact, of the 170 previous times this lottery had been won, there had been multiple winners ten times, so the risk was real—though even if the jackpot had to be split with one other winner, it would still lead to a handsome profit.

The winning numbers on that day in February were 8, 11, 13, 15, 19, and 20, and, presumably after some anxious searching through 5 million tickets, they turned out to be a ticket the consortium had bought.

Unfortunately, the relief was short-lived. A state law, intended to prevent people from buying tickets and reselling them at a higher price, required that each ticket had to be paid for at the terminal which had actually printed it out. But the consortium had bought a $3 million batch of tickets from the headquarters of the Fresh Farm supermarket chain and had only *collected* those tickets from terminal sites. The consortium argued that although that was true, they'd also bought tickets directly from the Chesapeake outlet which had issued the winning ticket, and had no way of knowing if the winning ticket was one of those or merely one they'd had printed out there.

Eventually, the lottery operators recognized that proof would be difficult and that pursuing the issue would result in a protracted lawsuit whose outcome was not clear, so they finally agreed to pay out.

Stock Tipsters

Buying all of the tickets in a lottery is a way to try to use the law of inevitability to your advantage and win a great deal of money. A more reliable way to make money using this law is the following stock-tipping scam—though you might want to ponder the ethical questions involved before trying it out. The scam involves a combination of the law of inevitability and the *law of selection*. The latter, which is discussed in detail in chapter 6, is the idea that you can be certain of an outcome if you wait until it has happened.

What I'm going to (pretend to) do is correctly predict, for ten weeks in a row, whether a stock will go up or down. This is a difficult feat, and if someone came to you and did that, you might be inclined to take them seriously—perhaps to the point that you might even pay them money for their next tip. After all, if we assume that each stock has an equal probability of going up or down each week, then the probability of making such an accurate series of predictions by chance alone is just $\frac{1}{2} \times \frac{1}{2} \times \frac{1}{2} \times \ldots \times \frac{1}{2}$, ten times. Or 1 in 1,024—about one in a thousand.

Here's how I do it.

I'll begin by picking a stock—any stock will do. Then I'll choose 1,024 innocent potential victims, and I'll send them a prediction about what the stock will do over the next week. For half of them I'll predict that the stock will go up, and for the other half I'll predict that it will go down. Since the stock must go up or down, half of my potential victims, 512 of them, will receive the wrong prediction, and half the right one.

Now I'll forget about those who received the wrong prediction, and just focus on those who received the right prediction. For half of *those*, that is 256 of them, I'll now predict the stock will go up over the next week, and for the other half I'll predict it will go down. Once again, because the stock must go up or down, 256 of my victims will receive the right prediction and 256 will receive the wrong prediction. Then, as before, I'll drop those who received the wrong prediction and concentrate on the other half. And I'll continue in this way, each time writing a new letter just to those who received the right prediction the previous week.

At the end of the tenth week, I'm down to just one person. Everyone else at some point received an incorrect prediction, and I stopped sending them new letters. But what about this one person? They've seen me make ten correct predictions in a row. That sounds really impressive: it looks as if I really do have some clever method, perhaps an algorithm, that can predict how stocks will perform. And this is the point at which I ask them to pay for my next stock tip . . .

The fact is that over the course of the ten weeks, *some* combination of up and down movements must occur—it's the law of inevitability. Maybe the stock goes up in all ten weeks, or up the first and down in all the others, or up in the first, third, and seventh, and down in the others, or . . . But there are only 1,024 possible up and down sequences in ten weeks, and I have them all covered. It's as if I gave a different one of these possible patterns to each of the 1,024 people at the start, and gradually discarded patterns that didn't occur, until only the one that did occur was left—along with the lucky person who had been given that pattern.

As I said at the start of the chapter, *something must happen*. One of the set of 1,024 possible up/down configurations must occur. But to the person who's still around at the end, and who had no idea that there were originally another 1,023 people receiving (rather different) predictions, it looks as if I've simply told him or her how the stock price would move. Unless that person knows (or suspects) that there were others, he must assume that either I am indeed able to predict the future, or that I've simply been lucky with my predictions, to the tune of a 1 in 1,024 chance.

We've just encountered two strands of the Improbability Principle: the law of inevitability and the law of selection, which we'll explore in detail in chapter 6. Before that, we'll look at a third law: *the law of truly large numbers*.

5

THE LAW OF
TRULY LARGE NUMBERS

Fate laughs at probabilities.   —E. G. Bulwer-Lytton

You'd have to be very lucky to find a four-leaf clover. Most clover stalks have three leaves, and only about 1 in 10,000 has four. But people do find them. And if 1 in 10,000 seems unlikely, it's even more unlikely that 26 black numbers will come up one after the other in roulette—and yet that's what happened on August 18, 1913, at a casino in Monte Carlo. The roulette wheels there have 18 black numbers and 18 red numbers, along with one green slot for 0, so the probability of getting 26 black numbers in a row is about 1 in 137 million.

In contrast to those lucky events, you'd be very unlucky if you tossed a ball in the air and it landed in your wineglass. But again, these things happen. Fourteen-year-old Shannon Smith was killed by a bullet that landed on top of her head on June 14, 1999, in Arizona (after which Arizona made it illegal to fire guns into the air).

Remember Anthony Hopkins finding the very copy of *The Girl from Petrovka* that the author George Feifer had annotated? Well, in the 1920s, the writer Anne Parrish was browsing Paris bookshops with her husband when she came across a copy of *Jack Frost and Other Stories*. She showed the book to her husband, commenting that it had been one of her childhood favorites. He opened the book and saw written on the flyleaf, "Anne Parrish, 209 N. Weber Street, Colorado Springs, Colorado."

Perhaps there's something about books: more recently, the newspaper columnist Melanie Reid described culling her book collection at her home in Scotland. On the first shelf she tackled, she came across a 1937 cookery book inscribed "L. K. Beamish" that she'd found in one of the outbuildings of her house when she moved in. Amused by the coincidence of coming across such an unusual but still familiar name, she gave it to her friend Sally Beamish, the composer, who'd recently come to live nearby. And she learned that Lucia Katharine Beamish was Sally's grandmother, who had lived in England. The book had traveled hundreds of miles, from one country to another, from grandmother to granddaughter, over an eighty-year period.

Here's a final example that is more minor but personal. In early 2012, I received an e-mail with the subject heading "Catchup meeting with Muir," seeking to make arrangements for a date for a meeting with someone whose first name was Muir. The next e-mail was headed "Miur referees list." I assumed the first word was a misprint for Muir. However, this second e-mail turned out to be from the Ministero dell'Istruzione, dell'Università e della Ricerca (the Italian Ministry of Education, Universities, and Research), not a misprint for Muir at all, but something completely different. It was just a coincidence that the two e-mails had occurred one immediately after the other.

All of these are examples of events that would appear to be so unlikely that we shouldn't expect to see them—in accordance with Borel's law. And yet we do. Clearly some explanation is needed, and the explanation comes in the form of a third strand of the Improbability Principle:

> *the law of truly large numbers,* which says that, with a large enough number of opportunities, any outrageous thing is likely to happen.

This is (very) different from the *law of large numbers*, which we met in chapter 3, which says that averages of large samples fluctuate less than averages of small samples.

If you looked at just one clover stalk in your entire life, then you would indeed be surprised if it had four leaves—as we've seen, there's about a 1 in 10,000 chance that a random clover stem has four leaves. But if you are of a clover-leaf-inspecting disposition, it's likely that you've looked at more than one stem; that when you were looking at clover leaves you in fact carried out a small search, looking at several, perhaps many clover plants, hoping to find one of the rare four-leaf ones. More than this, it's likely that you don't search clover patches by yourself, but go with people who are similarly inspired by the possibility of finding a four-leaf one. And, of course, you and your small group are not the only people who have ever looked for four-leaf clovers. Many people, many times, all over the world (wherever clover grows) have carried out similar searches. Adding all these up, it's beginning to look very likely that someone, somewhere, at some time, would find one. In fact, given the large enough number of people searching a large number of times, the reality that some have been found doesn't seem surprising at all. It begins to look almost inevitable: the law of truly large numbers again.

A similar explanation accounts for the other examples above. My first reaction on seeing the successive Muir/Miur in my inbox was, "How strange." But then I thought: I get maybe fifty to a hundred e-mails a day, day after day, year after year, so occasional coincidences like this are to be expected. Similarly, croupiers spin roulette wheels time after time, day after day, in casinos across the world. There have been countless sequences of 26 successive spins of roulette wheels in history—certainly vastly more than 137 million—so we would *expect* to see an event with a 1 in 137 million chance occurring sometime, somewhere. The Anne Parrish coincidence occurred in the 1920s: if we allow a sufficient length of time in our search for such events we are providing ourselves with a truly large number of possible occasions for them to occur. Given enough possible occasions we shouldn't be surprised that we see coincidences.

Some mathematicians have appreciated the inescapable consequences of the law of truly large numbers. In the nineteenth century, Augustus De Morgan wrote, "Whatever can happen will happen if we make trials enough."[1] In the twentieth century, J. E. Littlewood presented various versions of it. In 1953 he wrote, "With a lifetime to choose from, [an outcome with odds of] 10^6 : 1 [against] is a mere trifle."[2] Lives are full of events, minor and major. With so many events to choose from, it's only to be expected that some surprises will occur, even though they are incredibly unlikely when taken by themselves.

Lotteries show the law of truly large numbers in action. Unless you're like the International Lotto Fund consortium of the last chapter, and buy up huge numbers of tickets, your chance of winning a lottery is minuscule. It follows that the chance of winning a lottery *twice* must surely be astronomically small. But Evelyn Marie Adams won the New Jersey Lottery twice in four months, first in 1985 and then again the next year, collecting a total of $5.4 million.[3] The chance of her winning twice in this time span was about one in a trillion.[4]

In the case of lotteries, the law of truly large numbers applies because the New Jersey lottery is not the world's only lottery, Ms. Adams was not the only player of the New Jersey Lottery, and she presumably didn't buy only two tickets in her life. When we look at the number of lotteries there are around the world, the number of people who play, the number of tickets they buy, and the number of weeks that they play, we rapidly approach a truly large number. Even if each event has a very small probability, if you have enough events the chance that one of them will happen can be very large. No wonder, then, that someone, somewhere, at some time won a lottery twice. We might even go so far as to say we should *expect* it to happen.

That being the case, it will come as no surprise to learn that a resident of the Whistler ski resort in British Columbia also won two lotteries, in the space of just two years: $1 million in the Surrey Memorial Hospital Lottery, and $2.2 million in the BC Cancer Foundation Lifestyle Lottery. Or to learn that Maurice and Jeanette Garlepy of Alberta won the Canadian Lotto 6/49 twice.

Second prizes pay out when just some of the numbers are matched (e.g., five instead of all six). If we include such prizes in what we mean by a "win" (the prizes can still be substantial), then the number of possibilities for a match is increased yet further. It's really a braiding together of two strands of the Improbability Principle: the law of truly large numbers and the *law of near enough*, which I'll discuss in chapter 8.

In April 2007, Robert Hong, of Kirkland Lake in Northern Ontario, won the second prize of $340,000 in the Canadian 6/49 lottery, and then, in November of that year, won the $15 million jackpot. In June 2011 Mike McDermott, from Gosport in the UK, won £194,501 with his regular lottery numbers 15, 16, 18, 28, 36, 49, matching five numbers and the bonus ball. And then in May 2012 he won again, with the same numbers, the same way, this time taking home £121,157. More recently, Virginia Pike had two tickets, each worth $1 million, which matched five of the six Powerball numbers on April 7, 2012, in the Virginia Lottery.[5] (I'm tempted to wonder about the probability of the Virginia lottery being won by someone called Virginia, but that's another story.)

People winning the lottery twice is one thing. But apparently stranger things have happened. In the next section I'll show how the *law of combinations* serves to magnify the law of truly large numbers, to the extent that the highly improbable becomes almost inevitable.

Making Numbers Truly Large

The law of truly large numbers says that given enough opportunities, we should *expect* a specified event to happen, no matter how unlikely it may be at each opportunity. But sometimes we're fooled. Sometimes when there really are many opportunities it can look as if there's only a small number. This leads us to grossly underestimate the probability of an event: we think something is incredibly unlikely, when it's actually very likely, perhaps almost certain. The *law of combinations* is a strand of the Improbability Principle which can lead to such a hidden explosion of opportunities. It says: the number of combinations of interacting elements increases exponentially with the number of elements. The *birthday problem* is a well-known example.

The birthday problem poses the following question: How many people must be in a room to make it more likely than not that two of them share the same birthday?

The answer is just 23. If there are 23 or more people in the room, then it's more likely than not that two will have the same birthday.

Now, if you haven't encountered the birthday problem before, this might strike you as surprising. Twenty-three might sound far too small a number. Perhaps you reasoned as follows. There's only a 1 in 365 chance that any particular other person will have the same birthday as me. So there's a 364/365 chance that any particular person will have a *different* birthday from me. If there are n people in the room, with each of the other $n-1$ having a probability of 364/365 of having a different birthday from me, then the probability that *all* $n-1$ have a different birthday from me is

$$364/365 \times 364/365 \times 364/365 \times 364/365 \ldots \times 364/365$$

with 364/365 multiplied together $n-1$ times. If n is 23, this is 0.94. Since that's the probability that *none of them* share my birthday, the probability that *at least one of them* has the same birthday as me is just 1 minus this. (This follows from the law of inevitability: either someone has the same birthday as me or no one has the same birthday as me, so the probabilities of these two events must add up to 1.) Now 1 minus 0.94 is 0.06. That's very small.

But this is the wrong calculation, because that probability—the probability that someone had the same birthday as *you*—is not what the question asked. It asked about the probability that *any* two people in the same room had the same birthday as *each other*. This includes the probability that one of the others had the same birthday as you, which is what I calculated above, but it also includes the probability that two or more of the others share the same birthday, different from yours. And this is where the combinations kick in. While there are only $n-1$ people who might share the same birthday as you, there are a total of $n \times (n-1)/2$ pairs of people in the room. This number of pairs grows rapidly as n gets larger. When n equals 23 it's 253, which is more than ten times as large as $(n-1) = 22$. That is, if there are 23 people in the room, there are 253 possible pairs of people, but only 22 pairs that include you.

So let's look at the probability that none of the 23 people in the room share the same birthday. For two people, the probability that the second person doesn't have the same birthday as the first is 364/365. Then, the probability that those two are different *and* that a third doesn't share the same birthday as either of them is 364/365 × 363/365. Likewise, the probability that those three have different birthdays *and* that the fourth doesn't share the same birthday as any of those first three is 364/365 × 363/365 × 362/365. Continuing like this, the probability that none of the 23 people share the same birthday is:

364/365 × 363/365 × 362/365 × 361/365 . . . × 343/365.

This equals 0.49. Since the probability that none of the 23 people share the same birthday is 0.49, the probability that some of them share the same birthday is just 1 minus this, or 0.51. This is greater than half.

For another example of the law of combinations, let's return to lotteries. On September 6, 2009, the Bulgarian Lottery randomly selected as the winning numbers 4, 15, 23, 24, 35, 42. There's nothing surprising about these numbers. The digits are all low values—1, 2, 3, 4, or 5—but that's not so unusual. Also, there's a consecutive pair of values, 23 and 24, but this happens far more often than is generally appreciated (if you ask people to randomly choose six numbers from 1 to 49, for example, they choose consecutive pairs less often than pure chance would). What was surprising was what happened four days later: on September 10, 2009, the Bulgarian Lottery randomly selected as the winning numbers 4, 15, 23, 24, 35, 42—exactly the same numbers as the previous week. The event caused something of a media storm at the time. "This is happening for the first time in the 52-year history of the lottery. We are absolutely stunned to see such a freak coincidence but it did happen," said a spokeswoman. Bulgaria's Sports Minister Svilen Neikov ordered an investigation.[6] Could a massive fraud have been perpetrated? Had the previous numbers somehow been copied?

In fact, this rather stunning coincidence was simply another example of the Improbability Principle, in the form of the law of truly large numbers amplified by the law of combinations. First, once again, many lotteries are conducted around the world. Second, they occur time after time, year in and year out. This rapidly adds up to a large number of opportunities for lottery numbers to repeat. And then third, the law of combinations comes into effect: each time a lottery result is drawn, it could contain the same numbers as produced in *any* of the previous draws. In general, as with the birthday situation, if you run a lottery n times there are $n \times (n-1)/2$ pairs of lottery draws that could match.

The Bulgarian Lottery is a 6/49 lottery, so the chance of any particular set of six numbers coming up is 1 in 13,983,816. That means that the chance that any *particular* two draws will match is 1 in 13,983,816. But what about the chance that *some* two draws among three draws will match? Or the chance that *some* two draws among 50 draws will match? There are three possible pairs among three draws, but 1,225 among 50 draws. The law of combinations is coming into play. Taking it further, among 1,000 draws there are 499,500 possible pairs. In other words, if we multiply the number of draws by 20, increasing it from 50 to 1,000, the impact on the number of pairs is much greater, multiplying it by almost 408, and increasing it from 1,225 to 499,500. We are entering the realm of truly large numbers.

How many draws would be needed so that the probability of drawing the same six numbers twice was greater than one-half—so that this event was more likely than not? Using the same method we used in the birthday problem results in an answer of 4,404. If two draws occur each week, making 104 in a year, this number of draws will take less than 43 years. That means that after 43 years it's more likely than not that some two of the sets of six numbers drawn by the lottery machine will have matched exactly. That puts a rather different complexion on the Bulgarian spokeswoman's comment that it was a freak coincidence!

And that's just for one lottery. When we take into account the number of lotteries around the world, we see that it would be amazing if draws *did not* occasionally repeat. So you won't be surprised to learn that in Israel's Mifal HaPayis state lottery the numbers drawn on October 16, 2010—13, 14, 26, 32, 33, and 36—were exactly the same as those drawn a few weeks earlier, on September 21. *You* won't be surprised to learn that, but scores of people flooded Israeli radio station phone-ins to complain that the lottery was fixed.

The Bulgarian lottery result was unusual, in that the duplicate sets of numbers occurred in *consecutive* draws. But the law of truly large numbers, combined with the fact that there are many lotteries around the world regularly rolling out their numbers, means we shouldn't be too surprised; and so we shouldn't be taken aback to hear that it had happened before. For example, the North Carolina Cash 5 lottery produced the same winning numbers on July 9 and 11, 2007.

Another, rather frustrating, way in which the law of combinations can generate lottery matches is illustrated by what happened to Maureen Wilcox in 1980. She bought tickets containing the winning numbers for both the Massachusetts Lottery and the Rhode Island Lottery. Unfortunately for her, however, her ticket for the Massachusetts Lottery held the winning numbers for the Rhode Island Lottery, and vice versa. If you buy tickets for ten lotteries, you have ten chances of winning. But ten tickets mean 45 pairs of tickets, so the chance that one of the ten tickets will match one of the ten lottery draws is over four times larger than your chance of winning. For obvious reasons, this is not a recipe for obtaining a vast fortune, since matching a ticket for one lottery with the outcome of the draw for another wins you nothing—apart from a suspicion that the universe is making fun of you.

The law of combinations applies when there are many interacting people or objects. Suppose, for example, that we have a class of 30 students. They can interact in various ways. They could work as individuals—there are 30 of them. They could work in pairs—there are 435 different pairs. They could work in triples—there are 4,060 possible different triples. And so on, up to, of course, them all working together—there is one set of all 30 students working together. In total, the number of different possible groups of students that could be formed is 1,073,741,823. That's over a billion, all just from 30 students. In general, if a set has n elements, there are 2^n-1 possible subsets which could be formed. If $n = 100$, this gives $2^{100}-1 \approx 10^{30}$, a truly large number in anyone's terms.

But if even 10^{30} isn't large enough for you, consider the implications of the World Wide Web. This has around 2.5 billion users, any and all of whom can interact with any of the others. This gives 3×10^{18} pairs and $10^{750,000,000}$ possible groups of interacting members. Remember Borel's definition of probabilities that were negligible on a supercosmic scale? Well, even events with probabilities that small become almost certain if you give them that many opportunities to happen.

Roll the Dice

As I've mentioned, I have a large collection of dice. One of them is rather unusual, in that it's symmetrical, with ten identical faces. Now, if you're an expert in solid geometry, you might suspect that I'm being economical with the truth here, since there is no symmetrical three-dimensional shape with ten identical faces. So to reaffirm your faith in me, I should tell you that the die is in fact *cylindrical*, with a ten-sided polygon as its cross-section and rounded ends, so that it has to land on one of its ten identical faces. The faces of this die are numbered 0, 1, 2, 3, 4, 5, 6, 7, 8, and 9. (And if that doesn't convince you that I have a die that will produce one of ten outcomes with equal probability, then I should tell you that in my collection of dice I also have several that are *icosahedral*: they have twenty faces, all of the same shape and size. I could put the same numbers on two faces, so that again I would have a die that produced 0, 1, 2, 3, 4, 5, 6, 7, 8, and 9 with equal probabilities.)

Now suppose I threw this die twice and the same numbers came up. You might be a little surprised, but you wouldn't fall off your chair: it happens.

But now I'm going to throw my ten-faced die another time, and another—say six times in all. The probability that my first two throws will have the same value is just 1 in 10: whatever value came up on the first throw, there's a probability of 1 in 10 that the second throw will be the same. The same sort of argument then says that the probability that my six consecutive throws all have the same number is just 1 in $1 \times 10 \times 10 \times 10 \times 10 \times 10$ (that is, 10 times itself five times; 10^5 for short). This number is 1 in 100,000, or 0.00001. That's a pretty small probability. If you saw such a sequence of the same number coming up six times in a row you might begin to suspect that there was something funny going on. Maybe the die *always* comes up showing the same value. (Recall my "beginner's dice" from chapter 2, which have the number 6 on all six faces.) In any case, you'd look for an explanation.

Here's another way of looking at it. I've no reason to expect any particular sequence of numbers to come up more often than any other sequence. So the sequence of six numbers 786543 should come up just as often as 225648, and just as often as 111654, and so on. This also means that we should expect the sequence of numbers 000000 to come up as often as any other sequence. Likewise, the sequences 111111, 222222, etc. How many sequences of six numbers are there altogether? Well, the first number can occur in ten ways. And the second number can occur in ten ways. So there are $10 \times 10 = 100$ possible ways in which the first pair can occur. Ten of these have identical values: 00, 11, and so on up to 99. Ten out of 100 is 1/10, so this is the probability of getting the same values in a pair of throws, as we've already seen. A similar calculation for six throws shows that there are 10^6 possible sequences, and just 10 sequences that have identical values (they are identically 0 or 1 or 2, and so on up to 9). So there's a probability of just 10 out of 10^6 that all the values will be identical. That is, 1 in 100,000, again as we've already seen.

So much for the theory. The fact is that, however you look at it, if you saw me throw my ten-sided die six times and get the same result each time, you'd wonder how I did it.

But now consider this variant. Suppose that, instead of just me, there are 100,000 people, each throwing a ten-sided die six times. We can imagine repeating the exercise, each time requiring our 100,000 willing volunteers to throw their die six times.

Sometimes nobody gets a set of six identical numbers. Sometimes several among the 100,000 do—perhaps two people produced a string of six 7's, and one person a string of six 1's. Since the probability of getting six identical values is 0.00001 it follows that, *on average*, one person among our 100,000 will produce such a string. This is an average: sometimes when we all throw our dice six times no one gets such a string, sometimes exactly one person does, sometimes more than one does. But we shouldn't be at all surprised when it happens. The law of truly large numbers tells us that if there's a large enough number of people throwing the dice, then we should expect to see such an outcome.

On the other hand, imagine what could happen in practice. We're gathered in a great hall, all 100,000 of us, throwing our dice six times. For most people, a rather uninteresting set of numbers comes up. These wouldn't attract attention. But what about somebody who by chance threw all the same digits—all 0's or all 1's or all 2's, and so on? That would certainly attract attention. It would look as if that person had an uncanny ability to throw the same number. The TV camera crews would cluster around. Conjectures would be made about how he or she did it. Was it a miracle? Did the person cheat? Humans, being inquisitive animals, would seek an explanation.

If the other volunteers, those who didn't get such striking results and had no reason to stay, left the hall so that it looked as if there was just this one outcome, people might well think that something extraordinary had occurred. The newspapers and the television shows, the blogs and Twitter, would report only the extraordinary result (no doubt inflating it to a "one-in-a-billion chance"). The 99,999 others, who produced patterns of numbers which appeared "random," would be forgotten. (The selective forgetting of some of the results is another aspect of the Improbability Principle, called the *law of selection*—the topic of chapter 6.)

However, taking a more scientific approach to questions of

chance, we might want to test our new media star's dice-throwing prowess. We might ask him to throw the die again, another six times. What do you think is likely to happen then? Since in fact he obtained his outcome purely by chance—he was just the one lucky person among the 100,000—the boring truth is that his next six throws have equal probabilities of producing any possible configuration of the ten numbers. It's overwhelmingly more probable that he *won't* produce another set of six identical digits. In fact, the probability is 0.99999 that he won't and only 0.00001 that he will. This effect is called *regression to the mean*. It describes the fact that he's much more likely to disappear back into the mass of undistinguished dice throwers when he makes his next six throws. Regression to the mean is an aspect of the law of selection.

You might think that example was rather unrealistic, but later I will describe some ESP experiments which look very much like it. However, here's a real example, not quite so extreme as the dice-throwing one, but of life-and-death interest.

One of the weapons used by Germany during the Second World War was the V-1 "doodlebug" flying bomb. These were small jet-propelled pilotless aircraft, packed with explosives, launched across the English Channel toward London. Often the points where the bombs landed seemed to lie in clusters, many near each other. This raised the question of whether they could be precisely aimed. The fact is, given enough such bombs, we'd expect some to fall near to each other just by chance—the law of truly large numbers (though in this case even a moderately large number was sufficient to raise the question). So was it targeting or was it chance?

In 1946, R. D. Clarke, a Fellow of the Institute of Actuaries, tackled the question by dividing a map of 144 square kilometers of London into 576 small squares of ¼ square kilometer each, and counting the numbers of bombs that fell into each small square. If the bombs fell at random places, the approximate number of squares that had no strikes, one strike, two strikes, and so on should be predictable (based on a statistical distribution called the *Poisson distribution*   after the great mathematician Siméon Denis Poisson). Clarke concluded that there was no deliberate clustering, and hence that the bombs were not precisely aimed.[7] The apparent clustering that people thought they detected was purely because of the number of bombs, and could be accounted for by the Improbability Principle.

Scan Statistics and the Look Elsewhere Effect

I began the last section by throwing the ten-sided die six times, and we saw that the chance of getting the same number on all six of those throws was just 1 in 100,000. Now I'm going to take that further: instead of stopping after throwing it six times, I'm going to keep on throwing it. Not just six times, but twenty times, a thousand times—keeping going until I have a sequence of 600,000 digits (I have a lot of spare time on my hands). Now what's the probability that we'll see six consecutive values *somewhere* in this sequence of 600,000 digits?

This sort of question—what's the chance that a particular pattern will occur *somewhere* in a large data set?—crops up in many contexts. It's asked by people who are attempting to detect fraud in credit card transactions, intrusions into computer networks, abnormalities in cardiac traces, faults in engines, and a host of other areas. But we have to be careful. The law of truly large numbers means we should *expect* peculiar patterns to occur. The key question thus is, what's the chance that we'll get particular patterns in large series of numbers purely by chance? And then— are we seeing more than we'd expect? If so, we have reasons for suspecting some non-chance cause.

One way to start to answer the question would be to group the 600,000 throws into 100,000 consecutive blocks of six numbers.

For example, if my sequence of 600,000 numbers started with 98837777770322611287 . . . I could split it into blocks of six: 988377, 777703, 226112, 87 . . . , and so on, and we've already seen that we would *expect* to see a set of six identical consecutive values somewhere among these 100,000 blocks. In fact, we saw that on average we'd expect one such set among our 100,000 blocks.

The trouble is that splitting the sequence up in this way doesn't allow for the fact that when we simply throw the die 600,000 times there might be a set of six identical values overlapping from one block of six throws to the next. In fact, that happens in my example above, where there *is* a block of six consecutive 7's, but they overlap from the first to the second block. Our procedure for estimating the probability of six identical values in a row fails to allow for such occurrences, and will seriously underestimate the chance that somewhere there's a sequence of six consecutive identical values in the 600,000 throws. When we allow for overlaps between blocks, the chance of getting a set of six consecutive identical values is much greater than when we ignore the possibility of such overlaps, simply because there are then many more opportunities for such sets of six consecutive identical values to occur.

The basic strategy for checking whether strings of six consecutive identical digits occur at *any* point in the sequence is to slide a window six digits long from the beginning to the end of the 600,000 digits and see how often it includes six identical values. Statisticians have developed methods for estimating how often you'd expect this to happen if the 600,000 digits were generated randomly. They're called *scan statistics* because of the way the window scans over the data.

Now, if that dice example strikes you as artificial, consider the following.

On February 23, 1996, *USA Today* carried a headline: "Another F-14 crash prompts stand-down." The article described how three F-14 fighter aircraft had crashed within a 25-day period, leading the U.S. Navy to suspend flights of that type of plane. The Grumman F 14 Tomcat, a supersonic two-seater fighter aircraft used by the U.S. Navy, flew between 1970 and 2006, and 712 of them were built. In all, beginning with a crash on December 30, 1970, 161 of them crashed. The average time between crashes was 70 days.

Now we shouldn't be surprised that such aircraft crash occasionally. After all, they're frequently flying at their limits, often in hostile and unpredictable environments, where the unexpected can happen. However, three in such a short period looks suspicious. Maybe there was more to the crashes than met the eye. Perhaps they had some common cause.

To investigate this, we could divide the period between 1970 and 2006 into months, say, and then use the Poisson distribution of the last section to estimate the chance of seeing three crashes within a one-month period. That's all very well, but like the dice example, it would miss closely spaced crashes which overlapped the month divisions. A better approach would be to scan a month-long window over the period from 1970 to 2006 and count the number of crashes occurring within it as we slide it along. This count could be compared with what would be expected by chance to see if more crashes occurred in any window than chance would lead us to expect. In fact this has been done for the F-14 crashes. It turns out that the chance of having three crashes within some month over a five-year period is well over one-half. Despite the suspicions leading the U.S. Navy to suspend F-14 flights, there were no grounds for thinking the three crashes in quick succession were anything but chance.

The dice and F-14 examples are *one-dimensional*. They involve consecutive events. But the same ideas can also be applied in two or more dimensions.

Imagine studying a map that shows the locations of everyone suffering from a specific disease. Some of these cases will be caused by external factors—perhaps a pollutant. In such situations we might expect to see a local cluster of cases. A terrible example of this was the Minamata Bay incident in Japan. Over some 36 years, methylmercury in waste water from the Chisso Corporation's chemical factory worked its way up the local food chain, building up in shellfish and fish, and then in the animals and humans who ate those fish. Several thousand people were afflicted with nightmarish symptoms and, at the extreme, death.

So you might think that the way to detect such environmental disease risks is to look for clusters of illness.

The Huffington Post ran a piece about disease clusters: "In December [2010] reports emerged of a 12-mile radius in Clyde, Ohio, that had been addled by 35 cancer diagnoses over a 14-year span. Residents described being scared by a simple cough; parents worried over a mere sinus-infection or stomach ache." The article went on to say that "On March 29, the Natural Resource Defense Council (NRDC) and National Disease Clusters Alliance identified 42 such disease clusters throughout 13 U.S. states."[8]

This is all very well, but there's a complication: just as in the one-dimensional examples above, we should *expect* to see local clusters of sick people purely by chance. Again we have the question of how to tell if they are chance or have an underlying cause. Again a solution is through scan statistics, which can tell us whether the number of clusters we are seeing is what we'd expect purely by chance or not.

In this case, since the problem is two-dimensional, instead of an interval we slide a small two-dimensional window, say a square ten miles by ten miles, over a map of the United States. As we slide this square over our map, we count the number of disease cases we see. This number will change as the square moves. If we see a number at any position that's much greater than the maximum we'd expect to see by chance, we can suspect a common underlying cause (like the pollution in the shellfish in Japan).

The cancer diagnoses example in the *Huffington Post* article illustrates that sometimes both time and geographical location are involved, so that the problem is essentially three dimensional. In such situations we're looking for an excess number of disease cases in a small geographical area and in a limited interval of time. This is particularly important in detecting the early stages of epidemics such as the Severe Acute Respiratory Syndrome (SARS) outbreak which occurred in 2002–2003, in which over eight thousand people contracted the illness and more than seven hundred died, and the 2009 H1N1 "swine flu" pandemic. Here it's especially important to spot the cluster early on, to decide if it represents a *real* outbreak with a common cause and is not just a chance co-occurrence of random events.

For my final example I'll turn to cutting-edge big physics, which often involves searches for anomalously dense clusters in very large data sets. If you know where the cluster is likely to be, then the analysis is straightforward, but if you don't know where the clusters may occur, you're in the same kind of situation we've just looked at. The search for the Higgs boson illustrates this perfectly: it involves massive amounts of data that must be trawled through to detect evidence of the phenomenon. For example, a *mass spectrum* from these searches contains counts of the numbers of particles of each mass observed from a series of experiments. Theory may tell us that there'll be a peak—an unusually large number of particles—at some specified mass, making the analysis relatively easy. But perhaps we are not sure where the peak should be. So now we have to search over the range of masses looking for peaks in the number of particles. And, just like the search for disease clusters or groups of doodle-bug strikes, this opens up the possibility of getting peaks purely by chance.

Particle physicists, who are very good at coming up with eye-catching names for phenomena, have coined the term "the look elsewhere effect" for this detection of clusters which have been generated purely by chance as a consequence of the large number of candidates examined.

The Bible Code, Geller Numbers, and the Inevitability of Pi

Questions of the kind we've just looked at crop up all over the place. Other examples include several suicides occurring in a particular place or in quick succession, clusters of silver specks in photographic film, birth-date clusters of people with inflammatory bowel disease in Sweden, clusters of flaws in mineral crystals, dense clusters of phone calls in telecommunications networks, and clusters of close galaxies in astronomical databases.

All those examples are concerned with clusters of events, but the idea generalizes to other patterns. Given enough opportunities, you'd expect to see any pattern eventually—the law of truly large numbers.

A rather fantastical case is the so-called "Bible code," which refers to the claim that the Hebrew Bible contains hidden messages forecasting future events. An example is the observation that the Hebrew word *torah* is spelled by taking every fiftieth letter of the Book of Genesis, beginning with the first *t*. It's an old observation, and similar ones have been made about other sacred texts, including both Christian and Islamic scriptures, but interest in these phenomena skyrocketed in the late 1990s with the publication of the book *The Bible Code* by Michael Drosnin. Unfortunately for Drosnin, the law of truly large numbers suggests that there are no hidden messages—only that the Improbability Principle is at work.

Since the Bible has many letters, there are a great many places to look for meaningful series of them. I could put my finger on any letter in the Bible, and, starting from there, try out many different types of pattern. In the "equidistant letter sequence" approach, for example, I would take equally spaced letters, in horizontal lines following the text, or in vertical or diagonal lines if the letters in successive lines on the page were aligned. The number of potential sequences and patterns which could be examined is unlimited, so it would be extraordinary if no supposedly meaningful sequences were found (indeed, finding *no* such sequences would be evidence either of something odd going on, or of the fact that you just hadn't looked hard enough!).

I doubt that Charles Dickens was trying to convey some secret information by concealing the word "fate," with the letters each separated by three other characters (counting spaces as a character) in chapter 4 of *The Pickwick Papers* ("the most aw-*f*ul *a*nd *t*remendous discharge that ever shook the earth"), or the word "doom" in chapter 5 in the phrase "close*d* up*o*n your *m*iseries." For entertainment, I searched this book as I was writing it and found the concealed message "help" in the words "t*h*an h*e* coul*d* ex*p*lain by chance" in the section Synchronicity, Morphic Resonance, and More, in chapter 2, with the letters *h*, *e*, *l*, and *p*, each separated by four other characters. Then the word "help" appears again, with the letters separated by four characters again, buried in the words "t*h*at w*e* wou*l*d ex*p*ect to see." in the previous section of this chapter. So, "help, help." Clearly there is someone hidden in my book crying out to be rescued!

Searching for hidden patterns in ancient (or even modern) texts is one way of looking for purported secret messages. Another is through the methods of numerology.

"Numerology" is the study of the mystical or magical properties of numbers. Unfortunately, it's a futile enterprise, because the rather banal truth is that numbers don't have any such properties. In fact, it's intrinsic to the very definition of "numbers" that their magnitude is their only property. That's the whole point of numbers: they extract what is common to three sheep, three minutes, three shouts, and so on. Nonetheless, throughout history people have attached mystic significance to numbers. Indeed, we still speak of "lucky" numbers.

Much of numerology is based on coincidences in which identical numbers occur. But we've seen that if you look long and hard enough, the law of truly large numbers means that such coincidences are to be expected.

I'll give just one illustration of the absurdity of numerology. Uri Geller, whom we encountered in chapter 2, has a fascination with the number sequence 11:11, and he's given many examples of how this sequence keeps appearing in his life.[9] The trouble is that, as a consequence of his public outreach, there is a huge opportunity for the law of truly large numbers to come into effect. He says: "I have been absolutely inundated over the recent years with emails about others who are noticing exactly the same. For example, I have received an email from a friend, with a picture of his boarding card number which was 111—and just out of 'coincidence' on the plane in front of him, was a code printed on the wall in front of him 11:11—and then the bay that the plane was towed to—was number 11. This was all on the same flight to Cyprus." But readers will recognize that the number of opportunities for such configurations to occur is vast—and that Geller's friends do not bother to send him e-mails about all the configurations that do *not* conform to this pattern.

The attack on the World Trade Center occurred on 9/11, giving Geller scope for further numerology (though I don't quite follow his reasoning when he says that "the 11.11 references surrounding this horrific tragedy, fill me with hope that the people who tragically lost their lives in this attack may not have died in vain"). He notes:[10]

- the date of the attack: 9/11. $9 + 1 + 1 = 11$
- After September 11th there were 111 days left to the end of the year
- September 11th is the 254th day of the year: $2 + 5 + 4 = 11$

- The Bali bombing occurred 1 year, 1 month, and 1 day after the September 11th attacks
- The first plane to hit the towers was Flight 11 by Ameri can Airlines or AA-> A = 1st letter in alphabet so we have 11:11
- Flight #11—had a crew of 11
- Flight #175—65 on board—6 + 5 = 11
- State of New York—11th State added to the Union
- Construction of the Pentagon began . . . September 11th, 1941
- The World Trade Center was built from 1966 to 1977 . . . taking 11 years

As Geller says, this is "bizarre, weird & unbelievable," but perhaps not in the way he thinks. He adds, "It baffles me how anyone can see all of these references and not be intrigued." But the scope to search for ways of combining numbers and for situations in which particular numbers can occur means that the law of truly large numbers has effectively become a law of unlimitedly large numbers. It's very clear that if we were *not* able to find such examples, it would merely reflect a lack of imagination in searching. If you wish to while away an idle moment or two, you could do exactly the same with any other set of numbers. Google would be an ideal tool to use.

To regain our balance after that short excursion into the realm of numerological fantasy, let's look at the digits of the decimal expansion of pi.

Pi is an extraordinary number, about which entire books have been written, but for our purposes we can simply regard its decimal expansion as a random series of the ten digits 0, 1, 2, . . . , 9.[11] Here are its first 100 digits:

3.14159265358979323846264338327950288419716939937
51058209749445923078164062862089986280348253421
17067

Now, since the digits seem to be random in the sense that it's not possible to predict what digit will follow any given sequence of digits, there's a nonzero probability that any particular string of digits will arise somewhere. Of course, we may have to search for a long time before finding that string, especially if it's a long one. In fact, we can work out the probability of finding a given string of length t in the first 100 million digits of pi. For example, the probability of finding any particular string of length $t = 5$ among the first 100 million digits of pi is 1 (that is, it turns out that *all* possible strings of five digits actually do occur among the first 100 million digits). Similarly, 63 percent of all strings of length $t = 8$ occur among the first 100 million digits, so the chance of a randomly chosen 8-digit string being there is 0.63.

Treating the first digit of pi after the decimal point as position 1, the second as position 2, and so on, then the digits of my birth date, expressed in the form DDMMYYYY, where D stands for day, M for month, and Y for year, occur at location 60,722,908.[12]

A more subtle phenomenon—and one which will doubtless excite numerologists, but which will impress *us* with the power of the law of truly large numbers—is the so-called "self-locating" string. Using the same definition of position as above, "self-locating" strings are strings of digits that are to be found at their own position in the decimal expansion of pi. Examples of self-locating strings can be found at

1 (since pi is 3.*14159* . . .)
16470 (that is, the string 16470 starts at position 16,470
    in the expansion of pi)
44899
79873844

I'll come back to numerical coincidences in chapter 10, where I discuss the origin and nature of the universe, but first, here's an

example showing that numerical coincidences *can* be meaningful—
that they do sometimes reflect an underlying structure.

There's a branch of mathematics called *group theory* and it's
concerned with the study of symmetries, of how making certain
changes to an object results in an object indistinguishable from
the one you started with. If you rotate a square by 90 degrees,
for example, you end up with what looks like the same square.
Likewise, if you flip a square over one of its diagonals, you again
end up with something indistinguishable from the original
square. Group theory has taken this study to extreme lengths,
looking at such symmetries in different mathematical objects.
One of these has the fanciful name "the Monster." This mathematical object, which involves symmetries between some 8×10^{53}
components (about equal to the number of elementary particles
in the planet Jupiter), was predicted to exist in the early 1970s.
By 1978, study had revealed that if it existed, this strange structure would do so in a very large number of dimensions—196,883
in fact.

The mathematician John McKay had studied the Monster,
but in November of that year he was reading about another subject entirely: number theory. This isn't the same as numerology,
but is concerned with the mathematics of whole numbers. It's a
completely different area from group theory, so McKay was as-
tonished when he encountered the number 196,883 in number
theory, too. It looked as if there was some previously unsuspected
link between these two entirely different areas of mathematics—
and his discovery sparked a mathematical treasure hunt for an
explanation of the coincidence.

If there was a link, it was hard to pin down. The eminent
mathematician John Conway, who was taking part in the search,
coined the name "Moonshine" to describe what was going on—
"It had the feeling of mysterious moonbeams lighting up dancing
Irish leprechauns." (Who says mathematicians don't have a touch
of poetry in their souls?)

The mathematician Mark Ronan has written a book about the discovery of the Monster and the resulting quest for an explanation of the link between the two apparently disconnected areas of group theory and number theory. As he explains: "The method leading to its discovery, brilliant though it was, gave no clue to the Monster's remarkable properties. It was only later that the first hints arose of odd coincidences between the Monster and number theory, and these were to lead to the connections with string theory. The Moonshine connections between the Monster and number theory have now been placed within a larger theory, but we have yet to grasp the significance of these deep mathematical links with fundamental physics. We have found the Monster, but it remains an enigma. Understanding its full nature is likely to shed light on the very fabric of the universe."[13]

So, sometimes coincidences do have an underlying cause: a pollutant resulting in a disease cluster, an anomalous particle count revealing the Higgs boson, or *something* yielding the Monster. But the law of truly large numbers tells us that more often than not (and sometimes *far* more often than not), if we have looked in enough places, the curious matches we have found will be a consequence of the Improbability Principle.

Lightning, Golf, and Animal Magic

Although lightning is an awesome and frightening display of nature's power, the chance of actually being hit by a bolt is very small, and the chance of being killed is much smaller. In fact, meteorologists have estimated that on average, each person's probability of being killed by a lightning strike in one year over the entire Earth is around 1 in 300,000. That's a pretty small probability. But the population of the Earth is around 7 billion. That 7 billion is a large number—perhaps even a *truly* large number. And that allows the law of truly large numbers to sneak in.

With so many people, each with a probability of 1 in 300,000 of being killed in a year, the chance that *no one* will be killed by lightning is about $10^{-10,133}$, more than cosmically improbable on Borel's scale. With such a small probability that no one will be killed, we should expect to see *someone* killed, and estimates show that around 24,000 deaths do indeed occur each year due to lightning strikes, with about ten times that many people being injured.[14]

I'll return to lightning strikes and the probability of being killed by a lightning bolt in chapter 7, when I talk about the *law of the probability lever*. This is another strand of the Improbability Principle, concerned with how small differences in circumstances can mean huge differences in probabilities. It's particularly important for lightning because the 1 in 300,000 figure above is a *global* average. In other words, the average includes people from urban and rural areas, people who spend their time underground in coal mines (not many lightning strikes there), and also people who spend their time herding cattle in open plains. It also includes different countries: for the population of the more developed United States, the probability of being killed by lightning is a reassuringly low 1 in around 4 million. The use of an average here brings to mind the old joke that your average temperature is fine if you have your feet in the oven and your head in the refrigerator.

As with lotteries and lightning, golf is a rich source of stories about improbable events, like the example in the first chapter of the two golfers who made consecutive holes in one. But there's a difference between golf, on the one hand, and lotteries and lightning on the other. In a sense the *aim* in golf is to hit a hole in one. So people train to develop the ability to do so—that is, to shift the odds to increase the probability of hitting a hole in one. It follows that different people will have different probabilities of hitting a hole in one. For example, while it's not all that surprising when Tiger Woods hits a hole in one, it would definitely be something worth writing home about if I did. Woods has in fact made 18 holes in one. Likewise, Jack Nicklaus recorded 21 in his career, while Arnold Palmer and Gary Player each recorded 19. Even so, and as we can see by the relatively small numbers of holes in one scored by these leading professionals, it's a rare event. So rare, in fact, that the U.S. Professional Golf Association regards it as sufficiently noteworthy to maintain an archive listing details of the holes in one people have hit,[15] and there is at least one website devoted to such events.[16]

The probability of hitting a hole in one is about 1 in 12,750, and if that probability is roughly correct, the law of truly large numbers tells us that such events should be expected: there are many golf courses around the world, many people play each day, they play time after time, and each full round they play they hit 18 tee shots. It all adds up to a truly large number of opportunities for holes in one to occur, to the extent that the law of truly large numbers means we should *expect* to see such events occurring, perhaps with an almost tedious regularity.

And we do. The oldest golfer to score a hole in one appears to be Elsie Mclean, aged 102, from Chico, California, and the youngest, five-year-old Keith Long in Mississippi in 1998.[17] At the time of writing, the record number of holes in one is claimed by an American amateur, Norman Manley, with 59.

In fact, the law of truly large numbers can lead to even more apparently improbable golfing events. It can lead, for example, to the *same* person hitting two holes in one on consecutive days. Here's an extract from an article written on August 2, 2006 by Tim Reid, Washington correspondent of *The Times*:

> An amateur golfer became the talk of clubhouses in America yesterday after hitting holes in one on the same hole two days in a row at a tournament in Texas. Danny Leake, 53, followed up his first hole in one at the 6th hole on Saturday—a 174-yard shot with a five-iron—with an-

other at the same hole on Sunday, using the same club from 178 yards.[18]

And here's an extract from the website of the Hunstanton Golf Club:

A feat of incalculable odds also occurred at Hunstanton. In 1974, the amateur Bob Taylor holed in one during a practice round for Eastern Counties Foursomes. The following day, in the actual competition, he again holed in one. The very next day in the same competition, he once more holed in one. If a hole in one on three consecutive days is not enough, you'll be amazed to hear that it was achieved each time on the same hole, the 16th, a 191-yard par three![19]

The impact of the law of truly large numbers is also illustrated by the phenomenon of psychic animals. These are animals that appear to be able to predict the future, or tell when some event has occurred.

During the 2010 FIFA football World Cup, "Paul the Octopus," from his tank at the Sea Life Center in Oberhausen, Germany, successfully predicted the outcome of the seven matches of the German national team and the final. "Prediction" took the form of Paul picking one of two boxes, each marked with the flag of one of the competing teams, and each containing food. The probability of getting all these predictions correct is 1 in $2^8 = 256$—so not that startling. And it's even less startling when we take into account the law of truly large numbers. In fact, in this case, because 1 in 256 is not so small a probability, the numbers don't even need to be "truly" large. Nonetheless, Paul's apparent "power" made him an instant media star. He was made an honorary citizen of a town in Spain, and ambassador for England's 2018 World Cup bid. Unfortunately, as the Oberhausen Sea Life

Center reported, he won't make it to that World Cup, having been found dead in his tank on the morning of Tuesday, October 26, 2010. "We are consoled by the knowledge that he enjoyed a good life," said Stefan Porwoll, the Center's manager. Paul's "agent" Chris Davies commented, "It's a sad day. Paul was rather special but we managed to film [him] before he left this mortal earth."

And Paul wasn't the only one. Look at enough animals, matching them against enough sporting events, and you're opening the door to the law of truly large numbers.

Mick Power refers to Mani the Parakeet, of Singapore, which predicted the outcomes of the first seven matches but then failed on the eighth (so he's not quite in Paul's league).[20] One side effect of the law of truly large numbers is that you'd expect even more animals to fail in some of their predictions than succeed in getting them all right. And at Chemnitz Zoo in Germany, Leon the porcupine, Petty the pygmy hippopotamus, Jimmy the Peruvian guinea pig, and Anton the tamarin all unfortunately incorrectly predicted the outcome of the final. Octopuses Xiaoge in China and Pauline in the Netherlands both got the final wrong, as did the Estonian chimpanzee Pino and red river hog Apselin, along with the Australian crocodile Harry.

There seems to be no end to this sort of thing. It clearly strikes some sort of psychological chord. From an article in *The Sunday Times* of May 27, 2012, we learn that "A llama in Ashdown, East Sussex, has already correctly tipped Chelsea to win both the FA Cup and the Champions League. But he faces competition for next month's Euro 2012 from Kiev, one of the host cities, which has unveiled a telepathic pig. A spokesman described it as 'a unique oracle hog, a real Ukrainian pig and a psychic that knows the mysteries of football.' At 4pm each day it will predict the results of the next day's game . . . The Polish co-hosts prefer to rely on Citta the elephant, who was chosen over a donkey, a parrot and another elephant after correctly predicting the results of the

Champions League final, using apples painted in team colours . . . At last year's world ice hockey tournament in Slovakia, the results were predicted by a 'psychic' two-headed tortoise called Magdalena, who picked winners by moving around a scale model of a hockey rink." I rather like the Citta the elephant story, as it reminds me of the stock-picking strategy I described in chapter 4: get enough animals, all making different predictions, and one will match what actually happens. Citta happened to be the lucky one.

Sports predictions aren't the only situations where "psychic" animals crop up. Just a moment surfing the Web will show thousands of other cases, ranging from animals acting strangely before earthquakes to dogs that appear to know when their owners are about to arrive home.

There have been speculations that animals might be able to detect some kind of terrestrial vibration preceding an earthquake, but the International Commission on Earthquake Forecasting for Civil Protection essentially concluded that there was no credible evidence for such predictive powers.[21] We might have referred the Commission to the law of truly large numbers, and to the fact that the news media need eye-catching stories.

As for the dogs, there have been very few tests, but here's an account of one involving the terrier Jaytee, whose owner claimed he could predict when she would return home: "Matthew and Pam . . . used a random number generator to select a time to head back—9 p.m. Meanwhile, I continuously filmed Jaytee's favourite window so that we would have a complete record of his behaviour there. When Pam and Mat returned from the bar we rewound the film and eagerly observed Jaytee's behaviour. Interestingly, the terrier was at the window at the allotted time. So far, so good. However, when we looked at the remainder of the film, Jaytee's apparent skills started to unravel. It turned out that he was something of a fan of the window, visiting it 13 times during the experiment. During a second trial the following day, Jaytee visited the window 12 times."[22] The law of truly large numbers is coming into play—in terms of the amount of time the dog spends at the window. If he spends enough time there, it would be odd if he wasn't often waiting when his owner returned.

Less Than You Think

The law of truly large numbers says that if there are enough opportunities for an event to happen, then we should expect it to happen, even if the probability that it will happen on any particular occasion is tiny. Furthermore, as in the birthday problem, often the number of opportunities is far greater than at first meets the eye, so that the impact of the law can be unexpected and deceptive.

But we've also seen situations where it wasn't necessary for there to be a *truly large* number of opportunities for the effect to arise. Paul the Octopus had a 1 in 256 chance of getting it right, so if we had 256 animals all giving different predictions we would be *certain* that one would be right—the law of inevitability. So numbers near to 256 would give a high probability of finding an animal which made the right predictions. And 256 is quite a small number.

The critical point here is the proportion of outcomes which are covered. The effect is amplified if we are wrong about how many possible outcomes there are. If our first glance suggests there are a billion possible outcomes, only a hundred of which are in our favor, we'd be surprised if we got lucky. But we'd be less surprised if, on looking more closely, we saw that there were really only a thousand possible outcomes—still with a hundred in our favor. A one in ten chance is rather different from a one in ten million chance!

An example of how incorrectly estimating the number of potential outcomes can have an effect occurred in the 1997 Spanish

Grand Prix, when Michael Schumacher, Jacques Villeneuve, and Heinz-Harold Frentzen all completed laps in exactly the same time, 1 minute 21.072 seconds.[23] This seemed a remarkable coincidence. But if we assume, considering the usual margin of victory, that the three fastest times are all likely to fall within the same $\frac{1}{10}$th-of-a-second interval, and note that the time of 1 minute 21.072 seconds is measured to an accuracy of $\frac{1}{1,000}$th of a second, then the probability that these three drivers would finish in the same $\frac{1}{1,000}$th of a second is just $\frac{1}{100} \times \frac{1}{100}$, just 1 in 10,000. Not such a very small probability—at least when we factor in the number of races each year and the number of years over which motor racing has been a sport. Plenty of opportunity for the law of truly large numbers to operate.

Given Enough Opportunities . . .

Your chance of being involved in a train crash is small, but that chance clearly depends on how much rail traveling you do. Someone who travels on a train just once a year is far less likely to be involved in a crash than someone who commutes on one every day. Likewise, it's more likely that someone in your family will be involved in a train crash if you have a big family, and more likely if a longer period of time is taken into consideration: Bill and Ginny Shaw, from chapter 3, had a fifteen-year gap between their accidents.

Similarly, while it may be unlikely that some unfortunate event will happen to you, or to any other *particular* person on the earth, we need to remember that there are around 7 billion people alive at present. If each person has a probability p of having an accident on a given day, and if the accidents are independent of what has happened to anyone else, then the probability that no one will have an accident on that day in a population of size N is $(1-p) \times (1-p) \times (1-p) \times \ldots$ a total of N times. With N equal to 7 billion, the size of our global population, and p equal to a one-in-a-million chance, the probability that *no one at all will have an accident on that day* is about 1 in $10^{3,040}$, a really tiny probability. It's overwhelmingly more likely that someone, somewhere, will have an accident—so likely that Borel's law comes into play and makes it essentially *certain*.

6

THE LAW OF SELECTION

Who cares if you pick a black ball or a white ball out of the
bag? . . . don't leave it to chance. Look in the damn bag and
pick the color you want.
— Stephanie Plum, in *Hard Eight* by Janet Evanovich

Walnuts, Archery, and Stock Market Fraud

When I was young I was very impressed by how food producers
could fill jars with whole walnuts. Somehow they could crack the
shells while leaving the nuts intact. Most of the times I tried it, I
ended up with mixed pieces of shell and nut, managing to get the
nut out whole only once every ten times or so. Later, however, I
learned that although the manufacturers had a better success
rate than I did, they often ended up with mixed shell and nut
pieces, too. But I also learned that they did something else: they
selected their results. On those occasions when they were successful,
they'd take the whole nuts and stick them in a jar labeled "Whole
Walnuts." And on the other occasions, they'd separate the nut
pieces from the shell and stick them in a jar labeled "Walnut
Pieces." (They also had a way of softening the shells so it was
easier to get the nut out whole, but I won't let that get in the way
of a good story.)

The point here is that I wasn't seeing the entire picture. I'd assumed that the "whole walnut" jars were the results of *all of* their efforts, rather than of just a selected subset of them. Indeed, they could have obtained the same results—jars of whole walnuts— even if they'd had only a tiny success rate, one in a thousand, say—by choosing only the successful outcomes to package as whole walnuts.

My walnut story illustrates the law of selection, which says that you can make probabilities as high as you like if you choose *after* the event: the manufacturers made it *certain*—probabilities equal to 1—that the walnuts in their jars were whole by choosing only the whole nuts after cracking the shells.

Here's another old story illustrating the same idea. You're walking along a country lane and you come across a barn. On the side of the barn there are many painted targets, and right in the bull's-eye of each target is an arrow. "Wow!" you think. "This guy must be a really good archer." You carry on walking past the barn. Then, turning around to look at the other side of the barn, you see that it, too, has many arrows sticking in it. And busy painting bull's-eyes and targets around each of them is a man.

Again the point is that if we select the data after the fact, we can make probabilities look very different from the way they looked before. The chance of getting each arrow in the bull's-eye by the conventional method of shooting them at the target is much smaller than the chance of getting them in the bull's-eyes if you shoot first and paint later!

Although the target story might sound rather fanciful, it bears a close resemblance to something that happened in the world of stocks and shares, and which led to a Pulitzer Prize. Here's the story.

One widely used way of remunerating company directors is by awarding them stock options. These options take their initial value at the time they are given, so that if the stock price subsequently rises, the options become more valuable. In an article

published in the *Wall Street Journal* on March 18, 2006, Charles
Forelle and James Bandler identified six companies where the
stock options had dramatically increased just after the options
had been awarded. For example:[1]

> [T]he 1999 grant [to William McGuire] was dated the
> very day UnitedHealth stock hit its low for the year. Grants
> to Dr. McGuire in 1997 and 2000 were also dated on the
> day with those years' single lowest closing price. A grant
> in 2001 came near the bottom of a sharp stock dip. In all,
> the odds of such a favorable pattern occurring by chance
> would be one in 200 million or greater . . .

> One grant [to Kobi Alexander, chief executive of Converse
> Technology] was dated July 15, 1996, and carried an exer-
> cise price of $7.9167, adjusted for stock splits. It was priced
> at the bottom of a sharp one-day drop in the stock, which
> fell 13% the day of the grant and then rebounded 13%
> the next day . . . Another grant, on Oct. 22, 2001, caught
> the second-lowest closing price of 2001. Others also cor-
> responded to price dips. The odds of such a pattern occur-
> ring by chance are around 1 in six billion, according to
> the *Journal*'s analysis . . .

> [A]ll six of [CEO Jeffrey Rich's] stock-option grants [in
> Affiliated Computer Services Inc.] from 1995 to 2002 were
> dated just before a rise in the stock price, often at the bot-
> tom of a steep drop . . . a *Wall Street Journal* analysis sug-
> gests the odds of this happening are . . . around one in
> 300 billion . . .

> Brooks Automation Inc. . . . gave 233,000 options to its
> CEO, Robert Therien, in 2000. The stated grant date was
> May 31. That was a great day to have options priced.

Brooks's stock plunged over 20% that day, to $39.75. And the very next day it surged more than 30%.

(To give us some context for these probabilities, recall from chapter 4 that the chance of picking the winning ticket in a 6/49 lottery is around 1 in 14 million.)

There are various possible explanations for such highly improbable events. One is that they did indeed just happen. After all, a one-in-a-billion-chance event should be expected to happen if there are a billion opportunities for it. But a billion stock option awards is a lot of stock option awards.

Or perhaps those tiny probabilities are misleading. Perhaps the probabilities of hitting those highly remunerative dates by chance are actually much bigger than we thought. The fact is that the stock prices and options awards showing those dramatic increases were picked from the thousands of stocks and stock option awards which were made over the time of the study reported in the *Wall Street Journal*. If we randomly awarded options to company directors, we'd expect *some* of them to be made on great days, just before the stock price skyrocketed. And the article draws our attention to just those for which the stock price did skyrocket, ignoring all the others. So perhaps the apparently improbable events are really a consequence of the law of selection, with authors Forelle and Bandler selecting, *after the fact*, those options which increased dramatically in price.

That possibility certainly needs to be kept in mind, but it's difficult to see this effect leading to the 1 in 200 million, or in 6 billion, or in 300 billion probabilities mentioned above.

A third possible explanation was suggested by Erik Lie, from the University of Iowa.[2] His explanation is also a consequence of the law of selection, though working in an entirely different way. Using his analysis, Lie commented, "Unless executives possess an extraordinary ability to forecast the future marketwide movements that drive these predicted returns, the results suggest that at least some of the awards are timed retroactively." The selection here is not a question of picking those stocks to write about which happened to show the effect, and ignoring all the others. Instead, it's a consequence of company boards looking back in time and retrospectively picking dates just prior to a dramatic price increase. That is, they might have backdated the stated time of the awards to dates which were financially propitious.

The role of the law of selection here is just like its role in the targets-on-the-barn example. If you paint the target after shooting the arrows, it's easy to have the arrows in the bull's-eyes. And if you look back in time at stock market prices, it's easy to identify when they were about to shoot up—much easier than trying to predict future dates at which they will shoot up. (The great physicist Niels Bohr made a pertinent comment about this: "Prediction is very difficult, especially of the future.") By looking back at what *actually* happened, instead of looking forward and trying to see what *will* happen, we can change our probability of being right from uncertain to certain. This practice has been called *postdiction*, paralleling the word "prediction."

The striking contrast between prediction and postdiction arises all over the place. After a major disaster, for example, people often ask, "Why didn't we see it coming?" and suggest that the signs were there from the beginning. This was true of the 9/11 atrocity, for example. The trouble is that the warnings are often hidden among thousands of other signs and events. After the fact it's easy to put the pieces together, and show how they form a continuous chain leading to the outcome. Before the fact, however, there are many pieces and potential chains and it's just not possible to know which events fit together. This isn't because there are too many pieces, but simply because they can be put together in a vast number of possible ways, and there's no reason to select out any one of them. Our innate tendency to retrospectively adjust a recollection as new information becomes available, to identify the chain which led to the disaster, and to say, *after the fact,* "Look, it was staring us in the face!" is called *hindsight bias.* It's an old idea, and it's one way the law of selection manifests itself.

Like the other aspects of the Improbability Principle, the law of selection creeps into our lives in all sorts of unexpected ways. Think of a man arriving at a railway station and examining a map of the local area with a large red dot on it labeled "You Are Here," and being amazed that the railway company knew he'd be there at that time. I'm reminded of a friend who received one of those unsavory spam e-mails offering penis enlargement to men who feel insecure in that department—"How did they know?" he asked. Another, slightly surreal, example is that of a man asking "How come, when you misdial a telephone number, it never seems to be busy?" The map-reading man forgot that only people at that location could read the map, my friend forgot the millions of others who had also received the spam e-mail, and the man dialing the wrong phone number forgot that you discover you've dialed a wrong number only if someone picks up and tells you so.

These are all rather trivial instances of the law of selection. A more exalted example is the process of natural selection driving evolution, which progressively selects offspring to found the next generation. Yet another is what's been called the *anthropic principle,* which addresses the very question of why the universe is the way it is. I discuss both of these in detail in chapter 10.

The famous American psychic Jeane Dixon, whom we met in chapter 2, was renowned for making many correct predictions. But she was less well-known for making even more predictions which didn't come true. We saw that the trick is to draw attention to the predictions you get right, and conveniently forget about those you get wrong. And we can see now that this "Jeane Dixon effect" is simply an example of the law of selection. The same principle is also what lies behind the wealth of the stock tipster I described in chapter 4. Since he predicts *all* of the possible patterns of stock price outcomes, one pattern each to a different person, the law of inevitability tells us that one of his prediction patterns must turn out to be right. Then, applying the law of selection, he presents that correct one as "evidence" of his ability to predict the future—at least to the person who received that pattern of "predictions."

We've already seen that a coincidence is an unexpected concurrence of events—like two consecutive holes in one. But coincidences don't require that each of the separate events be highly improbable. In chapter 2, for example, we saw that both Caligula and Lincoln had dreamed that they would be assassinated, and they were. Now, scientists know that we each have at least four to six periods of dreams a night and that we forget most of them. We're much more likely to recall a dream if something happens the next day which reminds us of it. This is simply an aspect of how the brain works, linking and connecting disparate events. So it's not a case of having one dream which was a precursor of the one event in question. We have many dreams, and each is followed by many events, and we notice those which happen to match, tending to forget all the others. After all, why would we remember them? They're just part of the random background fluctuation of dreams, memories, and events, with nothing special to mark them out. It's the rare *concurrence* of dreaming that something would happen and then it actually happening which is striking.

Caligula was the emperor of Rome from A.D. 37 to A.D. 41 His real name was Gaius Julius Caesar Augustus Germanicus, and Caligula was a nickname meaning "little soldier's boot" given to him by his father's soldiers. He'd been the target of several previous unsuccessful assassination attempts, which surely must have made him more likely to have dreams of being assassinated. On the other hand (and this is where the law of selection comes in), unsurprisingly, history doesn't relate how many assassination dreams he'd had when he was *not* killed the next day. Caligula's advisers recalled that he told them of his dream and then indeed was assassinated—but of course dreaming of assassination and then not being killed wouldn't make much of a story. The law of selection also enters when we balance people who have dreamed that they would be assassinated and then indeed *are* against the (one would think) millions of people who have had such dreams and then *not been* assassinated.

Exactly the same applies to Lincoln's dream. We have to put it in the context of the number of assassination dreams he'd probably had previously, which he didn't bother to mention to his friends, or which they forgot, and after which he was not assassinated. The law of selection again.

"Precognitive" dreams like these also illustrate other strands of the Improbability Principle. For example, Caligula's dream was ambiguous. Caligula saw himself standing before the throne of Jupiter, king of the gods, but then being cast back down to Earth—and he interpreted this as a warning of imminent death. It seems to me that he might equally have interpreted it as indicating that his time had not yet come, and he was being cast back to continue his life on earth. Now, if you recall the principles for successful prophecy suggested in chapter 2, you'll recognize that ambiguity lies at the heart of many mistaken probability assessments. And in fact, it's the core of another strand of the Improbability Principle which I call *the law of near enough*, and which I'll discuss later. This law essentially says an event may not be *exactly* what you said it would be, but if it's not far off we can count it as a match. So, for example, Lincoln described his dream to Ward Hill Lamon and others three days before his assassination and began his description with *"About ten days ago . . ."*[3] Now, how near in time to the event does a dream have to be to count as prophetic? The day before, a week, a year? Stretch "near enough" sufficiently and you can guarantee a match—and that's the essence of the law of near enough.

The law of truly large numbers also comes into play here. We need to consider how many dreams, altogether, are dreamed by everyone in the world every night. What would be really extraordinary is if *none* of these happened to coincide with a matching event happening the next day.

The misleading effect of the law of selection is not a recent discovery. Francis Bacon gave a beautiful example four hundred years ago, in 1620, in his book *The New Organon*, which we met in chapter 2 when I talked about confirmation bias. Bacon wrote: "[I]t was a good answer that was made by one who when they showed him hanging in a temple a picture of those who had paid their vows as having escaped shipwreck, and would have him say whether he did not now acknowledge the power of the gods—'Aye,' asked he again, 'but where are they painted that were drowned after their vows?' "[4] Only those who survive shipwreck are able to tell you that they prayed beforehand.

Winning a Lottery

Up until now, the examples of the law of selection show it having an impact by choosing what data to use *after* the event has occurred. The walnut producers chose only the whole walnuts to put in their jar after cracking the nuts. But the law of selection can manifest itself in other ways. Here's an example showing how it can lead to lottery fortunes vanishing before your very eyes. It's not about your chance of winning the lottery, but about how *much* you might actually win.

There's not much point in picking the winning ticket in a lottery if thousands of other people pick the same numbers. Your vision of millions of dollars when you realize you have the winning ticket will evaporate into a puff of disappointment when you realize you're just one of a thousand winners. But surely, you might quite reasonably say, if the chance of choosing the winning ticket is so small (like the 1 in 14 million in a 6/49 lottery), then the chance of two people choosing the same set of numbers, let alone thousands of people choosing the same set, must be *incredibly* small.

That would certainly be true—except for two things. One is the law of truly large numbers. If enough people buy lottery tickets, the chance that someone else will buy the same ticket numbers as you becomes arbitrarily large. The second is the matter of how people choose their numbers—because people often don't choose their ticket numbers at random. They often choose numbers which have some special significance, like birthdays. So someone born on June 18, 1948, might code that date as the three numbers 06, 18, 48. So two birth dates—of a husband and wife, for example—would give us the six numbers we'd need for a 6/49 lottery ticket. Since months have 31 days or less, and years have only 12 months, if you restrict your choice to birth dates coded in this way you're not choosing from 49 numbers but from a smaller set: you could never pick the ticket 33, 36, 37, 45, 48, or the ticket 1, 4, 18, 35, 38, 43, for example.

Restricting the set of tickets people might choose increases the chance of picking the same ticket as someone else—partly because there are fewer to choose from, and partly because if you follow such a rule you can be sure others will also.

Other people, aiming to choose "randomly," base their choice on a pattern of numbers on the lottery form. For example, they might work down a diagonal, or keep away from the edge. Still others follow some rule such as starting with 1 and repeatedly adding 3 to give 1, 4, 7, 10, 13, 16, or using squared numbers, 1, 4, 9, 16, 25, 36, and so on. But, again, any such pattern is likely to be chosen by other lottery players, so that the odds of matching someone else's choice are increased.

Another popular strategy is to choose the same numbers that came up on the previous draw. That obviously produces a choice which randomly varies from draw to draw, but it's also a rule that other people might choose. You'll recall how the Bulgarian lottery numbers which came up on September 6, 2009, also came up four days later. Well, eighteen people chose those numbers the second time! The total jackpot of $137,574 plummeted to just $7,643 each. Nice to have, sure, but hardly life changing.

A surprising number of people do choose their numbers based on patterns. For example, in the New York State Lottery of June 7, 1986, 14,697 people chose the same six numbers 8, 15, 22, 29, 36, 43. The most popular combination of numbers for the California Lotto 6/49 on October 29, 1988, was 7, 14, 21, 28, 35, 42; this combination was chosen by 16,771 people. The regularity of these sequences (the values in both sequences are all separated by 7) makes them look suspiciously as if they were based on a regular grid of numbers—the layout of the lottery forms, presumably. In the Finnish 7/39 Lotto on August 27, 1994, 5,066 people chose the numbers 1, 2, 3, 4, 5, 6, 7, and 3,225 chose 5, 10, 15, 20, 25, 30, 35. If their thinking was that any one of these sequences had the same chance as any other, they were right. It's just that these sequences were also likely to be picked by other players.

In my walnut and arrows examples, by choosing outcomes after the event had happened we gained a misleading idea about the *chance* of an outcome. In our lottery examples, the law of selection works in a different way: it distorts the outcomes themselves. The *chance* of any particular ticket remains unchanged, but the *amount* you get if you win can change dramatically.

Incidentally, there's a lesson in this for all lottery players. While the only way to increase your *probability* of winning is to buy more tickets, you can increase the average *amount* you win by choosing combinations of numbers that others are unlikely to choose. This means avoiding using rules for picking your numbers. And, since you can't predict all the rules that people might think of so that you can avoid them, one strategy for decreasing the chance of picking the same numbers as someone else is to pick your numbers at random. Lottery operators typically make this approach easy, through options such as *quick pick* or *lucky dip*.

Regression to the Mean

Traffic enforcement cameras or "speed cameras" were first introduced in the United States in Friendswood, Texas, in 1986. In the UK they were introduced in the 1990s. Now they're ubiquitous. Those in fixed locations are often brightly colored so that approaching drivers can see them and (if necessary!) slow down. That makes sense because the aim, contrary to what some activists believe, is not so much to catch speeding drivers as to encourage them to drive more slowly. The misunderstanding is perhaps promoted by the fact that they often have an associated "cost recovery" scheme, so that they are, at least in part, self-financing. This can make it look as though they're yet another way to tax motorists, and explains why they remain controversial even though they're really a tool to encourage motorists to drive responsibly.

The issue of cost recovery is only one reason why they're controversial. Another is the fundamental question of whether or not they're actually effective in reducing accidents. The answer to this question is entangled with the law of selection, which acts to exaggerate the apparent effect of the cameras in reducing accident rates. We briefly encountered the form of the law which produces this effect in chapter 5—it's called regression to the mean. Sir Francis Galton was the first to describe this form of the law, in the nineteenth century, though he initially called it *regression to mediocrity*.[5]

Galton was an extraordinary character, one of the founders of modern science. He was a cousin of Charles Darwin, and, characteristic of the age in which he worked, when science wasn't as divided into distinct disciplines as it is today, he made huge advances in a number of areas, including statistics, meteorology, criminology, psychometrics, anthropology, and genetics.

Galton spotted that characteristics which are extreme in parents are likely to be less extreme in their children. For example, two very tall parents will tend to produce children who, while also being tall, will typically be nearer the average than their parents. Likewise, short parents will tend to produce children shorter than average but taller than them. The same phenomenon occurs in other inherited characteristics, so that it looks as if there is some biological mechanism pulling generations back toward the average height. Galton's genius lay in recognizing that this apparent force attracting things back toward the average was the result of a purely statistical selection phenomenon—a manifestation of the law of selection (though he didn't call it that).

To illustrate, let's take an abstract example, stripping away all the psychological implications of behavior, changes in road traffic safety measures, and underlying biological mechanisms. This abstract example is based on the throws of standard six-sided cubic dice.

Imagine we've thrown 3,600 such dice. Purely by chance we'd expect about 600 of them to show a 1, about 600 a 2, and so on up to about 600 showing a 6. Now let's pick all those showing a 6, ignoring the others. Since each of these shows a 6, the average value they show is obviously also a 6. We then throw all these again. By chance again, we'd expect about 100 of them to show a 1, about 100 a 2, and so on up to about 100 of them showing a 6. The overall average of the numbers showing on the dice on this second set of throws will be about 3.5 (it's just $[100 \times 1 + 100 \times 2 + \ldots + 100 \times 6] \div 600$). Now the average has decreased from 6 the first time we threw these particular 600 dice to 3.5 the second time we threw them.

The explanation for this reduction from 6 to 3.5 is straightforward enough. Each of the outcomes, 1 to 6, was equally probable. So, when we picked those (approximately) 600 that had come up 6 on the first throw, we were selecting the ones which *purely by chance* had shown a 6. But there was nothing special about those dice: at the next throw they'll behave in the normal dice way and produce an average of about 3.5.

It's a manifestation of the law of selection: we chose the dice on the basis of a chance outcome (they had come up 6), but there's no reason to expect that chance outcome to be repeated the next time we throw them.

Now let's translate this into a model for the speed cameras, so we can see why it's relevant. Suppose, for the moment, that the accidents occur purely by chance. We can think of each of the 3,600 dice as equivalent to a potential camera location, and the values given by throwing the dice as corresponding to the number of accidents (from 1 to 6) at those locations. Suppose we have only 600 cameras, and have to decide at which of the 3,600 sites to locate them. Clearly we'll choose to position the cameras at the sites which show the worst accident rates—there is, after all, little point in placing the cameras where there are very few accidents. So we install a camera at each of the (about) 600 sites where there were 6 accidents.

Now we follow developments over the next year to see what happens to the accident rate at each site where we've placed a camera. The accident rate over this second year will be equivalent to the results of throwing for the second time the 600 dice that originally showed a 6. As we saw, simply by chance, about 100 of the locations will show 1 accident, about 100 will show 2 accidents, and so on, all the way up to about 100 of the locations showing 6 accidents. The average of the second-year accident rate over all of the 600 locations will consequently be about 3.5, calculated as before. It looks as if the accident rate has dramatically decreased. But the reduction has nothing to do with whether or not the cameras are effective. It's just due to the law of selection, through regression to the mean.

Unfortunately, there are also further complications with real-life speed cameras. In life, as in our simplified model, speed cameras *are* placed at the locations which seem to need them most—where accident rates are highest. But in real life it isn't just chance which causes those places to have the highest accident rates: some locations are intrinsically dangerous (for example, a long straight stretch of road which encourages speeding). So, if the accident rate drops after the cameras are put at those places, it might be due to a combination of regression to the mean *and* a genuine effect of actually encouraging people to drive more slowly.

Careful statistical analysis of road traffic accident data, taking account of increased traffic, improved driving tests, continuing enhancements to vehicle safety (such as anti-lock braking systems), anti-drunk-driving campaigns, and so on, shows that there is a real effect due to the placement of cameras beyond the law of selection. For example, in one study of 216 cameras, the average annual number of fatal and serious accidents before and after the cameras were put in place was 226 and 103 respectively—an average decrease of 123 per year.[6] However, the analysis showed that about 78 of these could be attributed to the law of selection, in its regression-to-the-mean form, while the overall general trend toward decreasing accidents arising from changing traffic conditions and other measures accounted for another 21. So, of the average reduction of 123 per year, only 24 could be attributed to the cameras.

The bottom line is that while cameras reduce the number of accidents and save lives, we'll overestimate their effectiveness if we fail to allow for the law of selection.

This "regression to the mean" variant of the law of selection pops up in all sorts of unexpected places. For example, film studios, naturally, make sequels only to particularly successful films. But films are particularly successful because of a combination of their intrinsic merit and random effects. Any sequel, even if it is of comparable intrinsic merit, is unlikely to see the same positive random influences. So sequels are likely to be less successful than their predecessors.

Likewise, in chapter 1 of his book *Synchronicity*, Carl Jung outlines some of the extrasensory perception experiments of the parapsychologist J. B. Rhine, commenting, "One consistent experience in all these experiments is the fact that the number of hits scored tends to sink after the first attempt." Well, what would you expect? Regression to the mean tells us this is exactly what should happen.

The regression-to-the-mean effect has also led to confusion in treating diseases whose severity fluctuates over time or from which people naturally recover in time. Doctors give treatments when symptoms are more severe, and if the severity fluctuates over time, then we should expect patients to improve without treatment, simply by waiting. Many quack treatments and pseudo-scientific approaches capitalize on this. You wait until someone's symptoms are bad and then give them the medicine. And, lo! The symptoms ease up, and the quack claims it's all due to the medicine.

This is why randomized controlled trials are so important. In such a trial, there are two equivalent groups of patients. One group receives the purported treatment and the other receives a placebo, or nothing at all, with neither patients nor researchers knowing which group received which. If the symptom alleviation is purely due to regression to the mean, and not to the treatment, then the two groups will recover at the same rate.

An almost comic example of how regression to the mean can be misunderstood, and alternative explanations conjured up to explain something we should in fact expect to occur, is given by Arthur Koestler in his book *The Roots of Coincidence*. He wrote: "Even the most enthusiastic experimental subjects showed a marked decline in hits towards the end of each session, and after some weeks or months of intense experimenting most of them lost altogether their special gifts. Incidentally, this 'decline effect' (from the beginning to the end of a session) was considered as additional proof that there was some human factor at work influencing the scores, and not just chance."[7]

The regression-to-the-mean effect is ubiquitous. Once you've been alerted to the phenomenon, you can see it everywhere. It occurs whenever the score, outcome, or response has a random component. Take performance, for example—in an examination, a test, a workplace, sports, or whatever. While performance clearly does depend partly on intrinsic ability, preparedness, and other factors, it also owes something to chance. Perhaps you were feeling particularly good on the day, or the questions on the exam just happened to be on the topics you'd anticipated, or the representatives from the prospective client turned out to be old high school friends. The chance aspect of your good performance is likely to fade away the next time, so that it looks as if you have deteriorated. Regression to the mean signals that caution must be exercised in taking the results at face value: an extreme score may well be so primarily because of chance.

There's also a flip side to this. If extremely good performance owes something to favorable chance, then particularly poor performance likewise owes something to unfavorable chance.

All of this has obvious implications for just about any kind of ranking (of sports teams, surgeons, students, universities, you name it): if a high position owes much to chance, it's likely to be followed by a lower position next time.

Psychologist Daniel Kahneman illustrated these concepts in his autobiographical essay written on winning the Nobel Prize in Economic Sciences in 2000. He said:

> I had the most satisfying Eureka experience of my career while attempting to teach flight instructors that praise is more effective than punishment for promoting skill-learning. When I had finished my enthusiastic speech, one of the most seasoned instructors in the audience raised his hand and made his own short speech, which began by conceding that positive reinforcement might be good for the birds, but went on to deny that it was optimal for flight cadets. He said, 'On many occasions I have praised flight cadets for clean execution of some aerobatic

manoeuvre, and in general when they try it again, they do worse. On the other hand, I have often screamed at cadets for bad execution, and in general they do better the next time. So please don't tell us that reinforcement works and punishment does not, because the opposite is the case.[8]

This is regression to the mean in action!

Selection Bias in Science

The law of selection manifests itself in science in what is called "selection bias," which I mentioned in chapter 2. For example, in the late eighteenth century William Withering discovered that the plant foxglove was effective in alleviating what was then called dropsy, describing it in *An Account of the Foxglove and Some of Its Medical Uses*. He wrote, "It would have been an easy task to have given select cases, whose successful treatment would have spoken strongly in favour of the medicine, and perhaps been flattering to my own reputation. But Truth and Science would condemn the procedure. I have therefore mentioned every case in which I have prescribed the Foxglove, proper or improper, successful or other-wise."[9] He understood how selecting cases could be misleading, and was at pains to avoid the error.

In my book *Information Generation: How Data Rule Our World*,[10] I described several incidents in which very well-known figures in the history of science appear to have selectively chosen their results to support preconceived ideas. These figures include Louis Pasteur, who discovered that most infectious diseases were caused by microorganisms, and Robert Millikan, who measured the charge on the electron. Millikan was very explicit about having selected his data: "I would have discarded [the lower-quality results] had they not agreed with the results of the other observations."[11] The fact that he discussed this suggests he might have appreciated the dangers.

If selecting from the results is one way of distorting conclusions, another is *to decide what hypothesis you are testing after you've carried out the experiment and collected the data*. This procedure has been called "harking," an acronym for *h*ypothesizing *a*fter the *re*sults are *k*nown. It's clear that if you do this then you can easily come up with hypotheses which are supported by the data! Put like that, the dangers probably seem obvious, but the effect typically manifests itself in much more subtle ways. For example, researchers might sift through the data, observe a hint of a trend in a particular direction, and then carry out a more elaborate statistical analysis and test *of the same data* to see if the trend is significant. But any conclusion will be distorted by the initial observation of the hint of a trend.

Another version of selection bias which has attracted a great deal of attention also came up in chapter 2: publication bias. This is the tendency for scientific journals to preferentially publish studies which show a phenomenon rather than those which *fail* to show the phenomenon. It's also sometimes called "the file drawer effect," describing the fact that the unpublished studies will end up confined to the file drawer and never written up as papers appearing in the scientific literature.

It makes perfect sense. Studies which conclude a drug is effective are intrinsically more exciting than studies which conclude that the drug does not have an effect. So authors will be less inclined to submit papers describing results of the latter sort than the former, and editors will be more likely to accept the former sort for publication. After all, what editor would want to stuff his journal with papers showing that drugs didn't work? But the consequence is to give a misleading impression of whether the drug works.

Unfortunately, it gets worse. When testing drugs, typically several such trials will be carried out (it's a requirement by the medicine regulatory authorities that multiple trials should have been conducted). But the fact is that symptom severity fluctuates over time. Even if the drug doesn't work, some of the patients will appear to get better, purely by chance. As a result, in some of the trials the drug will appear to be effective, even if it really isn't. And now publication bias kicks in. Papers describing the results of the trials have to be written up and submitted to journals for publication. And, as we've seen, those papers which appear to show an effect are more likely to be written up, submitted, and accepted. A selection process is occurring, in which those papers that showed an effect *purely by chance* are disproportionately submitted and accepted for publication. The others disproportionately tend to fall by the wayside.

One interesting consequence of publication bias is a tendency for published "discoveries" to be refuted later. This follows by direct analogy with the dice and traffic-accident examples, by regression to the mean. If the apparent effect of a treatment is attributable to chance, then we should expect that effect to vanish when the treatment is used again later, or the study is replicated. John Ioannidis, an epidemiologist from Stanford, has taken this observation to an extreme. He writes, "There is increasing concern that most current published research findings are false."[12]

Yet another illustration of the distortion which can arise from the law of selection is given by many of the self-selected surveys which are carried out by the popular press and on the Web. To produce reliable results, any survey should choose the sample of respondents carefully, so that any deductions based on it are likely to represent the overall views of the target population. In particular, the surveys mustn't be arranged so that people more likely to answer the questions a certain way are also more likely to reply to the survey. Put bluntly like that, it probably seems blindingly obvious. Nonetheless, every week magazines, newspapers, and the Web are full of such things. The absurdity is illustrated by imagining the extreme case of such a "survey" being carried out to discover if the readers of a magazine replied to surveys by asking them the single question, "Do you reply to magazine surveys?"—and then basing the conclusion on the proportion of answers which were "Yes."

One of my favorite examples appeared in *The Actuary* of July 2006. A note to the reader said, "a couple of months ago I invited you—all 16,245 of you—to participate in our online survey concerning the sex of actuarial offspring . . . Well, I'm pleased to say that a number of you (13 in fact) replied to our poll." *The Actuary* recognized the absurdity of basing conclusions on such a small sample, though apparently not the dangers of conducting such a self-selected survey in the first place. (The note went on to say: "The one thing we can conclude from this is that actuaries do not contribute to online polls.")

We need to be on the alert for the distorting influence of the law of selection, especially as a potential cause for apparently low-probability events. Here are some more examples of how the law can manifest itself in subtle ways—the first shows how greater uncertainty can work to your advantage.

Imagine we want to choose the most able person for a job and aim to do this by testing the candidates. Now, test scores aren't perfect measures of ability (think of the exams you took in school: sometimes you did better than expected, sometimes worse, depending on exactly what questions were asked, how well you slept the night before, and so on). Suppose we have twenty candidates, all of the same ability—so that, *on average*, if we tested them lots of times, their average test scores would be the same— but ten of whom produce much more variable scores than the others.

So, for example, ten of the candidates might produce scores ranging from 45 to 55 while the other ten might produce scores ranging from 20 to 80. People in both sets have averages of 50, but those in the second set are much more variable. To fill the job, we're going to choose the one candidate with the highest score. It's clear that this candidate is much more likely to be from the second, more variable, set. There's a bias favoring greater variability, even though the candidates' average abilities are the same. From our perspective, with the aim of choosing someone for the job, this has a pointed downside: if the test really is measuring ability to do the job, then the candidates we are most likely to pick are also likely to have the most erratic performance on the job.

Next, imagine we are comparing ten medicines, and we evaluate them by giving each to a different group of 30 patients. Even if all the medicines are equally effective, one of the groups of patients will do best (there has to be a largest in any set of numbers). But if we simply take the score of that group as the expected future efficacy of the medicine, we're capitalizing on chance: the largest of the scores is likely to overestimate the efficacy. If we were to give that same medicine to another group of 30 patients, regression to the mean tells us that the new score is likely to be lower.

Another example of the law of selection in clinical trials is *dropout bias*. It's not at all uncommon for patients to drop out from a study, so that there's gradual attrition in numbers over time. They might drop out because they move house, or die, or simply get fed up with taking the medication. But suppose this attrition is happening because some of the patients are starting to feel better (the medicine is working), so they no longer feel motivated to continue to attend the clinic for tests. We would be preferentially left with the patients for whom the treatment did not work. Unless we somehow allowed for the dropouts in our analysis, it would look as if the medicine was ineffective when in fact the converse was true.

Length-time bias is another distortion arising from the law of selection. It arises when the probability of selection depends on a length of time. To illustrate, suppose we wanted to know how long cases of the common cold last, on average. To explore this, we might pick people (who come to the medical center) suffering from a cold on the 1st of January and ask them when it started, and follow up to see when it ends. The trouble is that people whose cold lasts a long time are more likely to be included in our count. People whose cold started at any time in the previous year and lasted for a whole year would certainly be included in our count. But anyone whose cold started at any time in the previous year, but lasted for just one day, would be unlikely to be included. Indeed, if colds have an equal chance of starting on each day, then we would include only $\frac{1}{365}$ th of the people whose cold lasted just one day. So our count would dramatically underestimate the number of people whose cold lasted only a short time. When we calculate the average length we would mistakenly obtain a value much longer than it should be.

Though I could have chosen countless others, my final example is one you may have experienced: coming across a new word for the first time and then encountering it again very soon afterward. There are various reasons that this can happen, and we'll examine some others later, but one is the law of selection. Consider words that are sufficiently rare that, *on average*, they each occur in your reading material only about once every ten years. This is an *average*, so some of these words will take longer—perhaps the entire length of your reading life to date—before you encounter them for the first time. But once you've read them, since on average they recur every ten years, there's a good chance that they'll recur much sooner than in another ten years, and you'll be surprised to see them again so soon. It's the law of selection again.

The law of selection can be looked at in various ways. It tells us how to change probabilities by making a choice after something has happened. It tells us how to make predictions come true by waiting until we know the outcome. It tells us how to increase our lottery jackpot—if not our chance of actually winning. The regression-to-the-mean version of the law tells us that what goes up must come down. If, partly by chance, we've done very well at something, we should expect to do less well the next time. And this law crops up all over the place. Once you're familiar with it, you'll see examples of it almost every day.

In the next chapter we'll look at a very different strand of the Improbability Principle: the law of the probability lever. This law tells us how slight differences in our thinking can have truly massive effects on probabilities.

7

THE LAW OF
THE PROBABILITY LEVER

Chance favors only the prepared mind.   —Louis Pasteur

From Tiny Acorns

You're driving along the highway, following the route you planned. You've passed several of the landmarks you noted. But suddenly something seems amiss. You don't recall seeing *that* village name on the map. You carry on, but more and more unfamiliar names flash past. Now you have no idea where you are. Nothing is as you expect. (You begin to wish you had bought that GPS navigator system after all.)

This chapter is about the causes of such jarring discrepancies. It's about world models and improbability.

In his history of hedge funds, *More Money Than God*, Sebastian Mallaby wrote: "a plunge of the size that befell the S&P 500 futures contracts on October 19 [1987] had a probability of one in 10^{160}—that is, a '1' with 160 zeroes after it. To put that probability into perspective, it meant that an event such as the crash would not be anticipated to occur even if the stock market were to remain open for twenty billion years, the upper end of the expected duration of the universe, or even if it were to be reopened for further sessions of twenty billion years following each of twenty successive big bangs."[1]

Borel's law tells us that we simply shouldn't see events as improbable as Mallaby's example. It says that events with a sufficiently small probability never occur, and surely a 1 in 10^{160} probability is "sufficiently small" in anyone's terms. So what's going on? We shouldn't see such improbable events, and yet on October 19, 1987, we did.

The answer has its roots in a strand of the Improbability Principle that I call "the law of the probability lever."

In mechanics, the law of the lever describes how objects of different weights balance on a beam—like two people on a seesaw. A lighter person sitting far from the balance point can counterbalance a heavier person sitting close to the balance point. If the heavier person moves slightly farther out, or if his weight is slightly increased, then the beam tips, and the lighter person shoots skyward.

In a similar way, the law of the *probability* lever tells us that a slight change in circumstances can have a huge impact on probabilities. The shift can, for example, transform tiny probabilities into massive ones.

However, at this point I must confess to having slightly misled you. I omitted something from my quotation from Sebastian Mallaby above. The full quotation begins: "In terms of the normal probability distribution . . ." We met the normal distribution in chapter 3. It showed us the probability, for some situations, of getting any particular value when we took a measurement or made an observation.

So, what the full quotation actually means is, *if you assume that the sizes of fluctuations in market prices follow the normal distribution*, then a plunge in the S&P 500 futures contracts of the size observed on October 19, 1987, had only a 1 in 10^{160} probability of occurring. Now, when scientific theory fails to match the observations, there are several possible reasons. One is that there's something wrong with the data—that there were errors of some kind in the measurements. Another is that the theory itself is mistaken in some way (that, for example, the assumptions on which it is built are not quite right).

The assumption that fluctuations in market prices are normally distributed is an attractive one: the normal distribution has very nice mathematical properties, which make theory and predictions that use it relatively easy to work out. Furthermore, as I've already commented, measurements *are* often approximately normally distributed. But that word "approximately" is important. Indeed, financiers now recognize that the fluctuations of financial markets, while *approximately* normally distributed, are not *exactly* so. And the law of the probability lever can worm its way in to capitalize on those very slight departures from normality, amplifying them and resulting in a huge effect further down the line—with consequences as dramatic as the one Mallaby described.

To see how the law does this, we first need to take a closer look at the normal distribution.

The Normal Distribution Again

In chapter 3, I remarked that the normal distribution is often described as "bell-shaped." In fact, mathematicians define its shape much more precisely than that. They have a specific formula which gives the shape of the normal distribution in terms of its average value and how widely dispersed its values are about that average. Once we know the average value (also called the *mean*) and the spread (also called the *standard deviation*), the mathematical expression of the normal distribution means we can work out the exact probability that a randomly drawn value will lie in any interval. For example, we can work out the exact probability that a randomly drawn value will lie between 0 and 1, or between −1 and +2, and so on.

Figure 7.1 illustrates this idea, with three normal distributions.

Measurement

Figure 7.1. Three different normal distributions. A has mean 10 and spread 1. B has mean 10 and spread 2. C has mean 16 and spread 1.

If it helps, think of these as test scores for three different groups of children—perhaps children taught by three different methods. The center of each distribution is its average value. The height of a curve at any particular score shows the probability of obtaining a value very near that score. We see that the probabilities are highest around the centers of each distribution, so that if we randomly chose a child from any group we would be most likely to find they scored near the average of that group. We would be unlikely to find they had an extremely large or extremely small score. The heights of the distributions also get lower the farther we go from the center, in a symmetric way. That means that the child is equally likely to have a score three points above the average or three points below the average, for example.

Distribution A has a mean value of 10 and a spread of 1. Distribution B also has a mean of 10, but a larger spread of 2. Because it has a larger spread, B is higher than A for values farther from the mean. At values of 6 and 14, for example, A has a height of virtually zero, while B is relatively high. So B has a higher probability of giving extreme values compared to A.

In our example, children in the group with test score distribution B tend to have more extreme scores than those in A. (And lest you think this is fanciful, it's a curious fact that on some psychological tests the scores of boys appear to be more widely dispersed than those of girls: boys have more high scores and more low scores, with relatively fewer near the average.)[2]

Distribution C has the same spread as A, but a different average. On average, the test scores from C will tend to be higher than those from A or B. But the spread of C's values around its average is the same as the spread of A's observations around *its* average: the chance of someone from the C group getting a value three points above C's average is the same as the chance of someone from the A group getting a value three points above A's average.

The key point here is that, although there are differences between the three distributions shown in Figure 7.1, with C shifted to the right and B being squashed, they all have the same basic *shape*—this shape is given by a specific mathematical formula, and this shape is what is meant by the normal distribution.

Money, Money, Money

With that discussion of the normal distribution under our belt, let's return to the crash of '87. On October 19, "Black Monday" as it was called, the Dow Jones Industrial Average dropped by 22.6 percent, the largest one-day drop in its history, and by the end of the month stock markets around the world had fallen dramatically:

in the United States by 23 percent, in the UK by 26 percent, and in Australia by 42 percent.

Then about ten years later, in 1998, the hedge fund Long-Term Capital Management collapsed. Roger Lowenstein described the probability of such an event: "[T]he odds against the firm's suffering a sustained run of bad luck—say, losing 40 percent of its capital in a single month—were unthinkably high . . . Indeed, the figures implied it would take a so-called ten-sigma event . . . for the firm to lose all of its capital in one year."[3]

A "ten-sigma event" is another way of describing an extremely improbable outcome. It's based on the spread of the normal distribution. The spread, or standard deviation, of a normal distribution is typically denoted by the Greek letter *sigma*. The expression "ten-sigma event," or "10-sigma event," then simply means a value so large that it's at least 10 standard deviations larger than the mean. (Sometimes it's taken in either direction, a value at least 10 standard deviations larger than the mean, *or* at least 10 standard deviations smaller than the mean. Because of the symmetry of the normal distribution, the probability of observing a value smaller *or* larger will be twice the probability of observing a value at least 10 standard deviations larger than the mean.) We've seen that because of the shape of the distribution, the probability of observing extreme values gets smaller and smaller the farther you go away from the mean, so the probability of a 10-sigma event is much smaller than that of a 5-sigma event. In fact, Table 7.1 shows just how much smaller. This table shows the probabilities of observing 5-, 10-, 20-, and 30-sigma events. A 5-sigma event (a value at least five standard deviations above the mean of a normal distribution) has a probability of about 2.867×10^{-7}, or about 1 in 3.5 million. A 10-sigma event corresponds to about 1 in 130,000,000,000,000,000,000,000.

TABLE 7.1.

The probabilities of 5-, 10-, 20-, and 30-sigma events from a normal distribution

A 5-sigma event has probability	1 in 3.5 million
A 10-sigma event has probability	1 in 1.3×10^{23}
A 20-sigma event has probability	1 in 3.6×10^{88}
A 30-sigma event has probability	1 in 2.0×10^{197}

About ten years after the collapse of Long-Term Capital Management, in August 2007, another financial shock occurred, which Goldman Sachs's CFO characterized as "25-standard-deviation events, several days in a row." Bill Bonner, writing in *MoneyWeek*, said, "Things were happening then that were only supposed to happen about once in every 100,000 years."[4]

These financial shocks are beginning to have a painful familiarity. Stepping forward a further three years from 2007, Dennis Gartman, writing in *The Gartman Letter* of Friday, May 7, 2010, said: "What we witnessed yesterday was a series of movements of utterly unprecedented proportions, with currency price changes that are at the 6th and 7th and 8th standard deviations from the norm . . . a 12th 'sigma' event if there is such a thing . . . We are told that such massive shifts in prices that are 'out there' on the edges of the bell-shaped curve can occur only once every several thousand years."[5]

You'll probably agree with me that, far from being "utterly unprecedented," as Gartman put it, such events are beginning to look singularly *precedented.* And the crashes I've singled out are just recent events from a whole *series* of financial crashes. In fact, the economists Carmen Reinhart and Kenneth Rogoff have looked at the history of events just like these, going back some eight centuries.[6] How, then, do we reconcile the improbability of the events, the fact that they should be extraordinarily unlikely, at least according to the authors cited above, with the fact that they just keep on happening?

Well, as Bill Bonner added after his remark that things were happening which should happen only about once every 100,000 years, "Either that . . . or Goldman's models were wrong." Exactly: the models were wrong. In fact, they were based on the assumption that price changes followed the normal distribution, the same distribution that Mallaby drew to our attention. If that's not right, if price changes are distributed in some way other than normal, then perhaps such crashes should be expected. This is the essence of the law of the probability lever: slight changes to a model, or slight inaccuracies in what we believe, can have massive consequences in terms of differences in probabilities.

What If Normal Isn't Normal?

If the distribution of market fluctuations isn't normal, it must have some other shape. One other shape, a subtly different one, is shown in Figure 7.2. Here the continuous line shows a normal distribution with mean 10 and spread 1, the same as we saw before, while the broken line shows a shape called the *Cauchy distribution*[7] (named after the nineteenth-century French mathematician Augustin Cauchy, who is said to have more mathematical ideas named after him than anyone else). The two shapes, the normal and the Cauchy, are different—they're described by different mathematical expressions, and they give different probabilities of observing each value. But, as you can see, they're not *very* different. It would be very easy to confuse the two—it would be easy to think you were dealing with a normal distribution, when in fact the distribution was Cauchy.

To see if such a difference would matter, let's examine how changing from a normal distribution to a Cauchy distribution with a similar shape impacts the probabilities of observing values greater than 20. In terms of our children's-test-score example, you could describe this as the probability that a child has a "genius" score.

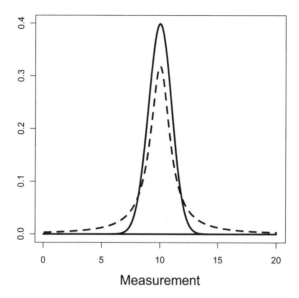

Figure 7.2. A comparison between a normal distribution (continuous line) and a Cauchy distribution (broken line).

For the normal distribution, the probability of getting a score above 20 is just 1 in 1.3×10^{23} (as we saw in Table 7.1). That's equivalent to the chance of getting heads in all your first 77 tosses of a fair coin. Pretty small! So small, in fact, that by Borel's law, we wouldn't expect it to happen.

For the Cauchy distribution, on the other hand, the probability of getting a score above 20 is 1 in 31. This is equivalent to the chance of getting heads in all your first *five* tosses of a fair coin. Quite likely! In fact, about 3 out of every 100 children would have such a score (so maybe, while bright, not quite genius level).

If the true distribution of the test scores is Cauchy but we've assumed it to be normal, we've underestimated the probability of getting a genius score by a factor of some 4.2×10^{21} or 4,200,000,000,000,000,000,000. A serious underestimate!

This shows the law of the probability lever in action. Slight shifts in the *shape* of a distribution—the change from the shape of one of the curves in Figure 7.2 to the other—can alter probabilities from being incredibly small to being part of the familiar course of events: the probability of your train being late, or of you dropping a pencil, or getting caught in a rain shower. Under one assumption, the event is so improbable that you'd not expect it to happen in the entire history of the universe. Under the other, almost imperceptibly different assumption, you might expect to see it happen every day.

Table 7.2 below is an expansion of Table 7.1, in which I've added the corresponding Cauchy probabilities. Remember that a 5-sigma event is the probability of getting a value five times larger than the mean. Now we see that we should actually expect such "rare events" quite often.

TABLE 7.2.

The probabilities of 5-, 10-, 20-, and 30-sigma events from a normal distribution and a Cauchy distribution

	NORMAL	CAUCHY
A 5-sigma event has probability	1 in 3.5 million	1 in 16
A 10-sigma event has probability	1 in 1.3×10^{23}	1 in 32
A 20-sigma event has probability	1 in 3.6×10^{88}	1 in 63
A 30-sigma event has probability	1 in 2.0×10^{197}	1 in 94

Why Not Normal?

I opened the discussion of the law of the probability lever by referring to financial crashes, but there's nothing special about finance in this regard. Slight changes to a distribution can lead to huge consequences in any domain. Now, while the distribution of the probabilities is often assumed to be normal, you'll recall that I pointed out in chapter 3 that the normal distribution doesn't actually exist in nature—observed distributions are never *exactly* normal. And now we've seen that assuming the distribution to be normal when it's just slightly different can have massive implications.

One common way distributions can differ from normality is by being contaminated. This can happen in many ways. For example, we could be studying a population that actually consists of distinct subpopulations. Take the distribution of weights of loaves of bread, for example. The baker has a target weight, but is unlikely to hit that exactly. Instead, his loaves will sometimes weigh slightly less and sometimes slightly more. Extreme departures from the target will be rare for the baker, and the weights of his loaves might well be roughly normally distributed. But suppose the baker's assistant made a few of the loaves, and he had a tendency to underestimate the amount of flour for each loaf. Now the distribution of weights of the loaves which appear in the shop would be a combination of the distribution of weights of the baker's loaves and the distribution of weights of the assistant's loaves. The baker's normal distribution will be distorted by the assistant's contaminating distribution.

Another way departures from normality can occur is as a consequence of the law of selection. For example, while in theory some property of stars might follow a normal distribution, in practice we're less likely to detect more distant and dimmer stars because less light reaches us from them. This will lead to fewer observations from the left side of the normal distribution, which correspond to smaller values. It will change the distribution's shape so that it is no longer symmetrical—and no longer normal. As before, this is a subtle effect when we're collecting our data, but one with a potentially big impact on our probability estimates, because of the law of the probability lever.

Catastrophes, Butterflies, and the Far Ends of the Universe

The law of the probability lever is related to many other phenomena. One is *catastrophe theory*. A system is said to be in a *stable* state if slight perturbations of it lead to only small changes in its state. However, there are systems which can undergo sudden massive changes to completely different states when the conditions change slightly. For example, imagine heating and cooling a glass of water over a temperature range of 10–20 degrees Celsius. All that happens is that the water gets hotter and colder, along with some imperceptibly slight increase or decrease in volume. But now suppose we extend the temperature range, cooling the water down to −4 degrees Celsius. As we pass through 0 degrees we'll observe a dramatic change: the water will freeze. A very slight change in the temperature around 0 degrees changes the material from being a liquid to being a solid. Catastrophe theory elaborates on such dramatic changes, showing how they can arise in different ways.

Another related phenomenon is that of the *domino effect*, where a system is intrinsically unstable, so that a small initial change precipitates a massive further change, often via a long sequence of small intermediate events. The effect is named after a line of standing dominoes, of course, in which toppling the first causes it to knock over the second, which in turn knocks over the third, and so on.

I mentioned chaos and the butterfly effect earlier on in the book. We saw how uncertainty about the system's initial conditions, or very slight changes to them, could mushroom to produce huge effects later on. The eminent physicist Michael Berry gave a beautiful example of this.[8] He pointed out that all the objects in the universe are linked by gravity, so that, in principle, a perturbation of one will impact all the others, albeit in an absolutely tiny way for distant objects. Berry imagined removing just one electron at the edge of the universe (that is, about 10^{10} light-years away), and looked at the gravitational effect of this change on the angle at which two oxygen molecules on earth are deflected when they collide.

He showed that after about 56 collisions between molecules, the angle of deflection could be completely different from what in fact occurred when the electron was present. Now imagine following the paths of oxygen molecules as they bounce around in the air, bumping off each other and off walls and other objects. If we follow one such molecule, then its path will be completely different, after less than 60 collisions, according to whether that one electron is or is not present at the edge of the universe.

For air, each gas molecule goes from one collision to another in about two ten-billionths of a second on average, and each molecule is involved in about 5 billion collisions each second. This means that removing the electron at the edge of the universe would have completely changed the paths of oxygen molecules in the air *you breathe* after just a 100 millionth of a second.

Michael Berry also showed that the mass of the two human players is enough to completely alter the angle of deflection of two balls on a pool table after just nine collisions. The movement of the players around the table leads to dramatic shifts in the probabilities that the balls will follow particular paths: the law of the probability lever.

Other examples of the probability lever are easy to find, once you know what you're looking for. For example, it appears in experiments in the world of extrasensory perception.

The Alister Hardy ESP Experiment

A large experiment from the world of ESP is described in the book *The Challenge of Chance* by Alister Hardy, Robert Harvie, and Arthur Koestler.[9] In the experiment, 200 people sat in a large hall, with 20 "receivers" separated from 180 "senders." The researchers showed pictures to the senders, who concentrated on mentally transmitting them to the receivers, who in turn sketched what they thought they had received. Hardy's book reproduces a large number of the pictures and sketches used in the experiment.

The experiment was extremely elaborate. All 200 of the volunteers played roles of both sender and receiver in turn, with 20 at a time being selected for the receiver role, making ten "runs" in all. Two of these runs were carried out on each evening that the experiment took place, and it was repeated on seven evenings in all, over the course of seven weeks. The 20 receivers sat in cubicles, screened at the front and sides, and arranged in a four-by-five array, like the desks in a classroom. The 180 senders were seated to the front and to either side of the block of receivers, so that they could see drawings and photographs displayed at the end of the hall, while the receivers were unable to see either the senders or the displays.

At the start of each session Sir Alister Hardy "explained the procedure being adopted and stressed the importance of everyone remaining absolutely silent whilst any experiment was being conducted: to be careful, for example, not to allow oneself to make even the slightest involuntary sound such as a sigh, a gasp of surprise or a little laugh which might indicate something of the nature of the drawing or photograph being displayed."[10]

Hardy's assistants walked up and down behind each row of receivers, as if they were proctors during a test, to check that no collusion was taking place, either among receivers or between receivers and anyone else.

Each of the receivers had a sheet of paper and a pen, and they were instructed to make a rough sketch or describe in a few words whatever came into their minds when a buzzer was sounded to indicate that a drawing or photograph was being shown. The drawings or photographs were randomly selected from a collection.

One of the difficulties with all scientific research is that you can never be one hundred percent certain that an effect you detect has the cause you think. Perhaps something else led to it. To overcome this problem, scientists use control groups. We've already seen this in the context of drug trials, where the two groups are equivalent except that one receives the medicine being tested while the other receives a placebo. Since the groups differ in only one way, any difference in response must be due to the fact that one group received the medicine.

Hardy was aware of this difficulty. He considered creating a control group (showing the senders blank screens instead of pictures or photographs, for example), but decided this was too problematic. You can see why: it was enough having 200 people working for seven evenings, without duplicating this effort but showing only blank screens. Instead he adopted a more sophisticated statistical method known as a "permutation test," in which target images were *randomly* paired with responses from other trials. Now any matches couldn't be caused by direct ESP, so this would give the proportion of matches expected to arise purely by chance.

Clearly a huge amount of thought went into designing this experiment and preventing the results from being affected by uncontrolled influences. And yet, we've already seen how even very small changes to a probability distribution can have major impacts on the probability of what ought to be rare events. And it takes only tiny influences to produce those small changes to a distribution.

At first glance, the results of Hardy's experiment looked promising: the proportion of matches was greater than when the images and responses were randomly paired. But simply being greater isn't enough. We have to ask the deeper question: *could the difference easily have arisen by chance?* After all, if I toss a coin ten times and it comes up heads six times, you'll hardly be convinced I have psychokinetic powers and can influence the coin to come up heads: you're more likely to attribute the fact that more heads than tails came up to chance. Statisticians Persi Diaconis and Frederick Mosteller described a statistical test to see how likely it was to get, purely by chance, the difference Hardy and his collaborators observed.[11] They concluded, "The experiment offers no strong evidence for ESP or a hidden synchronous force."

The presence of the patrolling assistants in the experiment by Hardy and his colleagues reminds me of "Clever Hans," the horse that appeared to be able to do arithmetic and tell time. Someone would ask Hans a question, which could be simple, like "What's four minus two?" or quite elaborate, such as "If the eighth day of the month comes on a Tuesday, what's the date of the following Friday?" and he'd indicate the answer by striking his hoof the correct number of times. He was able to give the right answer even if his trainer wasn't there.

But careful investigation by the psychologist Oskar Pfungst showed that Hans could get the answer right only if the person asking the question knew what it was: then he was right 89 percent of the time. But if the questioner didn't know the answer, Clever Hans was right only 6 percent of the time. It turned out that the horse was responding to subliminal cues subconsciously given by the questioner. So: if a horse can do it, what about Hardy's receivers, responding to subconscious cues from the assistants? Remember, it takes only a tiny shift in the background probabilities to have a large impact on the outcome probabilities.

Hardy's experiment was further complicated by feedback. Here's his explanation: "As soon as the [receivers] had finished making their drawing or written description, their papers were collected up by the supervisors and new sheets of paper appropriately numbered were issued for the next experiment. When all the papers from one experiment had been received, I then allowed the participants in the cubicles to stand up and look at the target drawing or slide to see if they had received any idea of it."

Now, providing feedback can often be an excellent idea. Even if you can't articulate what's needed to improve a skill, a simple "good/bad" mark can lead people to improve over time. Indeed, many practical skills are acquired in this way. But in this case it complicates matters. It's possible that it set the minds of the receivers on similar paths for the next trial, so that they were more likely to be thinking along the same lines as each other. This could explain a slight excess in triple and quadruple matches in the experimental compared to the control group. (That is, not matches between guess and target, but between guesses by different volunteers.)

Hardy had noticed this excess. He'd noticed that receivers in cubicles "in close proximity" often drew "remarkably similar" images, although their drawings frequently had little in common with the target drawing or photograph. (He also drew attention to the fact that "in close proximity" did not necessarily mean adjacent—they often had a gangway between them—so he could rule out the obvious explanation of collusion.) He described it by saying, "It was as if there were small pockets of thought common to two or three localised participants."

That last paragraph should have set alarm bells ringing in your head. Hardy had tested the hypothesis he set out to test, but then he'd started looking around for other interesting matches. We can see the doors of the law of selection, the look elsewhere effect, and the law of truly large numbers creaking open. The law of selection applies because he's looking at the data, spotting anomalous patterns, and saying, "Hey, look, an anomalous pattern!" He's finding the pattern first, and then drawing attention to it (like the farmer with the arrows in the barn), rather than saying what he's looking for and then seeking it. The look elsewhere effect applies because, having failed to find the pattern he was hoping for, he looks for other patterns. And the law of truly large numbers applies simply because the number of potential patterns among the results is truly large. Indeed, matters are even worse than this might suggest: the door of yet another aspect of the Improbability Principle is also beginning to swing open: *the law of near enough*, which I'll go into in the next chapter.

Hardy did a sterling job of trying to control for various possible influences in a situation where sound experimental design is especially difficult. It's an area where you're looking for very small effects—a proportion of drawings matching the targets only a little larger than chance would suggest. The trouble is that, as we've seen, the law of the probability lever requires only very small alterations in the base probabilities to have a large impact further down the line. A tiny undetected influence on Hardy's receivers could easily shift that proportion of targets into the realm of the statistically unlikely—without having anything to do with ESP.

If ESP experiments are vulnerable to incorrect conclusions because of the law of the probability lever, at least they're harmless. My next example shows a tragic consequence of ignorance being amplified by the law.

Dependence

In 1997, Christopher, the eleven-week-old child of a young lawyer named Sally Clark, died in his sleep: an apparent case of Sudden Infant Death Syndrome (SIDS, or crib death). Such events are terribly sad, but, even with the best of care, they happen. Only in this case, one year later, Sally's second child, Harry, also died, aged just eight weeks.

Sally was arrested, and accused of killing the children. She was convicted of murdering them, and in 1999 was given a life sentence. Now, this is not the place to go into the weakness of the case, the paucity of forensic evidence, or the disagreements about the causes of death. Rather, I want to show how a simple mistaken assumption led to incorrect probabilities.

In this case the mistaken evidence came from Sir Roy Meadow, a pediatrician. Despite not being an expert statistician or probabilist, he felt able to make a statement about probabilities in his role as expert witness in Ms. Clark's trial. He asserted that the probability of two SIDS deaths in a family like Sally Clark's was 1 in 73 million. A probability as small as this suggests we might apply Borel's law: we shouldn't expect to see such an improbable event. If we don't expect to see it, but we do anyway, then there must be some other explanation—such as, in the present case, that the mother had killed the children.

Unfortunately, however, Meadow's 1 in 73 million probability is based on a crucial assumption: that the deaths are independent; that one such death in a family does not make it more or less likely that there will be another.

On average, the chance of a given child dying of SIDS is about 1 in 1,300. Meadow instead (correctly) used the much smaller figure of 1 in 8,543, arrived at by taking account of the fact that Sally Clark was nonsmoking, affluent, and young, all factors which reduce the probability of this kind of infant death. He failed to take account of the fact that both of the Clark children were male, a factor which increases the probability of a SIDS death. Then he made the critical assumption. He assumed that the probability of having a second such death in a family was independent of whether there had already been one.

You'll recall from chapter 3 that if two events are independent, you can find the probability that *both* of them will occur by multiplying their separate probabilities together. And that's just what Meadow did. If you assume independence, then the probability of getting two such deaths in a family is $1/8,543 \times 1/8,543$; about 1 in 73 million, and this is the figure he presented to the court, describing it as the sort of event you would expect to see once every hundred years.

Now, you'll recall how slight changes to what we assume about the shape of a distribution can change probabilities by large amounts. In the present case, perhaps we shouldn't assume that

SIDS deaths within the same family are independent. And, in fact, that assumption does seem unjustified: data show that if one SIDS death has occurred, then a subsequent child is about ten times more likely to die of SIDS. Meadow's estimated probability of two deaths was wrong.

To arrive at a valid conclusion, we would have to compare the probability that the two children had been murdered with the probability that they had both died from SIDS. This would require us carrying out similar calculations for child homicide statistics. I won't go through the details here, but Professor Ray Hill of the University of Salford in the UK calculated that "single [SIDS] deaths outweigh homicides by about 17 to 1, double [SIDS] deaths outweigh double homicides by about 9 to 1, and triple [SIDS] deaths outweigh triple homicides by about 2 to 1."[12] There is a factor-of-ten difference between Meadow's estimate and the estimate based on recognizing that SIDS events in the same family are not independent, and that difference shifts the probability from favoring homicide to favoring SIDS deaths.

Professor Hill added, "[O]ne wonders whether the Clark jury would have convicted if, instead of being given the 'once in a hundred years figure,' they had been told that second [SIDS] deaths occur around four or five times a year and indeed happen rather more frequently than second infant murders in the same family." Later evidence also showed that at the time of his death, the second child, Harry, had a blood infection known to cause sudden infant death.

Following widespread criticism of the misuse and indeed misunderstanding of statistical evidence, Sally Clark's conviction was overturned, and she was released in 2003.

The episode attracted a vast amount of attention, and paved the way for other similar appeals, for example by Donna Anthony, who was jailed in 1998, and Angela Cannings, who was convicted in 2002, both for the murder of two of their babies. Both cases involved evidence from Sir Roy Meadow. And in both cases the convictions were later overturned and the women were released.

There is a tragic corollary to the Sally Clark story. She never recovered from her ordeal, and was found dead in March 2007, from acute alcohol poisoning. Slight changes to models can have big impacts on apparently small probabilities: it's the law of the probability lever.

My Probability or Yours?

The law of the probability lever can be a rather insidious law, sneaking into our lives in unexpected ways. One manifestation of it, straightforward in principle but often deceptive in practice, is when we apply the probability for an average person to someone who is actually anything but average. Here's an example.

In chapter 5, I talked about the risk of being struck by lightning, and we saw that the chance of being killed by a lightning strike in any given year is about 1 in 300,000. But that's an average. Some people will have a higher than average probability, and some a lower one. And you can guess the sort of lifestyle that will lead to a higher probability—it won't be an urban office worker.

Take Major Walter Summerford, who was knocked from his horse by a lightning bolt in Flanders in February 1918, and was temporarily paralyzed from the waist down. After that experience, Summerford moved to Canada, where he took up fishing—only to have the tree he was sitting under struck by lightning in 1924, paralyzing his right side. He recovered, until he was completely paralyzed by yet another lightning strike in 1930, while walking in the park. He died two years later, in 1932—but not from a lightning strike. But just to rectify the oversight, in 1936 his gravestone was struck by lightning. Clearly life would have been less risky for him if he had taken up knitting.

If you think Major Summerford was unfortunate, consider

the case of Roy Sullivan, a park ranger in Virginia. He was struck by lightning *seven* times: in 1942 (causing him to lose his big-toe nail), July 1969 (when he lost his eyebrows), July 1970 (his left shoulder was seared), April 1972 (his hair was set on fire), August 1973 (his regrown hair was set on fire and his legs were seared), June 1976 (his ankle was injured), and June 1977 (his chest and stomach were burned). All of those seven strikes were attested to by R. Taylor Hoskins, the superintendent of Shenandoah National Park, and confirmed by doctors. In fact, Sullivan claimed he was also struck when he was a child, out helping his father with the harvest.

We've seen earlier in this chapter how even a slight change in a probability distribution could have a very substantial effect on the chance of rare events. Being struck by lightning seven times would seem to be a very rare event. But it becomes far less unlikely if you spend your time wandering around parks in thunderstorms. Calculating the chance of someone being hit seven times using the probabilities referring to the average person is likely to be seriously misleading if you're referring to a park ranger. The law of the probability lever again.

Breaking the Bank

The financial markets aren't the only place involving money where the law of the probability lever has an impact. Another is gambling.

In roulette, for example, a player "breaks the bank" if they win more chips than the table has (not more than the wealth of the entire casino). Clearly breaking the bank is a rare event. But it happened to Yorkshireman Joseph Jagger in 1875. Behind his achievement lies the law of the probability lever.

Even a slight deviation from equal probabilities on a roulette wheel can give you an edge if you know what that deviation is, since the casino's probability calculations are based on assuming each number is equally likely to come up. But Jagger found himself such an edge. In 1873 he hired assistants to collect data on the fall of the ball on the six roulette wheels at the Beaux-Arts Casino in Monte Carlo. Analyzing his data (presumably no mean feat in the days before computers), he discovered that one of the wheels produced the numbers 7, 8, 9, 17, 18, 19, 22, 28, and 29 more often than the others. On July 7, 1875, he placed bet after bet that these numbers would win, yielding a small fortune. The casino reacted by shifting the wheels around, and Jagger started to lose. But then he remembered that the biased wheel had had a small scratch on it. This allowed him to track down the table the wheel had been moved to, and he started winning again. In response the casino shifted the metal dividers in the wheels around daily, and Jagger started losing again. At that point he gave up, leaving Monte Carlo with over $4 million in today's money, which he invested.

Although Jagger was able to stop when he was ahead, few gamblers have his control. Certainly Charles Wells, who also broke the bank in Monte Carlo, in 1891, didn't. He won a million francs, once getting 23 out of 30 spins of the wheel right, and once successfully betting on the number 5 five times in a row. But he died penniless after a string of convictions for fraud.

8

THE LAW OF NEAR ENOUGH

I'd rather be vaguely right than precisely wrong.
—John Maynard Keynes

The aspect of the Improbability Principle known as the law of near enough says that *events which are sufficiently similar are regarded as identical*. It accepts as a match things which are in fact merely similar. By doing so it expands the number of potential matches.

Suppose I try to predict the number which will come up when I throw the 100-sided die from my collection (I really do have such a die: it's basically a sphere with 100 flattened patches, numbered from 1 to 100). I would have a 1 in 100 chance of getting it right. But what if, instead, I claimed to have made the right prediction if the number I had in mind came up *or* a number near to it did—say, the number just one less or one more? Then if, for example, I predicted 13, instead of just a 1 in 100 chance of being right, I'd have a chance of 3 in 100 (any of 12, 13, or 14 would match according to my relaxed definition).

No doubt you'd regard it as a coincidence to discover that, unknown to you, one of your friends had been visiting Berlin at the same time you'd been there. But what if they were visiting a different part of the city? And what if their visit overlapped yours by only one day? And what if your friend hadn't actually been visiting Berlin, but a nearby town? Or, in fact, not Germany at all, but France—so he was in Europe at the same time you were? That's still surely a remarkable coincidence?

By relaxing the criteria for a match we can increase the probability of an apparent coincidence. Events which might seem extremely unlikely can turn out to be quite probable on closer examination.

The law of near enough complements the look elsewhere effect, which arises when we look to see if a particular match occurred in a particular place, and then relax the criterion to see if a match occurred *at any location*. Hence "look elsewhere." For example, in physics we might begin by seeing if there's an excess number of observations (a "bump" in the data) which have a particular value. And then, when it turns out that there isn't, we extend the search to accept as a bump an excess number of observations at *any* value. As we've seen, this "looking elsewhere" obviously dramatically increases the chance of finding such a bump. The law of near enough also increases the chance of finding such a "bump," but does so by enlarging what we mean by a bump. If we originally defined a bump as being ten times more observations than we expect, we could relax it by requiring only five times as many. Again, this will obviously increase the chance of finding a bump.

In chapter 5 I mentioned two successive e-mails I received, one with the subject "Catch-up meeting with Muir" and the other with the subject "Miur referees list." The law of near enough led me to regard Muir and Miur as a match. At the beginning of chapter 3, I described the case of Bill Shaw and his wife, who both survived train crashes in Yorkshire in which several people died. But they weren't the same crash and their crashes were fifteen years apart. No doubt the newspapers would have picked up on it had one of the crashes involved Bill and the other his brother, or sister, or children, or parents, and so on, and if the accidents had been four years apart, or twenty. The law of near enough expands the range of people who would be regarded as a match, as well as the time between the accidents. In doing so it increases, possibly by a very large amount, the probability that we'd see such an apparent coincidence.

In earlier chapters we explored some ways in which the Improbability Principle meant that apparent coincidences in lottery wins were actually almost inevitable. The law of near enough provides another way. You'll recall the case of Virginia Pike from chapter 5. She had two tickets matching five of the six Powerball numbers in the Virginia Lottery. There's a much higher chance of getting five out of the six right than there is of getting all six right, and if we relax our definition of a "win" to include matching five as a "win," as newspapers sometimes do, then Ms. Pike was a winner: the law of near enough. As was Mike McDermott, who won second prize in the UK National Lottery twice within a year, with five (out of six) matching numbers plus the bonus ball.

In the same way, we can generalize the birthday problem discussed in chapter 5. While it might be a surprising coincidence if I had the same birthday as you, it would be less of a surprise to find that my birthday was *within a week* of yours. Indeed, take this far enough by sufficiently relaxing what you mean by "near enough," and it's certain that our birthdays will be near each other (I was born on one of the days between January 1 and December 31— *and so were you!*).

In chapter 5 we also looked at the claimed discovery of coded messages concealed in the Bible—the so-called "Bible code." There are many places in the Bible where we could search for a specified series of letters. Moreover, as we saw, these places needn't be restricted to consecutive letters—they can also include other configurations: letters might be skipped in a regular way, the configuration might be based on the two-dimensional way the letters are displayed on the page, and so on. By expanding the search to allow such configurations, the probability of finding a matching set of letters can be made as high as we like. I gave a couple of examples (I still haven't found the person hidden in this book who was crying for help). But there's even more. The chance of a match can be made even greater by expanding the sequences we regard as a legitimate match. In my example, I searched for the word "help," but suppose I was prepared to accept as a meaningful match a slight misspelling: hlpe or hepl, for example. Since I now have three sequences of letters I regard as a match (help, hlpe, hepl), my probability of finding a match will be increased, so that I'd expect to find rather more matches. Indeed, there is (exactly) one match of each of these two extra sequences (with four characters between the letters). While the look elsewhere effect increases the number of places you look *at*, the law of near enough increases the number of things you look *for*.

Naturally, the law of near enough plays a role in pseudoscience as well. We've already encountered Carl Jung's synchronicity in chapter 2. Here's another story from his book of that name:

> A young woman I was treating had, at a critical moment, a dream in which she was given a golden scarab. While she was telling me this dream I sat with my back to the closed window. Suddenly I heard a noise behind me, like a gentle tapping. I turned round and saw a flying insect knocking against the window-pane from outside. I opened the window and caught the creature in the air as it flew in. It was the nearest analogy to a golden scarab that one finds in our latitudes, a scarabaeid beetle, the common rose-chafer (*Cetonia aurata*), which contrary to its usual habits had evidently felt an urge to get into a dark room at this particular moment. I must admit that nothing like it ever happened to me before or since, and that the dream of the patient has remained unique in my experience.[1]

Jung describes the beetle appearing at the window just as his patient was telling him about a dream of a beetle as an example of a coincidence which was "connected so meaningfully that [its] 'chance' concurrence would represent a degree of improbability that would have to be expressed by an astronomical figure."[2]

I don't know about you, but I've quite often heard large insects tapping at windows. I'd always assumed that they simply hadn't yet evolved to cope with the modern development of invisible physical objects such as sheets of glass, and so kept trying to fly through what appeared to them to be an empty space. But the phenomenon is sufficiently intrusive that I do notice when it happens—as Jung did. In Jung's case, he seems not to have taken account of the fact that the beetle was a common one (the failure to recognize baseline probabilities has been given a name—the *base rate fallacy*). Jung does acknowledge that the beetle was only a *close* match, "the nearest analogy to a golden scarab that one finds in our latitudes," not an exact one. But what if it had been a different kind of beetle? Or not a beetle at all? How far would he have been prepared to stretch the accuracy of the match? How far is near enough?

Sir Alister Hardy recognized that it would be very difficult to decide whether the receivers' sketches matched the picture being displayed in his ESP experiment. There is inevitably some judgment involved—someone would have to decide whether two images were similar enough to count as a match. Make it too lax, and it would seem as if many of his volunteers had psychic powers. Make it too strict, and you'd miss any effect that was there. When he described some of the drawings, Hardy said: "[I]t is tempting to suppose that the little guardsman drawn in the sentry-box outside the Palace in Experiment 74 has some relation to the drawing of the toy soldier; that the mountain and road drawn in Experiment 61 has a relation to the pyramids which were the target drawing; and that the railway station drawn in Experiment 125 is related to the target drawing of a Noah's ark for it is almost identical *except* for the fact that the ends of the platform of the station slope down whereas those of the hull of the ark slope up."[3] It's very clear from this passage that there's plenty of scope for the law of near enough to have an effect, and to dramatically increase the probability of an apparent match. It's the same phenomenon as when we mistake a young child's drawing of a cat for a picture of a dog.

Arthur Koestler described other parapsychology experiments that also opened the door to the law of near enough:

> In 1934 Dr. [S. G.] Soal, then a lecturer in mathematics at University College London, read about Rhine's experiments and tried to repeat them. From 1934 to 1939 he experimented with 160 persons who made altogether 128,350 guesses with Zener cards.[4] The result was nil—no significant deviation from chance expectation was found.

He continues:

> Soal was on the point of giving up in disgust when a fellow researcher, Whately Carington, suggested to him that he check his reports for 'displaced' guesses—that is, for hits not on the target card, but on the card which was turned up before it—or *after* it (Carington, who experimented with the telepathic transmission of drawings, thought that he had noticed such displacement effects in some of his subjects). Soal reluctantly undertook the tedious labour of analysing his thousands of columns of experimental protocols, and was both rewarded and disconcerted to find that one of his subjects, Basil Shackleton, had scored consistently on the next card ahead—i.e. precognitively—with results so high that chance had to be ruled out.[5]

We could continue this ad infinitum. We could look for predictions of cards two in advance, or three. We could look for an overabundance of predictions of the Zener cross when the target was the circle. And so on. All extending what we mean by a match, so that, eventually, the law of near enough makes it effectively inevitable that we will "discover" a volunteer who produces a high score.

Incidentally, Louisa Rhine suggested that one possible reason for Soal's failure to replicate Rhine's results was a lack of emotional involvement of his volunteers, because they'd simply come to him in response to advertisements. But surely the reverse is more likely to be the case. Someone who had gone to the trouble of responding to an advertisement, and who was willing to spend time on such an intrinsically rather dull exercise, must have had some desire to be involved. Contrast this with undergraduate students who might simply be roped into the task!

As if the role of the law of near enough was not sufficient, the law of truly large numbers and the law of selection then also come into play. The predictions of one of Soal's volunteers had consistently matched the card which would be drawn *next*. But he had 160 volunteers. It's hardly surprising that out of all those, someone would do reasonably well, just by chance, in matching the next predictions. It's the law of truly large numbers. Recall the parable of the 100,000 dice throwers: true, 160 is not quite 100,000, but then Soal's outcome is not as extreme as getting the same result on all six throws of the dice. And then the law of selection also takes effect: Soal takes the volunteer who'd produced the most extreme result and draws attention to that, ignoring all those who did worse. Once again it's like the 100,000 dice throwers, where all but the one who rolled the same values left the hall.

Encouraged by his results, Soal carried out more trials with Shackleton. The studies were monitored by over twenty eminent observers, and they appeared to be statistically significant[6]: the results would have been extremely improbable to obtain purely by chance, without precognition, telepathy, or some other parapsychological explanation. That seemed pretty definitive, and seemed to support Soal.

But there's a corollary: the results of Soal's experiments have proved extremely controversial. Soal was unable to replicate them in later studies, and, using more sophisticated statistical analyses, other parapsychologists concluded that the data had been manipulated, with some sequences being reused, and extra digits inserted.

The eminent parapsychologist J. B. Rhine was himself fooled by the law of near enough. Arthur Koestler describes how: "A number of researchers, starting with Rhine himself, were reluctantly made to realize that some of their star subjects produced results showing more or less the same odds against chance if the target cards to be guessed had *not* been previously seen by the agent." Rhine's "star subjects," the ones who appeared to do better than chance when "reading someone's mind," also appeared to do better than chance when asked merely to say which symbols were on successive cards in previously unopened decks. If this possibility, as well as the mind-reading possibility, is considered a demonstration of psychic powers, then there is greater chance for a "subject" to appear to possess such powers. Koestler continued: "This phenomenon was labelled 'clairvoyance' and defined as 'extra-sensory perception of objective events as distinguished from telepathic perception of the mental state of another person.' "[7] I like this example, because it illustrates how able people are to come up with "explanations" when the results do not conform to their expectations.

Numerology is another rich playground for the law of near enough. One aspect of numerology manifests in different formulae which appear to produce identical numbers. Such coincidences prompt suspicions about hidden causes. This is exactly what we saw in chapter 5, where the law of truly large numbers almost inevitably led to numerical coincidences: even randomly generated sequences of numbers will come up with any subsequence you want if you keep going for long enough.

Here's an example of how the law of near enough can mislead

us. It's based on Pythagoras's theorem, which you probably learned about in school. Pythagorean triples are sets of three positive integers $\{a, b, c\}$ which satisfy the relationship $a^2 + b^2 = c^2$. For example, the triple $\{3, 4, 5\}$ satisfies $3^2 + 4^2 = 5^2$ and the triple $\{5, 12, 13\}$ satisfies $5^2 + 12^2 = 13^2$.[8] However, there's a very famous theorem in mathematics, called *Fermat's last theorem*, which says that no three positive integers satisfy $a^n + b^n = c^n$ for any n that is an integer greater than 2. So, for example, the theorem says that there is no set of three positive integers $\{a, b, c\}$ which satisfy $a^3 + b^3 = c^3$.

The reason the theorem has this curious name is that Pierre de Fermat noted in the margin of his copy of the ancient Greek text *Arithmetica* in 1637 that he had a marvelous proof of it, but the margin was too small for him to write his proof out. The simplicity of stating the problem, along with Fermat's implicit challenge, led to generations of professional and amateur mathematicians unsuccessfully seeking a proof for over three centuries. It wasn't until 1995 that the theorem was at last proved, with the final steps being provided by the mathematician Andrew Wiles.

But with that theorem as context, what do you make of the statements that both $89{,}222^3 + 49{,}125^3$ and $93{,}933^3$ are equal to $828{,}809{,}229{,}597 \times 10^3$? This seems to suggest that the triple $\{89{,}222, 49{,}125, 93{,}933\}$ satisfies $89{,}222^3 + 49{,}125^3 = 93{,}933^3$, contravening Fermat's last theorem.

The answer is that $89{,}222^3 + 49{,}125^3$ and $93{,}933^3$ are actually only *approximately* equal to $828{,}809{,}229{,}597 \times 10^3$. The exact value of $89{,}222^3 + 49{,}125^3$ is $828{,}809{,}229{,}597.173 \times 10^3$, and the exact value of $93{,}933^3$ is $828{,}809{,}229{,}597.237 \times 10^3$. The two expressions are not actually *exactly* the same, though a difference of 64 out of $828{,}809{,}229{,}597{,}237$ would be *near enough* for most people to regard them as the same! Still, the fact that they are not exactly the same means Andrew Wiles can breathe again.[9]

By being less strict about what we mean by near enough we can find many such apparently matching triples, but it's an illusion, because the matches are not exact.

There's an infinite number of similar examples of apparently identical numbers arising in different areas, some of which are quite esoteric. For example, Ramanujan's constant is $e^{\pi\sqrt{163}}$, which is equal to

$$262,537,412,640,768,743.9999999999992500\ldots$$

If we had calculated this to "only" 12 decimal places, we might easily have concluded that it was equal to 262,537,412,640,768,744— an apparently extraordinary coincidence. But we would be wrong.[10]

Those examples show how the law of near enough manifests itself in relationships between numbers. In other situations, the matching arises from the properties of real physical objects. An example of this arises in the domain of *pyramidology*. In his book *The Great Pyramid: Its Secrets and Mysteries Revealed*,[11] Charles Piazzi Smyth, the Astronomer Royal for Scotland from 1846 to 1888, described numeric relationships between aspects of the Great Pyramid of Giza and astronomical measurements. For example, he claimed that the length of the perimeter, in inches, equaled the number of days in a thousand years. Take enough measurements, compare them with enough astronomical phenomena, and you have ideal ground for the laws of truly large numbers and the look elsewhere effect to combine synergistically with the law of near enough, so that you'd be hard put to avoid finding some coincidences!

Unfortunately, Smyth's elaborate theories about the structure of the pyramid weren't helped when William Matthew Flinders Petrie repeated the measurement with greater precision in 1880, and obtained a smaller value. (Petrie described his result as an "ugly little fact which killed the beautiful theory.") Smyth's predictions of the date of the Second Coming, as with everyone else's predictions of this event, have proved inaccurate.

Before ending this chapter, I feel I should redress the balance a little by acknowledging that, sometimes, apparent coincidences do represent an underlying truth. We've already seen this with the Monster Group and the number 196,883, but another example is the match between the shape of the eastern coast of the Americas and the western coast of Europe and Africa. The matching of the shapes of these coastlines, which make them look like parts of a jigsaw, is not simply a coincidence. The fact is that these two continental edges were once together—but have been pulled apart by convection currents in the magma of the earth's mantle and separated by new seafloor as lava welled up into the middle of the Atlantic Ocean.

To conclude, let's leave the realms of mathematics and physics for a moment, and switch to classical literature. In his novel *The Old Curiosity Shop*, Charles Dickens describes the conversation that ensues when the mothers of two characters, Kit and Barbara, meet for the first time:

> "And we are both widows too!" said Barbara's mother. "We must have been made to know each other" . . . tracing things back from effects to causes, they naturally reverted to their deceased husbands, respecting whose lives, deaths, and burials, they compared notes, and discovered sundry circumstances that tallied with wonderful exactness; such as Barbara's father having been exactly four years and ten months older than Kit's father, and one of them having died on a Wednesday and the other on a Thursday, and both of them having been of a very fine make and remarkably good-looking, with other extraordinary coincidences.[12]

A perfect illustration of the law of near enough.

9

THE HUMAN MIND

I wouldn't have seen it if I hadn't believed it.
                                        —Marshall McLuhan

In previous chapters we've looked at various ways in which the Improbability Principle manifests itself. They include the law of inevitability, the law of truly large numbers, the law of selection, the law of the probability lever, and the law of near enough. One thing is clear: many of these aspects of the Improbability Principle arise as a consequence of a failure to properly appreciate something about the way nature works. They arise because of common and natural idiosyncrasies in the way we think. Now, let's explore a few of these human aspects of the Improbability Principle in a little more detail.

What's the Probability?

The obvious starting point is to note that our intuitive grasp of probability isn't good. A simple illustration of this is the fact that we find it very difficult to behave in a random manner. If you ask people to produce a stream of random digits, they often produce series which are too homogeneous (for example, tending to avoid consecutive repetitions of the same number). Probability and chance often appear to be counterintuitive. Indeed, even professional statisticians can be fooled—until they sit down and go through the calculations.

Consider the following scenario:

John initially took a degree in mathematics, and followed it with a PhD in astrophysics. After that, he worked in the physics department of a university for a while but then found a job in the back room of an algorithmic trading company, developing highly sophisticated statistical models for predicting movements of the financial markets. In his spare time he attends science fiction conventions.

Now, which of the following do you think has the higher probability?

A: John is married with two children.
B: John is married with two children, and likes to spend his evenings tackling mathematical puzzles and playing computer games.

Many people answer B. In fact, the set of people described by the characteristics in B is a subset of those described by the characteristics in A: for John to have the characteristics of B, he has those of A *and more*. It follows that the probability that John is described by B *cannot be larger* than the probability that he's described by A.

One proposed explanation for the counterintuitive aspect of this illustration arises from the fact that B nicely matches the stereotypical depiction of John: those activities look like the sorts of things John would do, given his description. In contrast, consider the following scenario, which has exactly the same logical structure but a rather different description of John.

John is male.

Now, which of the following do you think has the higher probability?

A: John is married with two children.
B: John is married with two children, and likes to spend his evenings tackling mathematical puzzles and playing computer games.

Here it's clear that the probability that John has the characteristics of B must be smaller than the probability that he merely has those in A.

This failure of intuition is often called the *conjunction fallacy*, and it can be even more pronounced than in that illustration. Sometimes people perceive the *combination* of two independent events as more likely than either event: the probability that you will win the lottery *and* it will rain today may be seen as greater than just the probability that you will win the lottery.

Another proposed explanation for the conjunction fallacy is that sometimes people invert the probabilities. That is, they're given the description of John and asked for the probability that he has the characteristics in A or B, but they think of it the other way around: they start with the characteristics in A or B, and come up with the probability that John will be like the description.

This kind of mistake is an example of a very important and common confusion called *the prosecutor's fallacy*, or *the law of the transposed conditional*. In a trial, the jury might be told by the prosecutor that it would be highly improbable that the defendant's fingerprints would be at the scene of the crime if he were innocent. Since his fingerprints are there, this is taken as proof that he's not innocent.

But that's wrong. What we really want to know is the probability that he's innocent, given that his fingerprints were at the scene, not the probability that his fingerprints would be at the scene if he were innocent. These two probabilities can be very different.

We can see the error in this transposition if we look at an extreme example. At present, far more CEOs of blue-chip companies are male than female. So the probability of being male given that you are a CEO is considerably greater than ½. But that's very different from the probability of being a CEO given that you are male, which is very much less than ½ since very few men (or women, for that matter) are CEOs.

Let's put some imaginary numbers on our trial example to illustrate.

Table 9.1 shows innocent and guilty people, cross-classified by whether or not their fingerprints were found at the scene of the crime. Let's suppose there are nine people who are innocent *and* whose fingerprints were at the scene (the top left box of the table), one person who is guilty *and* whose fingerprints were there, and about 7 billion people (everyone else on earth) who are innocent and whose fingerprints were *not* found at the scene. Finally, since there's only one guilty person, there are no people who are both guilty and don't have fingerprints at the scene of the crime—the 0 at the bottom right of the table.

TABLE 9.1.
The trial

	INNOCENT	GUILTY
Fingerprints	9	1
No fingerprints	7 bn	0

Now what we'd like to know is the probability that the defendant is innocent when his fingerprints are at the scene. Well, ten people have fingerprints at the scene of the crime, and nine of these are innocent, so this probability is $9/10 = 0.9$.

And what about the probability that someone's fingerprints

will be there if he or she is innocent? There are 7 billion plus 9 innocent people, and 9 of these have fingerprints at the scene. So the probability that someone's fingerprints will be at the scene if the person's innocent is 9/(7bn + 9), which is a very small probability indeed.

The two probabilities we've calculated are very different: one's not far off 1 and the other's almost 0. We should be interested in the first of these: the probability of innocence, given the presence of the defendant's fingerprints. This is 0.9, a large probability. If, in error, we take the second (as did our imaginary prosecutor above), the probability of the fingerprints being there given that he is innocent, we have the tiny probability above. Instead of being very confident of his innocence, we are very confident of his guilt. Talk about a miscarriage of justice!

There are also slightly different versions of the prosecutor's fallacy, but they have the same confusion at their heart.

Another common failure of intuition in probability is called the *base rate fallacy*. This arises when people fail to take account of background probabilities. For example, they might not allow for the fact that the probability of contracting a rare disease is very small.

Here's an example.

Imagine we've developed an instrument to detect credit card fraud which correctly classifies 99 percent of legitimate transactions as legitimate, and correctly classifies 99 percent of fraudulent transactions as fraudulent. Sounds pretty good?

A credit card manager who was not aware of the base rate fallacy might decide to act on the predictions of this instrument. When it flagged a transaction as possibly fraudulent, he might block the card, preventing any further transactions. That's all well and good, but now suppose I tell you that a ballpark figure is that about 1 in 1,000 credit card transactions is fraudulent. This figure, the 1 in 1,000, is the base rate. Because the number of legitimate transactions is overwhelmingly larger than the number of fraudulent transactions, it's much more probable that a flagged transaction is actually a misclassified legitimate one than a correctly classified fraudulent one. In fact, the exact probability that the flagged transaction is actually a misclassified legitimate one is 91 percent. That means that despite the fact that the fraud detector labeled 99 percent of the fraudulent transactions correctly and 99 percent of the legitimate transactions correctly, 9 out of 10 of the times when it raised the alarm it was wrong.

The credit card example is straightforward enough because we have data on the base rate of fraudulent transactions—about 1 in 1,000. But where the base rate fallacy causes real difficulties is when we don't know the background probabilities. Then people have a tendency to estimate the probabilities purely on the basis of their subjective experience. In particular, if they have concrete examples of similar experiences which they can easily bring to mind, they tend to assess things as more probable.

Unfortunately, the ease of bringing something to mind is subject to various kinds of distortion. The Nobel laureate Daniel Kahneman, one of the creators of *prospect theory* (which has been defined as "a rational theory of irrational human behavior"[1]), gave an elegant illustration of this. He asked volunteers to imagine whether a word, randomly chosen from an English text, would be more likely to start with the letter *k* or on the other hand to have *k* as the third letter. People tended to choose the former—deciding that more words start with *k*. In fact, in a typical English text (whatever that is) there are about twice as many words with *k* for their third letter as for their first. The trouble is that words with *k* as the third letter are much more difficult to bring to mind.

In general, we tend to overestimate probabilities when it's easy to think of examples. Kahneman called this phenomenon the *availability heuristic*. Unfortunately, the readiness to bring examples to mind is highly susceptible to outside influences—like topical media coverage, for example. In fact, news coverage is one possible explanation for increased public anxiety about crime rates, even at times when crime rates are falling.

Even if you were confident that your past experience meant you'd seen a representative sample of events, so that in principle you could produce an accurate probability estimate, it would be complicated by the fact that memory is not like a blank piece of paper or a computer, with our daily lives being simply and faithfully recorded. Rather, memory is a dynamic processing system, which observes, evaluates, sifts, combines, restructures, reinforces, and selects our experiences. Vivid experiences create strong memories. Recent experiences are more readily recalled than older ones.

Psychologist Ruma Falk illustrated the malleability of probability assessments by showing that the extent to which a coincidence evoked surprise depended on the context. Adding even irrelevant detail made the coincidence seem more surprising. Furthermore, coincidences which happened personally tended to be regarded as more surprising than those which happened to other people—though this might be a subconscious awareness of the law of truly large numbers: "There are a lot of other people out there that this could happen to, but only one of me, so it's less surprising when it happens to someone else."

Predictions, Patterns, and Propensities

The malleability of memory is related to the confirmation bias I mentioned in chapter 2. This is the subconscious tendency people have to note evidence supporting their beliefs (or hypotheses, in science) but not the evidence against them. Here's an illustration:

I have in mind a rule for generating a sequence of numbers. The three starting numbers are 2, 4, and 6. You have to suggest the next three in the sequence, and I'll tell you if you're right. Then we'll do it again: you'll suggest three numbers to add to the end of the sequence and I'll tell you if you're right. We'll keep going until you're confident you know what my rule is.

In this example, people tend to look for successive sets of three numbers confirming their hypotheses about the sequence. So if, in that example, you suspect my rule is "generate even numbers," you might suggest 8, 10, and 12 as the next three. On being told those are correct, you suggest 14, 16, and 18 as the next three. Again being told those are correct, you might feel confident that my rule is that the numbers are indeed simply increasing by 2 at each step.

It's certainly true that such a sequence satisfies my rule, but in fact your suggestion wasn't the rule I was thinking of. My rule was: any increasing set of whole numbers. In that example, people have a bias to find triples of numbers which conform to their hypotheses, rather than testing the hypotheses with other sequences they think might refute it.

It's interesting that the idealized view of science is that scientists come up with a hypothesis and then conduct experiments to try to disprove it. The more such tests the hypothesis passes, the more likely it is to be right. But since scientific reputations are based on coming up with successful hypotheses—hypotheses that pass such tests—there's a natural human tendency to avoid making the tests of one's own hypotheses too difficult. Fortunately, since science is a competitive enterprise, other researchers are always keen to test your hypotheses, and prove you wrong!

The example of finding the rule behind the sequence 2, 4, 6, 8, 10, 12, . . . concerned the human (and indeed animal) mental need and ability to find patterns. We've touched on this earlier at various places. It's a natural product of evolution—if you can spot the signs of a tiger approaching, or members of a neighboring warlike tribe creeping up on you, or recognize the characteristics indicating that a certain fruit is good to eat, then you're more likely to survive and pass your genes on to the next generation. But, as we saw when we discussed superstitions, patterns of events can also occur by chance, without any underlying cause. The belief that two events are correlated (the occurrence of one being associated with the occurrence of the other) when in fact there's no such relationship is often called the *illusory correlation* effect. And this is where statistical inference comes in. The aim of statistical inference is to distinguish between configurations which have arisen by chance and those which are a consequence of some genuine underlying cause.

One kind of pattern is the *hot hand* in sports and games, which we've already encountered in chapter 2. The belief sounds perfectly reasonable, but careful statistical analysis suggests that it is a fallacy. The lengths of sequences of successful shots can be explained without assuming any temporary change in ability or luck. It's simply that people tend to underestimate the frequency with which little bursts of lucky shots occur. We've already seen that if you ask people to generate a series of random digits, they spread the numbers out too much, producing too few sequences of the same consecutive digit. It's the same phenomenon which leads people to underestimate the frequency with which pairs of consecutive numbers (like 8, 9 or 23, 24) occur in lottery draws. Likewise, if you ask people to mentally generate random sequences of 0's and 1's, of the kind you might get from tossing a coin with heads labeled 1 and tails 0, they have a tendency to avoid extremes: the proportions of heads and tails they produce tend to be closer to $\frac{1}{2}$ than occurs if you actually toss a coin.

Another counterintuitive effect which may help encourage the hot hand belief is that people underestimate the proportion of time that one or the other of two equally skilled players will be in the lead. This effect can be very striking. Suppose, for example, that we flip a fair coin once per second for 24 hours a day, 7 days a week, for an entire year, calculating the proportions of times it has come up heads and the proportion of times it has come up tails as we go along. You might think that about half the time there would be more heads and about half the time there would be more tails. After all, we know that the proportion of heads will be about 1/2 at the end of the year.

But you'd be wrong. The strange fact is that it's far more likely that either heads will be in the lead for most of the year, or tails will be in the lead for most of the year. Furthermore, the probability is ½ that one of heads or tails would have the higher proportion for the entire last six months of the year. So, if many people undertook such a year-long exercise, you'd see heads or tails remain in the lead throughout the last half of the year for about half of them. Even worse, calculation shows that on average for one out of ten of these people, the last change of leadership (from heads having the higher proportion, or tails having it) will take place within the *first nine days* of the year.

An important study debunking the hot hand belief was carried out by Thomas Gilovich of Cornell University and his collaborators Robert Vallone and Amos Tversky from Stanford.[2] They focused on basketball statistics, analyzing the shooting records of the Philadelphia 76ers and other teams, including a controlled experiment with the varsity basketball players (both men and women) of Cornell University. They concluded that the data "provided no evidence for a positive correlation between the outcomes of successive shots," attributing the continued belief in such a correlation partly to the fact that "long sequences of hits (or misses) are more memorable than alternating sequences, [so that] the observer is likely to overestimate the correlation between successive shots."

Other studies have reached similar conclusions. For example, while work by Christian Albright on baseball statistics concluded that "some players exhibit significant streakiness during a given season"[3] (that is, streaks of good or poor hits), we must remember that someone has to come at the top and someone has to come at the bottom in a league table. If we look at a large number of players (Albright looked at 501), we'd expect some of them to show apparent streakiness just by chance. Albright was aware of this, adding, "The proportion of batters who exhibited nonrandom behavior was reasonably close to that predicted by a random model."

The hot hand belief is very seductive, and our natural tendency to notice patterns such as a series of consecutive successful plays means that it's a difficult one to dispel. One consequence is that there will always be fresh researchers seeking to debunk the debunking. As I said, that's in the very nature of science, with other researchers testing and probing theories and explanations to see how well they stand up to new data. Such counterattacks sometimes claim that Gilovich and his colleagues didn't control for all relevant factors. The argument is that sports or games performance is not like the abstract model of coin tossing, and there are many influences which need to be taken into account to yield an unbiased analysis, such as the mental state of players, their health, minor injuries, and so on. Another such factor is the time between successive plays. If the hot hand phenomenon decays over time, then clearly this could influence the results of an analysis which does not allow for this.

Another suggestion made in attempted refutation of the conclusions reached by Gilovich and his colleagues is that they had insufficient data to detect the real, but small, positive correlations. This might be true, but a real correlation which is only infinitesimally above zero would probably not be of any interest. In general, the smaller the difference you seek to detect, the more data you need to detect it. For example, it wouldn't take many coin tosses for us to recognize that a coin which had a probability of 0.9 of coming up heads wasn't fair (that is, to detect that its probability of showing a head was different from 0.5). But it would take a great many if the probability was 0.501. How much data you need really depends on how small a difference you consider it worthwhile knowing about. But if the difference was only 0.001, would we care?

Jim Albert, commenting on Albright's negative conclusion about the existence of streakiness in baseball hits, illustrates how difficult it can be to convince those who believe in the existence of streaks.[4] He says: "I believe that it is wrong to conclude from this analysis that streakiness is not present in baseball data. Instead we should recognize that streakiness, like other situational variables, is a subtle characteristic of data . . . Streakiness is a characteristic of data that is not well understood by many people and is difficult to detect statistically."

You can't argue with that. All data, especially data about human beings, have their subtleties, and in general we should expect many of these subtleties to be hidden. But Albert's quoted passage does have the flavor of a rearguard action: "The data appear to show me wrong, but maybe the effect does exist under some circumstances." While this could be true, it reminds me of the comments made by the believers in ESP and parapsychology as successive experiments failed to demonstrate the existence of the phenomena.

Coincidences also illustrate the subconscious human need to find patterns in events. We saw some examples of this in chapter 2, when we looked at Carl Jung's ideas of synchronicity. Here are others from the same source. The passages are Jung's own words, quoted from *Memories, Dreams, Reflections*.[5]

The first involves a former patient of Dr. Jung, whom he claimed to have "pulled out of a psychogenic depression." Subsequently, the patient married a woman whom Jung "did not care for." Jung saw the "wife's attitude [as placing] a tremendous burden on the patient which he was incapable of coping with." The patient then relapsed, and didn't contact Jung again. Jung picks up the story:

> At that time I had to deliver a lecture in B. I returned to my hotel around midnight. I sat with some friends for a while after the lecture, then went to bed, but I lay awake for a long time. At about two o'clock—I must have just fallen asleep—I awoke with a start, and had the feeling that someone had come into the room; I even had the impression that the door had been hastily opened. I instantly

turned on the light, but there was nothing. Someone might have mistaken the door, I thought, and I looked into the corridor. But it was as still as death. "Odd," I thought, "someone did come into the room!" Then I tried to recall exactly what had happened, and it occurred to me that I had been awakened by a feeling of dull pain, as though something had struck my forehead and then the back of my skull. The following day I received a telegram saying that my patient had committed suicide. He had shot himself. Later, I learned that the bullet had come to rest in the back wall of the skull.

This experience was a genuine synchronistic phenomenon such as is quite often observed in connection with an archetypal situation—in this case, death. By means of a relativization of time and space in the unconscious it could well be that I had perceived something which in reality was taking place elsewhere.[6]

Indeed. Or it could also be that staying up until just before 2:00 a.m. had led to a headache, and then he woke with a start when someone slammed the door on entering a nearby room. You have to wonder how often he'd experienced such waking in hotel rooms in the past (I know I've experienced plenty), unconnected with "archetypal situations" (at least, mine are unconnected!), and which don't require explanation via "a relativization of time and space in the unconscious." The event may have seemed extraordinary to Jung, but the strands of the Improbability Principle explain it.

The second example is even more bizarre and contrived.

A year later I painted a second picture, likewise a mandala, with a golden castle in the center. When it was finished, I asked myself, "Why is this so Chinese?" I was impressed by the form and choice of colors, which seemed to me Chinese, although there was nothing outwardly Chinese about it. Yet that was how it affected me. It was a strange coincidence that shortly afterwards I received a letter from Richard Wilhelm enclosing the manuscript of a Taoist-alchemical treatise entitled *The Secret of the Golden Flower*, with a request that I write a commentary on it . . .

In remembrance of this coincidence, this "synchronicity," I wrote . . .[7]

With his unusual interests, I think it is a safe bet that Jung often received letters containing strange manuscripts (or was told strange stories, and so on—just how wide should we cast this net? Just how near is near enough?), and he does not say how long "shortly afterwards" is. The Improbability Principle tells us that the "coincidence" of these two events—Jung's subjective feelings about the picture he himself painted, and his receipt of the letter—is not surprising at all. The treatise is not even about a golden castle! Would a manuscript about a red castle have been just as surprising to him as one about a golden flower? Above all, here, Jung's interests are opening the door to the law of selection: he is noting and recognizing topics which are of particular relevance to him.

The law of the probability lever is also apparent in many situations like these. We might read an article about someone, then see them on television, and then overhear a colleague mention them at work. At first we might think it something of a coincidence, the way their name keeps cropping up. But presumably they've done something which merits them being in the news. That would mean that the probabilities of them being featured in a newspaper article, appearing on television, and being mentioned by a colleague, were all elevated. The events had a common underlying cause which had changed the probability distributions. This is a further illustration of how failing to take proper account of dependencies can lead to mistaken judgments of probability—as in the Sally Clark case.

We met a similar situation in chapter 6—the not uncommon experience of coming across a new word for the first time, and then encountering it again very soon afterward. We saw how the law of selection could lead to the experience, but other strands of the Improbability Principle can also explain it, perhaps working together to make the phenomenon even more striking. Maybe your behavior has changed—you might be reading a new kind of material where this word is not unusual, or a new author who uses this word—so that the law of the probability lever applies. Maybe you've read the word before, but it's become topical so that heightened awareness has now drawn it to your attention—the law of selection again. Or maybe the world has changed, so that the word was once rare but is now less so: words change their meanings, and become more widely used ("tweet," for instance), new words are coined ("google," for example), and words cross international boundaries. This is the law of the lever in another guise.

This kind of heightened awareness happened to me while I was finishing this book. I have an interest in the application of statistical methods in astronomy, but I'm also interested in how easily we can be misled, and I'd been reading books on magic. Now, as is its custom, on October 6, 2012, *The Times* included a short list of eminent figures who had been born on its day of publication in earlier years. This list included Nevil Maskelyne, who was Astronomer Royal from 1765 to 1811. But then, just a few pages later in the same edition, there was a description of the Second World War incident in which Montgomery fooled Rommel by misleading him about where an attack would take place. Montgomery achieved this by employing painters and carpenters to disguise 600 tanks as trucks, so that they appeared harmless, and to make mock-ups of guns and tanks somewhere else. One of those employed in this ruse, and who is explicitly mentioned in the article, was Jasper Maskelyne, a famous magician. Jasper Maskelyne claimed to be a descendant of Nevil Maskelyne. What a coincidence, I thought, that these two related people should be mentioned, on the same day, in entirely unconnected stories! But note that I noticed this only because of my interest in both of the topics—astronomy and magic. You can't help wondering how many other "coincidences" I missed, and how many would have been spotted in that very same issue by other people with other interests. It's the law of selection. Furthermore, since it's not the same Maskelyne mentioned in the two articles, the law of near enough is also at work.

Psychological Surprises

In the previous section I looked at patterns of events, and at how various psychological biases made it more likely that we'd encounter such configurations. Our tendency to underestimate the rate at which repeated numbers occur in a random digit sequence was an example. We also saw how changes in the world, or in ourselves, could make unexpected patterns more likely, taking us by surprise.

Sometimes this sort of effect works in an even more pronounced way through *feedback mechanisms*. Feedback occurs when a reaction to some event or phenomenon influences the chance that it will then happen. Such mechanisms are commonplace in biological systems, for example in what is called a *prey-predator* cycle. The Canada lynx preys on the snowshoe hare. An increase in the number of hares means that more lynx can find food and survive. The greater the number of lynx , the more hares are eaten, so their population declines. As a consequence, fewer lynx can find food, so *their* population declines. With fewer predators eating them, the hare population picks up. And so it goes on, round and round.

Economic fluctuations are another example. Rising stock prices encourage more people to buy, so the price rises even more.

This encourages more purchases, in turn pushing the price up further. That is, until someone suspects that the price has peaked. They sell. The price drops a little. Seeing the drop, others sell, driving the price down even further. And so on.

One form of feedback mechanism is the self-fulfilling prophecy I mentioned in chapter 2, where the belief that something *will* happen leads to an action that makes it *more likely* to happen. Remember Robert Merton's example of an anxious student who, convinced he would fail his test, spent more time worrying than studying, and as a consequence failed? It's been suggested that optimists, expecting good things to happen to them, are more likely to place themselves in situations where good things *can* happen. Certainly, someone who believed they were intrinsically lucky might well contrive opportunities where their luck could manifest itself. Liz Denial, from Stapleford, Nottingham, in the UK, has won a 37-inch LCD TV, a home cinema system, two Xboxes, a five-star holiday to Kenya, £16,500 on a TV game show, and many other prizes. What's revealing is that she says she won a prize every single day between October 2012 and June 2013 (when the newspaper article describing her success was written).[8] That means she entered a remarkable number of competitions. Remember the lottery sales pitch "You've got to be in it to win it" mentioned in chapter 4? The same principle applies here: "be in" enough competitions and the law of truly large numbers will do the rest.

In a like way, an optimist, believing they'd find whatever they were looking for if only they kept looking long enough, would be inclined to keep looking for longer than a pessimist who felt that they'd be unlikely to find it. And then the extra time spent looking would mean that the optimist would be more likely to find the object.

But remember the law of selection! Think of the familiar example of people battling a fatal disease who say, "I overcame it because I believed I could." Those who succumbed will not be around to tell you they'd failed to overcome it, even if they believed they could.

The phrase "You've got to be in it to win it" characterizes the line separating the impossible (probability of zero) from the possible (probability above zero; in fact *just* above zero in the case of lotteries). Unfortunately, we generally find it difficult to assess very small probabilities. We typically *overestimate* them (thinking the events more likely than they are) and *underestimate* very high probabilities. The *possibility effect* is the name given to this twist of human psychology for very small probabilities. The true probability might be one in a million, but we exaggerate it. A 1 in 14 million chance of winning a lottery is sufficiently small that Borel's law applies, and yet we still enter lotteries. Likewise, people are often prepared to pay above the odds to reduce or eliminate very small risks. To take an extreme example, you can buy insurance against alien abduction—which, you will be relieved to hear, also covers any medical expenses you incur while recovering from the effects of the abduction.

The possibility effect exaggerates the impact of Borel's law. Because of the possibility effect, we mistakenly think that highly improbable events are not so improbable. We might even think they're quite likely. But Borel's law tells us that if an event is highly improbable we won't see it happen. That means that we won't see such events happen even though we think they're quite likely. The mismatch between the world and our beliefs about it is amplified.

The effect at the other end of the scale is called the *certainty effect*: the tendency to underestimate the probability of events which are almost certain. It stands in interesting contrast to yet another psychological phenomenon, the *overconfidence effect*. When people are asked to predict whether an event will occur, they tend to be overconfident about their predictions. Events don't actually occur as often as people predict they will. And this in turn is related to *hindsight bias* (the tendency to see past events as being more predictable than they were at the time), which I'll discuss shortly.

Sorting out all these biases is complicated by the fact that the interpretation depends on our perspective. Imagine two medical tests, one of which is 95 percent accurate, and another which is 96 percent accurate. You might regard the tests as being essentially equally effective. But now look at it another way: the first test misclassifies 5 percent of the patients, and the second only 4 percent. The difference is $5\% - 4\% = 1\%$ out of 5%. So the second test misclassifies one-fifth fewer patients than the first. Now the second test looks *much* better than the first.

Likewise, if a probability is very small, then twice that probability is still very small. Suppose a drug company promotes a new medicine by claiming that only 1 in 100,000 people will suffer from a side effect, contrasting it with a competitor's product which has a 1 in 50,000 (equal to 2 in 100,000) side effect rate. The new medicine leads to only half as many people having side effects. Can't be bad? True, but the difference is only 1 in 100,000! That's a tiny number. Of all the risks to worry about in life, this should probably not be the most prominent on your radar. While not quite in the realm of Borel's law, it's still negligible. We can ignore the difference between the two risk rates.

A more subtle misconception is *denominator neglect*. Technical books on probability often describe constrained and artificial situations so they can focus on the probability essentials abstracted from the messy complications of the real world. Indeed, I've done this myself in places in this book by looking at dice throws and coin tosses. Similarly, probability texts sometimes imagine drawing marbles from urns. So, suppose we have two urns:

Urn number 1 contains 10 marbles, 9 white and 1 red.
Urn number 2 contains 100 marbles, 92 white and 8 red.

We're told which urn contains the 10 marbles, and which urn contains the 100 marbles.

You're now invited to blindly plunge your hand into one of the urns and pull out a marble. If the marble you draw is red, you win a prize. The question is, which urn should you choose, the one with 10 marbles or the one with 100 marbles?

Basic calculations show that the chance of picking a red marble from urn number 1 is 10 percent, and from urn number 2 it's 8 percent, so the rational answer is urn number 1. But about a third of the people given this test choose urn number 2. It seems that the larger number of marbles in the second urn leads many people to (correctly) conclude that the colors are more homogeneously mixed in the second urn. But then from this they make the incorrect inference that more-uniform mixing means a greater chance of drawing a red marble from the second urn.

In chapter 3 we met the law of large numbers (as distinct from the law of *truly* large numbers). The law of large numbers described how the average of a set of numbers randomly sampled from some population was more likely to be nearer to the overall average of the population if you took a bigger random sample. The phrase "law of small numbers" is sometimes used to describe the mistaken assumption that the law of large numbers applies to small numbers as well.

Suppose we toss a fair coin a hundred times. The law of large numbers tells us that we're very unlikely to see a proportion of heads which departs significantly from 1/2, that is, from 0.5. In fact, calculations show that the probability of observing a proportion which deviates from 0.5 by so much that it's smaller than 0.4 or larger than 0.6 is 0.035. By the law of small numbers, we might then also expect to see a similar small probability of observing a proportion less than 0.4 or greater than 0.6 if we toss the coin five times. But that would be wrong. Calculation shows that the probability is in fact 0.375. It's actually more than ten times as likely.

Here's a different variant of the same phenomenon. Suppose we're comparing two local anesthetics. We give one to a randomly chosen group of four patients, and the other to a second randomly chosen group of forty patients. To evaluate the effectiveness of the medicines we press a sharp instrument into the patients' skin, not quite hard enough to break the skin, and ask them to rate how uncomfortable it is, on a three-point scale: very painful, mildly uncomfortable, barely feel it.

Now suppose that, in the overall population from which we picked the patients, the two medicines are actually equally effective, and that some 30 percent of the population would have found the skin test "very painful," for both anesthetics. That means we'd expect around 30 percent to respond this way on average in both groups. That's an average, but we probably wouldn't be very surprised if, by chance, *all four* of the patients we randomly picked for the first group responded "very painful" (in fact, the probability is 1 in 123).

In contrast, we would be very surprised if *all forty* of the randomly chosen patients in the second group happened to respond "very painful" (in fact this probability is 1 in 8×10^{20}). Smaller groups lead to proportions which are more variable than larger groups—and consquently to a larger number of extreme proportions. The law of small numbers describes our tendency to fail to take account of this higher variability when there are small numbers of cases.

We saw the impact of greater variability in chapter 6, in an example where job applicants with more-variable test scores were more likely to obtain a high score than applicants with very homogeneous test scores, even if they would produce the same average if they were to be tested a very large number of times. This also applies here, but now the extra variability is due to the smaller sample size: smaller sample sizes lead to more-variable sample averages. So, of two equally skilled surgeons, the one who performs fewer operations is likely to have the greater variability in his success rate. That variability will manifest itself in a greater chance of scoring a high success rate—and also of scoring a low success rate. From the perspective of the Improbability Principle, it means that observations based on small amounts of data are likely to produce apparently rarer average values.

Incidentally, the expression "law of small numbers" has been used to describe other phenomena as well. One is simply the behavior of numbers drawn from the Poisson distribution. Another is Richard Guy's *strong law of small numbers*, based on his lighthearted observation that "there aren't enough small numbers to meet the many demands made of them."[9] He means that because there are so few small numbers, they crop up in many places, generating apparent coincidences. The question Guy raises is, when we see coincidences involving small numbers, are they merely chance or do they reflect deeper underlying truths? One way to answer this is to extend the examples to larger numbers, since then, if a match is purely coincidental, it will vanish. Here are two examples, the second being one of Guy's:

Example 1: We note that $3^2 + 4^2 = 5^2$ and that $3^3 + 4^3 + 5^3 = 6^3$, and wonder if such relationships between consecutive integers starting at 3 always hold (so, for example, does $3^4 + 4^4 + 5^4 + 6^4 = 7^4$?), or is it just a coincidence for these values?

Example 2: If you write down the positive integers (as in row 1 below), delete every second integer (as in row 2), and form the cumulative sums of those remaining (as in row 3: so $1 + 3 = 4$, $1 + 3 + 5 = 9$, etc.), you get a sequence of square numbers.

1	2	3	4	5	6	7	8	9	10	11
1		3		5		7		9		11
1		4		9		16		25		36

The question is, is it an intrinsic property of numbers that such a process will generate square numbers, or is it just a coincidence which happens to be true for the small numbers in the example?[10]

Guy describes the consequences which follow from his strong law of small numbers in various ways, including that "superficial similarities spawn spurious statements" and that "capricious coincidences cause careless conjectures."

This discussion wouldn't be complete without mentioning another aspect of the interaction between events and human aspirations. It's not part of the Improbability Principle, but *Murphy's Law*, which states that "anything that can go wrong will go wrong" is worth highlighting before we move on.

Murphy's law is an ironic comment on the perversity of the universe, although the irony has sometimes been expressed in stronger terms. The magician Nevil Maskelyne (not the former Astronomer Royal, but the father of the Jasper Maskelyne whom I mentioned earlier) wrote that "everything that can go wrong *will* go wrong. Whether we must attribute this to the malignity of matter or to the total depravity of inanimate things . . ."[11] I rather like the phrase "total depravity of inanimate things"!

Although it's sometimes claimed that Murphy's law is named after Captain Ed Murphy, who worked at Edwards Air Force Base in 1949, the idea behind the law is probably as old as humanity itself. You can think of Murphy's law as a special case of the law of truly large numbers, when that's expressed as "If it can happen, it will happen," or as a variant of the second law of thermodynamics, which says that the amount of randomness in a closed system increases.

There's also a more extreme version of Murphy's law, sometimes called *Sod's law*. This simply says that the worst possible outcome *always* happens. Traffic lights turn red when you're in a hurry, or your e-mail crashes just as you are about to hit "send" on that critical message. Or, at a more serious level, a composer such as Beethoven loses his hearing, or a drummer such as Rick Allen (with the band Def Leppard) loses an arm in a car crash. But then we'll recall the law of truly large numbers, which reminds us that some such incidents should be expected, and the law of selection, which means we'll bring them to mind.

Hindsight

Time moves in one direction, from the future to the past. The future is like a chaotic sea, bubbling and swirling from possibility to possibility, where things momentarily look as if they'll happen, only to be replaced by others that look more likely, and which then in their turn are replaced by yet others. The present acts like a freezing wind, solidifying events as it passes over them, crystallizing them so they can never change but become part of the fixed past.

We can study the steps through which the present appears to be progressing to try to predict what will happen next. But until the future becomes the past, we can never be certain: there's always the possibility that something unexpected will intrude and throw our predictions off. But *once the future has become the past*, then it's easy to look back and see the paths which led to it. This is the basis of hindsight bias.

It's especially difficult to predict the future when complex trains of events are involved. I've already mentioned the 9/11 atrocity, where *in retrospect*, it's possible to see the steps leading to the attack, but *in advance*, amid the maelstrom of everything else that was going on, it was not.

Leonard Mlodinow, in his marvelous book *The Drunkard's Walk*, describes how a series of signs had obvious implications, *in retrospect*, for the forthcoming attack on Pearl Harbor in 1941.[12] These included an intercepted message to a Japanese spy asking him to send information on how the warships were docked, the fact that the Japanese changed their call signs twice within one

month instead of every six months as they normally did, an instruction to Japanese diplomats to destroy their codes and ciphers
and burn confidential documents, and so on. In retrospect, and
looking at these as a string of signs in isolation from whatever
else was going on, you might think that only a fool would not
have spotted that something was up. But, again, retrospective vision
is perfect: at the time, these signs occurred in a seething turmoil
of other events and incidents. It wasn't possible to single them
out, to identify them as connected, and to predict the storm that
was about to follow. Hindsight is a wonderful thing.

There are many examples of leading authorities making confident predictions which *in hindsight* turned out to be hopelessly
wrong. Here are some examples:

- "I have not the smallest molecule of faith in aerial navi-
gation other than ballooning." (Often paraphrased as
"Heavier-than-air flying machines are impossible.")
Lord Kelvin, President of the Royal Society of London,
1896
- "We can close the book on infectious diseases." Wil-
liam H. Stewart, Surgeon General of the United States,
1969
- "Who the hell wants to hear actors talk?" H. M. Warner,
Warner Brothers, 1927
- "Groups of guitars are on the way out." Decca Record-
ing Co., rejecting the Beatles in 1962
- "There's no chance that the iPhone is going to get any
significant market share." Steve Ballmer, 2007

When the Queen of England visited the London School of
Economics in November 2008, she famously asked why nobody
had noticed that the credit crunch was on its way. The British
Academy explained that in fact many people *had* foreseen the
crisis. What they hadn't foreseen, however, and what would have

been impossible to predict, was the exact form the crisis would take, and exactly when it would occur. Indeed, I too can claim to have predicted change ahead. But my foresight wasn't particularly deep: it was simply based on noting that consumer credit in the form of credit card lending had been growing exponentially for some decades, and that this couldn't continue forever. But I had no idea of when or precisely how events would unfold.

The historian E. H. Carr presented a personal reminiscence of hindsight bias, and as it happens, of selection bias: "When I studied ancient history in this university many years ago, I had as a special subject 'Greece in the period of the Persian Wars.' I collected fifteen or twenty volumes on my shelves and took it for granted that there, recorded in these volumes, I had all the facts relating to my subject. Let us assume—it was very nearly true—that those volumes contained all the facts about it that were then known, or could be known. It never occurred to me to inquire by what accident or process of attrition that minute selection of facts, out of all the myriad facts that must once have been known to somebody, had survived to become *the* facts of history."[13]

In this chapter, I've moved from strands of the Improbability Principle which are a consequence of physics to strands which are a consequence of psychology; from strands which are an inevitable result of the way the world works, to strands which are a result of how we see the world. The two strands can interact, amplifying the principle, so that it becomes even more powerful.

10

LIFE, THE UNIVERSE, AND EVERYTHING

What does chance ever do for us?   —William Paley

Life and Chance

Human beings are extraordinarily complex organisms. We each contain about 10^{27} molecules. But even if you had all the right molecules, put them in a pot, and shook them up, the chance of them falling together in the right configuration to make a human being would be negligible on Borel's supercosmic level. It wouldn't happen. It's Borel's law.

Richard Dawkins carried out some calculations—not for an entire human being, but for a tiny part of a human, an enzyme molecule. He looked at the probability that such a molecule could "spontaneously come into existence by chance." He says: "There is a fixed number of amino acids available, twenty. A typical enzyme is a chain of several hundred links drawn from the twenty. An elementary calculation shows that the probability that any particular sequence of, say 100, amino acids will spontaneously form is 1 in $20 \times 20 \times 20 \ldots$ 100 times, or 1 in 20^{100}. This is an inconceivably large number, far greater than the number of fundamental particles in the entire universe . . . Professor Chandra Wickramasinghe . . . has quoted [Sir Fred Hoyle] as saying that the spontaneous formation by 'chance' of a working enzyme is like a hurricane blowing through a junkyard and spontaneously having the luck to put together a Boeing 747."[1]

Fred Hoyle's colorful illustration captures the point. The chance of the amino acids randomly moving around and configuring themselves into an enzyme is so small it's not going to happen. And yet not just enzymes, but entire humans, do exist. It certainly looks like a playground for the Improbability Principle. But first let's consider another possible explanation.

When we look at the world around us we see all sorts of complex structures: houses, aircraft, cars, computers, televisions, and so on. And they certainly didn't spring into existence by chance. They were in fact *designed* and *made*.

The eighteenth-century philosopher William Paley (who died in 1805) used exactly this analogy to support the notion that biological objects must have had a creator. He began his book *Natural Theology* with the words: "In crossing a heath, suppose I pitched my foot against a stone, and were asked how the stone came to be there, I might possibly answer, that, for any thing I knew to the contrary it had lain there for ever: nor would it perhaps be very easy to show the absurdity of this answer. But suppose I had found a *watch* upon the ground, and it should be inquired how the watch happened to be in that place; I should hardly think of the answer which I had before given, that, for any thing I knew, the watch might have always been there . . . [T]here must have existed, at some time, and at some place or other, an artificer or artificers who formed [the watch] for the purpose which we find it actually to answer; who comprehended its construction, and designed its use."[2]

The difficulty with this creation argument is that it can explain anything. We saw this in chapter 2 when we looked at miracles. The "it just is / someone put it there" argument can never be refuted, whatever evidence is provided. There's also the troubling question of who created the creator—where, and indeed how, does this chain of creation start? The creation argument is not so much an explanation as an evasion of the question.

And there's more. The existence of complex life-forms, such as human beings, is not the only thing needing explanation. Another is the fossil record. Over time, people learned that buried in rocks were fossilized remains of animals which could no longer be found in the living world. Doubtless such traces were the origin of some stories of dragons and other beasts which had existed in the past. But close study of these traces, matching the shapes of the fossils to the period in which they lived (evident from the strata of rock in which they were found), revealed a pattern to the forms. It was as if a developmental process had occurred, with different creatures existing at different times, and changes occurring over time in the types of creatures which had lived. To take just one example, there were no fossils of humans dating from millions of years ago, but there were remains of creatures which resembled humans in various ways. All of this has to be explained.

Science provides us with a strategy for searching for explanations—although not for finding absolute truth. Indeed, it has been said that if you want absolute truth then you must look to pure mathematics or religion, but certainly not to science. Pure mathematics yields absolute truth because it is simply the deduction of the consequences which follow from a given set of axioms when you apply a given set of rules. This means that in pure mathematics you define your own universe, so that you can certainly state the absolute truth within it. And religion as an expression of faith is a statement of belief in an absolute truth.

In contrast, science is all about possibilities. We propose theories, conjectures, hypotheses, and *explanations.* We collect evidence and data, and we test the theories against this new evidence. If the data contradict our theory, then we change the theory. In this way science advances, and we gain greater and greater understanding. But there is always the possibility of new evidence arising which contradicts the existing theories. It's the very essence of science that its conclusions can change, that is, that its truths are not absolute. The intrinsic good sense of this is contained within the remark reportedly made by the eminent economist John Maynard Keynes, responding to the criticism that he had changed his position on monetary policy during the 1930s Depression: "When the facts change, I change my mind. What do you do, sir?"

The laws underlying the Improbability Principle play a key role in helping us decide when to change our minds as new facts accumulate, in deciding when those facts can no longer be explained sufficiently well by our theories. We'll explore how to use it in this way in the next chapter. Here, let's look in detail at just two examples.

Evolution provides us with a prime example of how theories must change when new evidence appears. When Darwin published *The Origin of Species* in 1859, outlining his ideas on natural selection, the renowned physicist Lord Kelvin argued that the theory conflicted with the "fact" that the sun wouldn't have enough fuel to burn for the millions of years required for evolution to have occurred. This "fact" was a perfectly legitimate one, given the knowledge of the time. It was based on the supposition that the sun burned through some kind of chemical reaction, since nuclear reactions were unknown in those days. Once they were discovered it became clear that the sun would be able to burn for billions of years: plenty of time for life and humans to evolve. The facts changed, and the theories changed to accommodate the facts. Incidentally, had knowledge accumulated in a different order, then Darwin might have been able to suggest that Lord Kelvin must have been mistaken about his ideas of the age of the sun, because the *fact* of evolution would have required it to be older.

Tiny Steps and Billions of Years

Imagine standing blindfolded on the side of a large conical hill. Your aim is to get to the top, but you don't know which direction it's in.

One strategy might be to ask someone else to pick you up and carry you. This is equivalent to the creator "explanation." It's not really a strategy at all, not least because it requires the existence of someone else who knows where the top of the hill is, and has a strategy for getting there. This leads to the "Who created the creator?" question.

Another strategy would simply be to take jumps in random directions all over the hill hoping that one of them would land you on the top. This strategy is similar to the explanation that molecules coming together in random configurations would coalesce into the shape of a human being by chance. It might eventually work, but it could take a long time!

A third strategy is a little more complicated. This is to reach out your foot in a random direction and see if a step in that direction would increase your altitude. If it would, then you take that step. If it wouldn't, then you test a different random direction. Once you've taken a step you repeat the procedure, stretching out your leg in a randomly chosen direction, and so on.

By this process you'll gradually reach the top of the hill. Not directly, and not in a straight line, but in a sequence of many small steps, each of which led you a little higher. Your path might even circle the top in its random steps, though each would lead you to a higher position than the last. Mathematicians call this a process of *stochastic optimization*: "stochastic" because the steps are in randomly chosen directions, and "optimization" because you're getting nearer to the target. They use variations of this strategy to find the maximum and minimum values of mathematical functions.

Two strands of the Improbability Principle are coming into

effect here. One is the law of truly large numbers. Your steps are small, maybe a couple of feet at a time, and the hill is large, maybe thousands of feet high. (According to the local Chamber of Commerce, Cavanal Hill near Poteau, Oklahoma, is the tallest hill in the world, at 1,999 feet.) And your steps are in random directions; although each one increases your altitude a little, it might be by only inches or a fraction of an inch. *But put together enough of them*, each one moving you a little higher, and you will get to the top.

The second strand which makes the outcome inescapable is the law of selection. You test each step before taking it, rejecting those which wouldn't lead to improvement. That is, you *select* only those steps which increase your altitude. After each step, your situation is slightly better than it was before. So your next step already has a better starting point.

This step-by-step strategy for reaching the top of the hill has three main components:

- each step is in a randomly chosen direction;
- you take a lot of steps; and
- you choose to take a step if it increases your altitude, albeit perhaps only very slightly, so that your starting point for the next step is higher.

The second and third of these components are strands of the Improbability Principle: the law of truly large numbers and the law of selection respectively.

These three components are exactly what drive biological evolution, leading to life and human beings. To see this, let's look at an example.

Each spring, a certain kind of insect swarms and the queens fly off in random directions, to random locations, to start new nests. When winter comes, some of those nests turn out to be in locations which are susceptible to the cold. Those nests are likely to die out. Others, however, find themselves in places which have a slightly warmer climate: perhaps closer to the equator. Those nests are more likely to survive. Nests which survive are around to breed and swarm next year. By this means, the population of insects gradually shifts toward warmer regions, regions more conducive to survival.

We see that the randomness is built-in: each stage involves the intrinsically random aspect of where the queens settle. And a selection process operates: by chance, some insects have moved to a place which means they have a higher chance of survival to breed next year, so the next generation is more likely to begin life in a warmer place. We also see that it takes a lot of generations to make noticeable changes.

We can see the principles behind evolution in dog breeding as well. There are many different breeds of dogs, but they didn't start out that way. The different breeds were produced over a very long time period by choosing breeding pairs that had the desired characteristics. Some of the offspring also had these characteristics, some didn't. Those that did were chosen to form the basis for the next generation. Repeating this process, generation after generation, gradually led to the distinct breeds we see today. Randomness is built-in—you can't tell exactly what the offspring of any breeding pair will be like. In this example, the dog breeder decides which offspring to select to produce the next generation. In nature, however, the external environment will decide what offspring survive to found the next generation.

On a large scale, we might expect macroscopic climate change to drive evolution, and scientists have indeed observed such adaptation. Tim Sparks of the National Environment Research Council Centre for Ecology and Hydrology observed: "The number of species of migratory Lepidoptera (moths and butterflies) reported each year at a site in the south of the UK has been steadily rising. This number is very strongly linked to rising temperatures in SW Europe."[3]

A less familiar example is that of the Italian wall lizards. Ten such lizards were taken to the island of Pod Mraru in 1971. On their originating island, such lizards had a mainly insect diet, but in their new habitat they ate more vegetation. Nowadays the lizards on the new island have larger heads and stronger bites, as well as differently structured intestines, more suited to eating vegetable matter.

The case of the cane toad in Australia is a rather elegant case of evolution. Cane toads are not native to Australia, but were introduced there from Hawaii as a predator to control the beetles which damaged sugarcane. Unfortunately, the species has subsequently propagated extensively, having a dramatic effect on native wildlife. The toads spread out from the point of release, in a sort of wave, moving farther out with each passing year. Those at the front of the wave are, naturally, those that are able to move most rapidly. Those at the front thus tend to breed with others who move most rapidly. The consequence is that subsequent generations of cane toads at the front of the spreading wave are more active and able to move faster than those behind, and the rate of movement of the front of the wave is increasing with time. This is a natural consequence of evolution.

Many generations are required for evolution to occur, but for some creatures a generation is a relatively short period of time. This is true of bacteria, for instance. In fact, bacterial generations are so short that their evolution can be studied in the laboratory. Since 1988 the evolutionary biologist Richard Lenski has observed over 50,000 generations of the *E. coli* bacterium, studying how the genetic makeup of the populations evolves over time. Fifty thousand is enough for the law of truly large numbers to have an impact.

The zoologist Mark Ridley provides another way of looking at specific aspects of the evolutionary process. He's commenting not on evolution over time, but on how geographical location favors slightly different characteristics. He writes: "As we look at the herring gull, moving westwards from Great Britain to North America, we see gulls that are recognizably herring gulls, although they are a little different from the British form. We can follow them, as their appearance gradually changes, as far as Siberia. At about this point in the continuum, the gull looks more like the form that in Great Britain is called the lesser black-backed gull. From Siberia, across Russia, to northern Europe, the gull gradually changes to look more and more like the British lesser black-backed gull. Finally, in Europe, the ring is complete; the two geographically extreme forms meet, to form two perfectly good species: the herring and the lesser black-backed gull can be both distinguished by their appearance and do not naturally interbreed."[4]

Charles Darwin summarized the basic process of evolution very nicely: "[I]f variations useful to any organic being do occur, assuredly individuals thus characterised will have the best chance of being preserved in the struggle for life; and from the strong principle of inheritance they will tend to produce offspring similarly characterised. This principle of preservation, I have called, for the sake of brevity, Natural Selection."[5]

It's an idea of extraordinary simplicity, elegance, and power. It's driven by the law of truly large numbers coupled with the law of selection.

The Copernican Principle and the Principle of Mediocrity

And how about the most improbable thing of all: the existence of the universe and the occurrence of life within it? Some have argued that this is so improbable that the only explanation is that the universe had to be conjured into existence by the conscious effort of a superbeing or god. But this evades rather than resolves the issue.

As I said, science is all about *evidence*. We look around, measure the properties of things, look at the relationships between them, and seek explanations. A fundamental principle of science, known as *the principle of parsimony* or *Occam's razor*, says we should favor simpler explanations over more complex ones. Nicolaus Copernicus's theory that the earth and other planets orbit the sun offered a much more compelling account of observed planetary motions than the older theory that the sun orbits the earth, because the older theory requires a complex hierarchy of corrections (so-called epicycles), whereas Copernicus's *heliocentric* theory merely requires that the planets move in ellipses.

When Copernicus demoted the earth from being the physical center of the solar system in this way, he started a revolution. That demotion was followed by discoveries revealing that the sun itself is simply an ordinary star among some hundreds of billions in the galaxy, and that the galaxy itself is simply one of countless billions of galaxies in the universe. Just as Copernicus said that the earth is not special in the solar system, so the more general *Copernican principle* says that the earth is not special in the universe. You might say that Copernicus reduced humanity to the ordinary.

But that's not the end of it. The revolution Copernicus started has been extended far beyond this simple *geographical* demotion. In particular, it's been extended into the *principle of mediocrity*. This says that earth, and by implication humanity, is not located at a special position in the universe, *and moreover that there's nothing special about the condition of humanity in other ways.* We haven't, for example, been singled out and given unusual laws of physics: the same laws apply throughout our universe. (I should say that, obviously, conditions at the surface of the earth are very different from conditions of interstellar space or in the center of a star. However, the principle of mediocrity is talking not about local conditions, but about the laws of physics underlying them. It's a higher-level "Copernican principle.") The physicist Victor Stenger has elaborated on this concept, to what he calls *point-of-view invariance*, which says that the models used in physics can't depend on the point of view of the observer if we are to claim that they represent an objective reality.[6] Using this, he showed how "practically all of fundamental physics as we know it follows directly from the single principle of point-of-view invariance."

Now, the Copernican principle is an observational fact. We can look at the sun and the other planets and see that by far the simplest explanation for the way they behave is that the planets orbit the sun. But the extension to the principle of mediocrity—that humanity has not been specially singled out and that our circumstances are ordinary rather than unusual—might strike you as a great leap further. But consider: ordinary things are, by definition, much more common than unusual things. It follows that if we have no further information or evidence about what we're seeing, then it only makes sense to assume that what we see is common—and hence ordinary. If my dice collection has thousands of ordinary dice and two weighted dice (it does), and you randomly pick one, would you think it more likely to be an ordinary one or a weighted one?

Essentially what we've done here is assign a probability—in the subjective "degree of belief" sense—to the two possibilities, that humanity's circumstances are ordinary or that they're unusual (or, in my dice example, the two possibilities "you picked an unweighted die" or "you picked a weighted one"). This rule for assigning probabilities is called *the principle of insufficient reason* or *the principle of indifference*. Since we had no reason for supposing that you had picked any specific die, we should assume that each of the several thousand was equally likely, so it was overwhelmingly more likely that you picked one of the unweighted ones.

Likewise, it's the safer bet to assume that the physical laws we observe on earth are the ordinary laws which apply elsewhere in the universe, rather than special ones just for us. This is not a proof, and neither is it an observational fact. It's an inference based on a balance of probabilities and the principle of insufficient reason. So, we've gone from the earth not being the center of the solar system, to our everyday laws of physics not being special. But that's not the end of it.

Fine-Tuning

At the foundations of physics lie a number of *fundamental constants* which describe certain basic properties of the universe. They include the speed of light, Planck's constant (which is central to quantum mechanics), the universal gravitational constant, the charge on the electron, and the ratio of the mass of the electron to the mass of the proton, and so on.

Study of the laws of physics suggests that the values of certain relationships between these fundamental constants have to be *just so*, or at least must be very, very similar to what they actually are, in order for stars and planets, and hence human beings, to exist. This is the *fine-tuning* argument. It goes on to apply the principle of insufficient reason to conclude that the probability of getting values in the narrow range necessary for our existence is very low, because there are overwhelmingly more different values that they could have taken. The fact that such a low-probability event has occurred requires some explanation. It is as if you discovered that the die you chose was one of the two weighted ones. A priori this seems highly improbable, so you would seek an explanation.

Various explanations have been suggested, including creationist arguments. But as we've seen, the various strands of the Improbability Principle can bend chance in unexpected ways, so that what at first seemed an extraordinarily unlikely outcome is in fact quite probable. Before we look at how the implications of these strands of the Improbability Principle play out here, let's look at four examples of the fundamental constants of nature.

One is the *strong nuclear force*. This is the force which binds together the protons and neutrons inside an atomic nucleus. If this were just 2 percent stronger, then atomic nuclei formed from two protons would be stable. This would mean that the nuclear reactions inside stars would fuse hydrogen into "diprotons," instead of into deuterium and helium. As a consequence, the behavior of stars would change. Since the energy from the stars, or at least from one particular star—our sun—is responsible for driving all life on earth, that 2 percent change would mean that life of our kind could not exist.

A second example is given by the *cosmic microwave background radiation*. The early universe was a hot and dense place—so dense that it was opaque to electromagnetic radiation and photons were unable to travel freely. But, by the time it was some 400,000 years old, it had expanded and cooled enough (to around 3,000 degrees Kelvin) for protons and electrons to combine into neutral hydrogen. This reduced the thickness of the particle soup and permitted radiation to travel freely. We can observe this radiation today in the microwave range of frequencies (with the right sort of detector, of course), and since the early 1990s we've been able to detect variations in its intensity. These variations are very small—of the order of 1 in 100,000, and scientists think they have been caused by quantum fluctuations at a very early time in the universe's expansion called the *inflationary period*. But their size is critical: slightly larger, and concentrations of matter would be greater, resulting in many stars colliding; slightly smaller, and the aggregation of matter into stars and planets would slow down. In either case, the universe would be very different from the one we see.

A third example is the ratio between the mass of the neutron and the mass of the proton: 1.00137841917.[7] Slightly smaller and there would be far more helium in the universe and stars would burn out too quickly for life to evolve. Slightly larger and atoms could not form—so matter, and hence stars, planets, and life as we know it, would not exist at all.

A fourth example is the ratio between the strengths of two fundamental natural forces: the electromagnetic and gravitational forces. The equilibrium of stars is maintained by a combination of these two forces: gravity trying to pull them in on themselves, and radiation resulting from nuclear reactions trying to push them apart. This balance must be such as to allow heavier elements to form within stars, while also later allowing stars to explode in supernovae to spread these heavier elements across the universe— where they can later condense to form planets and living organisms. If the electromagnetic force were a little stronger than it is, relative to gravity, it could lead to planets being unable to form. If it were a little weaker, supernovae would be less likely to occur. The precise balance is critical.

If something is to be "fine-tuned," if it is to have a value within a specified narrow range, clearly its value cannot depend on the units you choose to measure it in. Take the speed of light in a vacuum. This can be measured in miles per second, kilometers per second, or in various other units. Its value in miles per second is 186,282.397 miles per second, its value in kilometers per second is 299,792.458, and its value in light-years per year is 1 (that last value follows from the definition of a light-year: it is the distance that light travels in one year). In fact, take any number you like and you can define a length unit and a time unit such that that value is the speed of light. So the speed of light, per se, can hardly be fine-tuned.

However, some of the fundamental constants, and some relationships between others, are *dimensionless*: they have the same numerical value whatever units of measurement you choose. The ratio between two attributes measured in the same units is an example. The ratio of the mass of the neutron to the mass of the proton is the same (1.00137841917) whether you measure mass in grams, kilograms, or ounces, in just the same way that my mother's height is 80 percent of my father's height whether I use inches or centimeters. The ratio of the strengths of electromagnetic and gravitational forces in my fourth example above is dimensionless because both numerator and denominator are *forces*, and hence measured in the same units

Contrast this with the statement that a friend of mine weighs the same as he is tall: he weighs 170 pounds and he's 170 centimeters tall. You can immediately see that this "relationship" would alter if you changed the units of measurement, since weight and height are measured in different types of unit. In fact, change just the units of height from centimeters to inches and he becomes a "mere" 67 inches tall (while still weighing 170 pounds). The $170 = 170$ is hardly "fine-tuning" since it's purely a consequence of the units we chose to use. Only dimensionless values can be fine-tuned in any meaningful sense. If a description is intended to signify something fundamental about the universe, it must not depend on the particular units you choose. It follows that if a dimensionless constant were to have a different value, the fundamental physics and the nature of the universe would be different.

The Law of the Probability Lever

One weakness of most fine-tuning arguments is that they focus on one constant at a time. It might well be that changing any one of them, *while keeping the others fixed*, does indeed lead to an overwhelming number of universes which would not permit stars to form or to have sufficiently long lifetimes for life to evolve. But what happens if we change two (or more) together? Recall the example of the finely tuned balance between electromagnetic and gravitational forces in stars which is necessary to create an equilibrium which ultimately leads to planets and life. We saw that changing the value of either one of these forces would mean that the universe would not be suitable for life. But what if we changed them both? What if we increased the electromagnetic force a little, to match the increase in the gravitational force? Do this appropriately, and the equilibrium within stars is maintained, so perhaps planets still form and life evolves. Fine-tuning, yes, but with much more scope for a pair of values which will lead to life than if the forces must separately take highly specific values. A slight change in the model, allowing more than one constant to change at a time, has increased the chance of a universe like ours: it's the law of the probability lever.

We can take this further. What if various fundamental constants are *related*, so that it's not *possible* to change one without changing others? The idea is illustrated by considering two hypothetical constants, which can each take values between 0 and 1. Suppose that both equal 0.5 in our universe, and we calculate that if one is changed by less than 0.01 then stars and planets can form and survive long enough for life to evolve, but if changed more than that, stars cannot form. But now suppose they're linked, so that changing the value of one necessarily leads to a change in the value of the other (in just the same way that increasing your speed means you reduce your travel time). And what if, again, it's not the fact that they both have values (near to) 0.5 which leads to a viable universe, but the fact that they have *very similar* values which does it? One of them having a value of 0.2 might lead to a viable universe, provided the other has a value near to 0.2, with the connection meaning that if one *did* have the value 0.2 then the other *must* be near 0.2. Now it's become much more likely that we'd get a pair of values permitting stars to form.

In this last example, the law of the probability lever is working in a way similar to the Sally Clark case. There, the assumption that two events were unrelated (the two events being SIDS deaths of two siblings) implied a very small probability that both would be observed. But the recognition that there was a dependence between them changed the probability, and it turned out to be quite likely.

Physicists and cosmologists have explored ideas like these. For example, Fred C. Adams, of the Michigan Center for Theoretical Physics, investigated varying the gravitational constant, the fine structure constant, and a constant determining nuclear reaction rates. He found that about *a quarter* of all possible triples of these three values led to stars which would sustain nuclear fusion—like the stars in our universe. As he said, "[W]e conclude that universes with stars are not especially rare (contrary to previous claims)."[8]

The Anthropic Principle and the Law of Selection

Some modern theories of the universe suggest that it's possible that our universe is simply one among a myriad of universes (the whole thing being called the *multiverse*). This is not an idle esoteric fantasy, but is a logical consequence of solid theory. It arises from profound considerations based on quantum theory and the uncertainty principle, and fits in with the way the universe is known to have expanded over time. To explore it would require deep mathematics, but one implication is that other universes would have different fundamental constants.

Let's take the analogy of water freezing. Initially the water molecules are zipping around at random, bouncing off each other and changing direction in entirely unpredictable ways. The liquid looks uniform and homogeneous, the same in every position and in every direction. But now let it cool down and freeze. As the water freezes, the randomly distributed molecules become locked in position. Crystals of ice begin to form. Within each such crystal, the water molecules are aligned in a specific orientation, interlocking in a regular matrix pointing in a certain direction. But neighboring crystals may have their molecules interlocking in a differently oriented matrix: they may point in other directions. And so it is with the laws of physics. Our universe corresponds to one way in which the fundamental constants have "crystallized," and settled on one particular set of values. But other neighboring universes in the multiverse may have constants which "crystallized" differently—they may have different values for the fundamental constants. The specific orientation of the ice crystals, and the specific values of the fundamental constants in our universe, are just the result of a random process. There's nothing special about them.

Nothing special about them, that is, *except* for the fact that the universe in which we live is one in which we *can* live. If the fundamental constants of nature were such that stars could not form, life as we know it would not exist, and we would not be here to see the stars. This truism is the ultimate example of the law of selection. Because it's so fundamental, it has been singled out for study and given its own name—the *anthropic principle*: "The observed values of all physical and cosmological quantities are not equally probable but they take on values restricted by the requirement that there exist sites where carbon-based life can evolve and by the requirement that the Universe be old enough for it to have already done so."[9]

You can see a more direct, albeit smaller-scale, example of the anthropic principle if you consider the earth itself. If the earth were much farther from our sun, or much closer to it, then it would be too cold or too hot for life to evolve. If the earth's magnetic field had not shielded us from bursts of radiation sleeting through the biosphere, plants and animals would not survive. If the ozone in the stratosphere had not provided protection from ultraviolet radiation, we wouldn't be here, or at least we'd be very different. Now contemplate the fact that there are some half billion stars in our galaxy, and billions of galaxies in the universe. Many of those stars will have planets. Many of those planets will be completely different from earth (they might be gas giants like Jupiter). Others will lie far from their star, or near to it. Others might have no protective magnetic field. And so on. On planets like those, no life (at least, of our kind) could have evolved. This means there would be nobody there to collect the data, to look at the facts, and to say "Hey, what an extraordinary coincidence. Our planet has just the right properties for life to evolve."

The anthropic principle simply says that if life is to evolve to see it, the universe must have the characteristics (that is, values of the fundamental constants) which will permit the evolution of life. There's nothing magic about it.

The anthropic principle has consequences, showing just how powerful the law of selection can be; it's not merely idle metaphysical speculation. Our universe is about 14 billion years old, and the anthropic principle tells us *it cannot be any younger than this*. This is because we are a carbon-based life-form. Carbon is formed from helium by a fusion process in the centers of stars. So for human beings to exist, enough time must have passed for the first generation of stars to form and explode, and then for carbon and other heavier elements to have spread throughout the universe, where they could condense to form planets on which carbon-based life could evolve. And calculations show that all this would have taken about 14 billion years. If the universe was any younger than this, we wouldn't be around to see it.

Of course, if there are life-forms that are not based on carbon, then the argument does not apply to them, but for us the universe is at least in the region of 14 billion years old: the law of selection.

The version of the anthropic principle I have just described is sometimes called the *weak anthropic principle*. There are other versions, which are of a much more dubious nature. One is the *strong anthropic principle*, which says that the universe *must have* properties such that life could develop. Another is the *participatory anthropic principle*, which says that "observers are necessary to bring the Universe into being."[10] And a third is the *final anthropic principle* (or what Martin Gardner has called the *completely ridiculous anthropic principle*—you can work out the acronym for yourself[11]) which says that "intelligent information-processing must come into existence in the Universe, and, once it comes into existence, it will never die out."[12] John Barrow and Frank Tipler do say, "We should warn the reader once again that both the [final anthropic principle] and the [strong anthropic principle] are quite speculative; unquestionably, neither should be regarded as well-established principles of physics." Indeed. These speculative versions of the anthropic principle doubtless have their place, but reservations about them should not be allowed to detract from the power of the weak form. It is the ultimate manifestation of the law of selection.

11

HOW TO USE THE
IMPROBABILITY PRINCIPLE

Coincidence is God's way of remaining anonymous.
—Attributed to Albert Einstein

Likelihood

We've explored the laws constituting the Improbability Principle, seeing why extremely unlikely events are in fact commonplace. In this chapter we go beyond the principle, to see how it is used in science, medicine, business, and other areas. The ideas are old ones, and they go under different names.

Borel's law says that we simply should not expect (sufficiently) improbable events to happen. But we've seen countless examples of situations where such events *have* happened—and the Improbability Principle tells us why. It tells us we see them because we've failed to take account of the fact that *something* must occur (the law of inevitability), or the fact that we explored a great many possibilities (the law of truly large numbers), or the fact that we chose what to look at after it had happened (the law of selection), or indeed any of the other strands of the principle. The Improbability Principle tells us that events which we regard as highly improbable occur because we *got things wrong*. If we can find out where we went wrong, then the improbable will become probable.

To explore how we can use this idea, I'll strip away all the potentially confusing ambiguity of the real world, and begin with a very simple idea indeed. Imagine I have a cloth bag which I tell you contains 1 black marble and 999,999 white ones (it's a big bag). You reach your hand in and, without being able to see the color, draw out one marble. And you see it's black.

Clearly the chance of this happening is very small—it's literally one in a million. You might think that this probability is sufficiently small for Borel's law to apply: it shouldn't happen. (If you think 1 in 1,000,000 is not small enough for Borel's law to apply, imagine the bag had a trillion marbles, or a quintillion, only one being black.) But, despite Borel's law, you get a black marble. In such cases, as we've seen, this typically means that we've failed to take account of something which would lead to a greater chance of you drawing out a black marble. Perhaps I lied when I told you the number of black marbles in the bag.

Note that we haven't explicitly said anything about the probability that the bag really did contain just one black marble, or the probability that I was lying. Instead we've said something about the probability of drawing out a black marble if you believed the bag was as I claimed, and the occurrence of the very-low-probability event has cast doubt on that belief. In scientific terms we might say that the occurrence of the low-probability event has cast doubt on our theory (in our example, the "theory" is that the bag really did contain only one black marble).

In his book *Duelling Idiots and Other Probability Puzzlers*,[1] Paul Nahin discusses the Pentagon claim that "the Patriot antiaircraft missile system had 'successfully engaged over 80 percent' of the Scud missiles Iraq had launched at Saudi Arabia" in the first Gulf War. Nahin refers to the skepticism of the MIT physicist Theodore Postol, who in watching the videotapes of fourteen Patriot-Scud engagements had seen thirteen misses and one probable hit. Postol had asked what would be the chance of seeing just one hit in fourteen attempts if the Patriot system really was successful 80 percent of the time. As Nahin shows, the calculations are straight-forward: the probability is less than one in a hundred million. This might be a small enough probability for you to invoke Borel's law—it shouldn't happen. But since it did, we might in-stead invoke the Improbability Principle and suggest that per-haps the 80 percent claim is overstated. I suspect that most people, choosing between explanations on the basis of the balance of probabilities, weighing the one in a hundred million probability against some more likely but unspecified probability, would pre-fer the second explanation (that the success rate was not really 80 percent).

The strategy is also illustrated by the financial-crash exam-ples in chapter 7. The examples there are all concerned with the occurrence of events which had a remarkably small probability, and which happened even though Borel's law says that we shouldn't expect such events. The fact that we see them suggests that some alternative explanation is possible—an explanation which would lead to the events being more probable. As we saw, a slight change in the shape of a statistical distribution leads to a situation in which such crashes are far more likely—we would expect to see them. Again we are balancing probabilities.

In all of the examples I've just given, the probability of get-ting the outcome was extremely small, so that a combination of Borel's law and the Improbability Principle led us to look for some mistake or oversight in our understanding of the situation. But in those examples we didn't explicitly say what the alternative the-ory was. Sometimes we do spell out the alternative.

Let's return to my bag of marbles. But now suppose I tell you (truthfully) that I have two bags, and that one contains a million (or a trillion, and so on) marbles, one of which is black and the others all white, while the other bag contains the same number of marbles, one of which is white and the others all black. You blindly reach your hand into one of the bags and pull out a marble. It's black. The question is, do you think that bag was the one which contained only one black marble or the bag which contained 999,999 black marbles?

I hope you'll agree that since it's much more likely that the second bag would yield a black marble, that's the bag you'd choose.

Here's a more realistic example.

Standard six-faced cubic dice have the faces arranged so that the numbers on opposite faces add up to 7. So 1 is opposite 6, 2 opposite 5, and 3 opposite 4. Among the dice in my collection, however, I have some which are misnumbered. In the place of the 1 face there's a 6, so these dice have two 6's. Since it's not possible to see opposite faces at the same time, you can't detect this just from looking at the dice on the table. Whereas a normal die has a probability of one-sixth of showing a 6, these fake dice have a probability of one-third. Skilled dice cheats—"dice mechanics," as they're called—can palm such dice to switch them in and out of a game at will, thus distorting the odds of winning. And such a fake die will form the basis for my next scenario.

We're shown a die, and told it might be fair or fake. Our task is to decide which. To help us make this decision, we'll collect some evidence: the results of throwing the die.

Suppose we throw the die 100 times, and a 6 comes up 35 times. The probability of obtaining this number of 6's with the fair die is 1 in about 220,000. That's a small probability, and you might be tempted to think it's small enough that you should search for some other explanation—such as that the die is not the fair one.

But wait. Remember the law of inevitability. *Some* outcome must occur and it's possible that *each of them* is highly unlikely (the probability that a golf ball falls on any particular blade of grass is very small).

If each of the outcomes is pretty unlikely, then we'll be suspicious about the die whatever outcome we get. That seems unhelpful. But there is a way around it—we can balance the probabilities of the outcome (35 out of 100 throws showing a 6) for the two explanations: the die is fair or the die is fake.

If the die is fair, we've just seen that the probability of getting 35 heads out of 100 throws is about 1 in 220,000. A similar calculation shows that if the die is fake (one with two 6's, as described above), the chance of getting 35 heads is about 1 in 13. Still a small probability, but nowhere near as small as 1 in 220,000. So if the chance of getting the 35 heads is nearly 17,000 times as large if the die is fake than if it's fair, do you think the die is fake or fair?

Balancing the probability of getting the observed outcome if one of the proposed explanations is true against the probability if the other is true is a fundamental principle underlying statistical methods. We look at the data, and calculate the probability that it could arise from each of the competing explanations. The explanation which has the greatest probability of having produced the observed data will be the explanation in which we have the most confidence. Statisticians call this the *law of likelihood*: we prefer the explanation that is most *likely* to have produced the observed data.

Here's another example, showing the law of likelihood being used to catch plagiarists.

It's easy to detect plagiarism with some material. If student A's essay is word-for-word the same as student B's, then the law of likelihood can be applied to the two possible explanations: (i) some copying has been going on (either one student copied the other or both copied some other source), or (ii) by chance they produced identical answers. This rapidly leads to a preference for explanation (i). But it's more difficult in other cases. Take, for example, mathematical tables (such as tables of logarithms or square roots, or the values of fundamental constants). These tables ought to be the same, whichever publishing house performed the calculations (the square root of two is the same whoever works it out), so it's difficult to argue that one publisher of such tables has simply copied another, not bothering to recalculate the figures.

Unless, that is, the first publisher deliberately introduces occasional very rare errors into their tables, changing a few values by only very small amounts, so that they won't materially impact any calculations based on them. Now, if we see those errors also cropping up in another publisher's tables, we might invoke the Improbability Principle. For another publisher to happen to get the same errors as the first, by chance, would be extraordinarily unlikely, so that we might look for another explanation under which it is more likely that the errors would match. One such explanation is that the second publisher didn't in fact recalculate the figures themselves at all, but simply copied those of the first. This explanation leads to a probability of 1 that they will have the same errors as the first publisher. The law of likelihood then leads us to strongly favor the explanation that copying has occurred (leading in turn to a successful lawsuit and expensive damages awards).

This strategy for preventing plagiarism was adopted in the 1964 *Chambers's Shorter Six-Figure Mathematical Tables*, and it has also been used in other similar situations, including the deliberate creation of fictitious entries in maps (with imaginary towns added), dictionaries (with made-up words), telephone directories (with fictitious numbers), and musical scores (superfluous notes added).

Comparing the probability that something will happen if one explanation is correct with the probability that it will happen if another explanation is correct can yield surprising results. Shakespeare aficionados will know that the playwright appeared fond of alliteration. This is the literary device in which the same consonantal sounds are repeated. Thus, in *Romeo and Juliet*, we find "Her traces, of the smallest spider's web" (Mercutio, in Act 1, Scene 4); "a rose by any other name would smell as sweet" (Juliet, in Act 2, Scene 2); "Life and those lips have long been separated" (Capulet, in Act 4, Scene 5); and "The sun for sorrow will not show his head" (Prince, Act 5, Scene 3). But Shakespeare wrote a lot. Could the sets of similar sounds in Shakespeare's sonnets simply surface serendipitously?

This means that we have two potential explanations for the occurrence of alliteration in the sonnets: the first, that it's merely due to chance, and the second, that it's a deliberate artifice. The behavioral psychologist B. F. Skinner investigated these explanations, using the ideas described above.[2] He aimed to estimate the probability that the observed alliteration would arise purely by chance. If this probability was small enough it would suggest chance was an unlikely explanation—and that the alternative, having a higher probability of producing the alliteration, would be preferred.

Skinner counted the number of times the same sounds appeared in lines in the sonnets. In fact, he found a good match between the actual counts and the numbers you'd expect by chance if there was *no* deliberate alliteration. He concluded that although Shakespeare might have alliterated on purpose, the chance explanation matched the data very well. According to Skinner, "Shakespeare might as well have drawn his words out of a hat."[3]

Bayesianism

The fictional detective Sherlock Holmes said, in *The Sign of the Four*, "[W]hen you have eliminated the impossible whatever remains, *however improbable*, must be the truth."[4] That's a fine aspiration, but deciding that something is impossible in the real world is rather difficult (I'm resisting the temptation to say it's impossible). Unless it's logically impossible (the realm of pure mathematics, as discussed previously), there's always some slight possibility. Perhaps mistakes made during data collection mean that the data are distorted, so that things only *seemed* impossible: the evidence contradicted the theory, but the evidence itself could be at fault. Indeed, in science it's relatively rare that data unambiguously contradict theories. It is, after all, in the very nature of scientific progress that we're bumping against the boundaries, where measurement is difficult and uncertainties abound. All too often the best we can do is talk in terms of probabilities.

So, a more realistic (if less euphonious) version of the Sherlock Holmes quotation might be something like, "When you have eliminated the more improbable, whatever remains is likely to be the truth." It's a weighing up of probabilities of explanations: not of the probabilities of getting the observed outcome if each of the explanations is true (as in the law of likelihood), but of the explanations themselves.

We've seen, in chapter 2, this idea of balancing probabilities of explanations from David Hume, who wrote: "[N]o testimony is sufficient to establish a miracle, unless the testimony be of such a kind, that its falsehood would be more miraculous, than the fact which it endeavours to establish."[5] He was explicitly balancing the probability that a miracle had occurred against the probability of some other explanation, and pointing out that if there were two alternative explanations then the one with the higher probability would be preferred.

Now this is all very well, but you might justifiably raise an objection: how can "explanations" have probabilities? Surely they are either true or false? Either the man witnessed a miracle, or he didn't, and if he didn't then there must be some other explanation (perhaps he's lying).

However, you will recall the "degree of belief" interpretation of probability in chapter 3. This took probability as a numerical measure of confidence. With this interpretation, it makes perfectly good sense to talk about "the probability of an explanation": if we assign a high probability to an explanation, it merely means we are confident that it's right.

Choosing between explanations based on the notion of probability as a degree of belief in your head, rather than an objective property of the real world, is known as the *Bayesian* approach.[6]

But Is It Significant?

The law of likelihood balanced the probability of getting the observed outcomes if one of two competing explanations was true against the probability of getting the observed outcome if the other was true. It led to us favoring the explanation with the higher probability of yielding the observed outcome—or, as we might say in this book, the lower improbability. Another strategy is based on controlling the probability that we make the wrong choice.

As an initial example, suppose we're very keen to avoid concluding that a die is fake when it is in fact fair (after all, incorrectly accusing someone of cheating can have all sorts of consequences). So, suppose that we regard a probability of 1 in 1,000 as sufficiently low to give us the protection we want. This means that if we were to repeat the exercise many times, we'd incorrectly conclude that a fair die was fake only once in every thousand times.

Calculations show that the probability of the 6 face coming up 30 or more times in 100 throws of a fair die is less than 1 in 1,000 (in fact it's 1 in 1,478, equal to 0.00068). So if the die is fair and we throw it 100 times and draw the conclusion that it's fake only if 6 comes up 30 or more times, then our probability of being wrong is less than 1 in 1,000. We have limited the chance of making the mistake of concluding that a fair die is fake.

If we want more protection against concluding that the die is fake when it's not, we could choose a smaller probability—for example, a probability of 1 in 10 million. We might also regard such a low probability as sufficiently small that we can invoke Borel's law: we wouldn't expect to see an outcome with so small a probability. The probability of the 6 face coming up 39 or more times in 100 throws of a fair die is about 1 in 10 million (in fact it's 1 in 11,699,824). So if we throw the die 100 times and 6 comes up 39 or more times, we might reasonably conclude that our assumption is wrong: that this outcome has so small a probability that it should not happen if the die is fair, and hence that the die cannot be fair.

That example considered the probability of getting a particular outcome (30 or more 6's in 100 throws) if the die is fair. We can also look at the probability of getting the same outcome if the die is fake. We know that if the die is fair, the probability of the 6 face showing is just 1/6, whereas if it is fake the probability is 1/3. So we'd expect to see 6 come up more often if it's fake than if it's fair. We've seen that the probability of getting 30 or more 6's in 100 throws of a fair die is 0.00068. For a fake die, the probability of getting this same number of 6's is 0.79073. This gives us a rule for deciding whether the die is fair or fake which allows us to control our probability of being wrong: we say it's fake if we get 30 or more 6's in 100 throws, and fair otherwise. If it's fair, our probability of incorrectly concluding that it's fake is just 0.00068; and if it's fake, our probability of incorrectly concluding that it's fair is $1 - 0.79073$ (about equal to 0.2). Either way, whether it's fair or fake, we have a low probability of being wrong, and we have a particularly low probability if it is actually fair. Just what we wanted.

The result (e.g., 30 or more 6's in 100 throws of a die) of an experiment to test a theory (e.g., that the die is fair) is said to be *statistically significant* if there's only a small probability of getting that result by chance if the theory is true. The smaller this probability, the greater the doubt it casts on the theory. With very small probabilities, we can reject the theory on the basis of Borel's law.

What exactly is meant by "a small probability" will depend on the context. In many areas—such as medicine or psychology—it's taken to be 0.05 (i.e., 1 in 20), or 0.01 (i.e., 1 in 100). Not especially small in terms of the Improbability Principle. But in other areas it's taken to be much smaller. In the high-energy physics search for new particles (based on observed events such as a shower of subatomic particles with particular energies and masses), a small probability is taken to be only 0.0000003. We saw in chapter 6 that, in finance, such small probabilities are often described as "*n*-sigma" events. The same terminology is also used in particle physics. Physicists searching for the Higgs boson, for example, described some of their results as 5-sigma events.

So statistical significance is a probability—the probability of getting data as extreme as or more extreme than those actually observed if a theory is right. It's an indication of whether the outcome is what we'd expect if that theory was true—or a sign that we should apply the Improbability Principle and look for another explanation.

Statistical significance is not the same as practical significance. Something might be very statistically significant indeed, so it casts great doubt on the theory, but that doesn't mean it matters. In a drug trial, a tiny difference between the effectiveness of two medicines might be highly statistically significant. That means we can be very confident that the effect is genuine. But the difference might also be so small that it's irrelevant to clinical practice, and nobody cares about it.

The above is all well and good, but complications can arise because of further factors related to the Improbability Principle. Recall the law of truly large numbers: if there are enough opportunities for something to happen, it's almost certain to happen.

In the dice example, we conducted a single test to see if the die was fair or fake. But what happens if we conduct many tests? To explore this, let's start by looking at two tests. For simplicity, we'll assume the tests are independent: the outcome of one test tells us nothing about the outcome of the other. One test might investigate whether a new treatment for asthma is better than the existing standard treatment, and the other might investigate whether a new treatment for depression is better than other treatments. Suppose we choose to limit the probability of mistakenly concluding that the new asthma treatment is better than the standard treatment to only 1 in 20—that is, we arrange matters so that our asthma test will have a probability of only 0.05 of concluding that the new treatment does work better when in fact it doesn't. Using the same idea with the depression treatment, we'll limit the probability of concluding that it's better than the existing treatment when in fact it's not to only 0.05. So in each case, 95 percent of the time we'll correctly conclude that the new treatment offers no improvement (since $1 - 0.05 = 0.95$) when it really offers no improvement.

But we're conducting *two* separate tests, one for asthma and one for depression. Using the ideas from chapter 3, the probability of *both* tests correctly concluding that the treatments are no more effective than the standard treatments is smaller than for one test alone. It's the product of the separate probabilities: 0.95×0.95. That is, 0.9025. That's the probability of correctly deciding that *neither* of the new treatments provides any gain over those we already have.

Since that's the probability of correct conclusions on both tests when neither treatment offers any improvement, the probability of at least one incorrect conclusion is 1 minus this. It's $1 - 0.9025 = 0.0975$. This is nearly 0.1. So we see that the probability of falsely concluding that *at least* one of the new treatments is superior is nearly twice the probability of reaching a false conclusion for either one of them alone.

That's what happens with two tests. But pharmaceutical companies test many drugs in their search for effective medicines. So let's see what happens if we want to test a thousand treatments. Let's again assume that all the tests are independent: that the outcome of any one of them doesn't affect the outcome of any of the others. And, as before, let's limit to just 0.05 the probability of mistakenly concluding that each treatment is effective when it isn't. Then, in exactly the same way as in the case of two treatments, the probability of correctly concluding that *none* of the thousand new treatments provides any gain when they really don't is the product of the separate probabilities: it's $0.95 \times 0.95 \times \ldots$

a thousand times: $0.95^{1,000} = 5.29 \times 10^{-23}$, or 1 in around 2×10^{22}. This is a tiny chance.

Since the probability of correctly concluding that none of the treatments provides any gain when they really don't is so small, it means that it's *overwhelmingly* likely (a probability of $1 - 5.29 \times 10^{-23}$) that we'll *falsely* conclude that one or more of the treatments is superior when in fact none of them are.

Now we can see the difficulties with scan statistics, the look elsewhere effect, and so on that we considered in chapter 5. These were problems in which we examined a very large number of possibilities (perhaps many more than 1,000), such as the many possible locations for a disease cluster. It means that it becomes very likely indeed that at least one of our tests will show a statistically significant result, even if really there are no locally elevated risks anywhere. That is, by the law of truly large numbers it becomes effectively certain that some disease clusters such as those described in the *Huffington Post* article will appear purely by chance, even if there is no underlying cause.

We can't avoid the problem, since it's a consequence of strands of the Improbability Principle. But perhaps we can alleviate it. One way is to set a much smaller value for the probability of reaching a false conclusion for each of the separate tests. Using our example, we could bend over backward to avoid saying a new treatment is superior when it isn't by choosing a probability of just 1 in 10,000, 0.0001 (instead of 0.05), of making that mistake. If we did this for the case of two treatments, the probability of mistakenly concluding that at least one of the two was more effective than the standard treatment would be about 0.0002. About twice 0.0001, but still highly improbable, which is a relief. When we have a thousand treatments, however, the probability of falsely concluding that at least one of them was more effective would be 0.095. That's not marvelous, but at 1 in 10, it's a great deal better than being *almost certain* you'll be wrong about at least one treatment.

Another way to ease the problem is to change the question. So far we've asked what the probability is of concluding that at least one of the treatments is better than the standard treatment, when in fact none are. Instead we could ask, among all those treatments we conclude are superior to the standard, what proportion actually are superior? If we could limit that proportion enough, this would be very useful.

Statisticians are very much aware of these problems. They're known as *multiple testing* or *multiplicity* problems. It's a hot topic of investigation, and is of great importance in a number of areas, including bioinformatics (where perhaps tens of thousands of genes are simultaneously tested to see if they're impacted by different conditions) and particle physics (where researchers look for phenomena at any of a great many values in a spectrum, as I mentioned in chapter 5). The large probabilities involved arise as a consequence of the law of truly large numbers: even if each event separately has a very small chance of occurring, take enough of them and it becomes overwhelmingly likely that at least one will occur.

Now we've looked at how we can evaluate and choose between explanations by weighing up probabilities. If something appears sufficiently improbable, then we have grounds for doubting it, and we look for an alternative explanation. This is the basis of statistical inference.

EPILOGUE

Chance has its reasons.   —Petronius

The Improbability Principle is not a single equation, such as Einstein's famous $E = mc^2$, but a collection of strands which intertwine, braiding together and amplifying each other, to form a rope connecting events, incidents, and outcomes. The main strands are the law of inevitability, the law of truly large numbers, the law of selection, the law of the probability lever, and the law of near enough. Any one of these strands is sufficient, by itself, to produce something apparently highly improbable—a multiple lottery winner, a financial crash, a precognitive dream. But it's when they combine and work together that their real power takes hold.

The law of inevitability says that something must happen. It says that if you make a complete list of all possible outcomes then one of them must occur. This law is so obvious that we often fail to notice it—just as we normally don't notice the air we breathe. This law says that even if each of the possible outcomes has a tiny probability of occurring, it's certain that one of them will: it makes the highly improbable certain.

The law of truly large numbers says that, with a large enough number of opportunities, any outrageous thing is likely to happen.

If you throw that handful of dice enough times, eventually they'll all come up 6's. It may be highly improbable that any one throw will produce all 6's, but given enough opportunities it becomes almost unavoidable.

The law of selection says you can make probabilities as high as you like if you choose *after* the event. My favorite example is painting the targets after the arrows have landed. The effect of selection in that example is evident; it makes the outcome certain. But often it's not obvious that a selection process is going on. If I select the students who do best in a test, I may not realize that I am also selecting those who are most likely to decline in performance at the next test.

The law of the probability lever says that a slight change in circumstances can have a huge impact on probabilities. We think of the earth as flat where we live, but if we keep going in one direction for long enough, we end up back where we started. The very slight, indeed imperceptible curve of the earth has major consequences. And in a similar way, the law of the probability lever bends probabilities, with the potential to increase them by huge factors.

The law of near enough says that events that are sufficiently similar may be regarded as identical. No two measurements are identical to an *infinite* number of decimal places, but in the real world, measurements are often so close that we regard them as the same. The probability that there will be a dead heat in a race depends on the accuracy of our stopwatch.

Putting these laws of the Improbability Principle together, we can hardly be surprised by "extraordinary" events like these:

- In July 2007 Bob Gould of Hayling Island, Hampshire, in the UK broke his leg falling from a ladder. Painful, you may agree, but nothing surprising in that. But in the same hour his son, Oliver, broke *his* leg jumping over a wall. And in both cases it was the left leg. Mr. Gould summed it up: "We are quite clumsy."[1]

- Mary Wohlford of Freeport, Illinois, wouldn't have had trouble remembering her daughters' birthdays. Her first four daughters were all born on August 3 of different years: Connie in 1949, Sandra in 1951, Ann in 1952, and Susan in 1954.[2]
- If you're planning a holiday, you might want to find out where Jason and Jenny Cairns-Lawrence, from Dudley in the UK, are planning to go—and avoid it. They were in New York on September 11, 2001, when terrorists flew planes into the World Trade Center; in London on July 7, 2005, when terrorists bombed the Underground metro system; and in Mumbai in November 2008, when terrorists attacked a number of targets.[3]
- Lawyer John Woods could share some stories with them. On December 21, 1988, he canceled his reservation on Pan Am flight 103 because he had been persuaded to attend an office party. That was the flight that exploded over Lockerbie. On February 26, 1993, he was in his office on the 39th floor of the World Trade Center when a car bomb exploded at its base. On September 11, 2001, he left his office just before the aircraft were flown into the buildings.[4]
- In 2010, when playing Scrabble on her computer, South African artist Raine Carosin drew the letters of her surname.[5]
- Lena Påhlsson, of Mora, Sweden, lost her wedding ring in 1996. Sixteen years later she pulled up a carrot in her garden and found the diamond-encrusted white gold ring encircling it.[6]

None of this is surprising at all. It's the Improbability Principle.

Appendix A: Mind-Numbingly Large and Mind-Bogglingly Small

The core of this book is the notion of a very small probability, a tiny chance. Now, one way of thinking about probabilities is to consider how often we'd expect an event to occur. For example, if I throw a standard six-sided die, the probability of a 5 showing is just one-sixth, or one in six. The probability of a fair coin coming up heads is one-half, or one in two. Likewise, if an event has a probability of one millionth it means that there is a one-in-a-million chance of it occurring: just one out of a very large number of possibilities. So to describe very small probabilities we need a way of representing really big numbers. In fact, we'll sometimes need to represent *mind-numbingly large* numbers.

Fortunately, there is a standard notation for conveying gigantic quantities—which you may already be familiar with:

The number x, when multiplied by itself n times, is denoted x^n.

So, for example, two multiplied by itself three times is $2 \times 2 \times 2$, and we represent this by the symbol 2^3 (and it is equal to 8, of course). Likewise, 2 multiplied by itself twenty times is $2 \times 2 \times 2 \times \ldots \times 2$, twenty times, represented by the notation 2^{20}. In fact, a little work with a calculator shows that $2^{20} = 1{,}048{,}576$, or just over a million.

Exactly the same idea applies to other numbers. So

$$100 = 10 \times 10 = 10^2$$

$$1,000,000 = 10 \times 10 \times 10 \times 10 \times 10 \times 10 = 10^6$$

and a 1 followed by a hundred 0's is 10^{100}.

That last example shows that this is a remarkably compact notation for representing very large numbers, since written out in full it becomes

100000000000000000000000000000000000000000000
000000000000000000000000000000000000000000000
000000000000000

This number, one followed by one hundred 0's, is called a googol. The name was invented by Milton Sirotta, the nine-year-old nephew of the mathematician Edward Kasner, when Kasner, who taught at Columbia University in the first half of the twentieth century, needed a name for a very large but nonetheless finite number.[1]

Appendix B: Rules of Chance

The *conjunction* of two events is the joint event that *both* of them occur. The conjunction of "My next throw of the die will show a 6" and "The throw after that will show a 6" is "My next two throws will both show 6's."

The *disjunction* of two events is the event that one *or* the other *or* both occurs. The disjunction of "My next throw will show a 6" and "The throw after that will show a 6" is "At least one of my next two throws will show a 6." Or, to put it another way, "One or the other or both of my next two throws will show 6's."

If two events each have a probability of occurring, then, since the conjunction and disjunction of two events are themselves events, the conjunction and disjunction also each have a probability of occurring. In my examples, there will be some probability that my next two throws will both show 6's, and some probability that at least one of them will show a 6.

The opposite of an event is called its *complement*. If my throw didn't yield a 6, then I could say the event "not a 6" happened. If an event has occurred, then its complement hasn't, and vice versa. If something is true, then its complement is false.

Now let's suppose we have a perfect die, so that each of its faces has a probability of one-sixth of showing. Then the probability that the die will show an even number is the probability that it will show a 2 or a 4 or a 6. This is just the disjunction of the events 2, 4, and 6.

The probability of this disjunction is the sum of the separate probabilities: it's the sum of the probability of showing a 2, and the probability of showing a 4, and the probability of showing a 6. This is the *addition rule* of probability. It also tells us that the probability that the die will show a number 4 or less is the sum of the probabilities that it will show a 1, a 2, a 3, or a 4. This probability is the sum of four one-sixths; that is, four-sixths, or simply two-thirds. And so on.

But there's a slight complication.

What if we want to know the probability of the disjunction of the two events "The die will show an even number" and "The die will show a number 4 or less"? So we want to know the probability that the die will show an even number, *or* a number 4 or less, *or* both of these events. Your first thought here might be that you just add together the probabilities of the two events "The die will show an even number" and "The die will show a number 4 or less."

But if you do this, you'll run into a problem. The probability of the die showing an even number is one-half, and the probability of the die showing a number of 4 or less is two-thirds. Adding these together gives us one-half plus two-thirds, or one and one-sixth, which is greater than one. And we know that probabilities can't be greater than one.

The problem here is that we're counting some outcomes twice. If the die shows a 2 or a 4, for example, it's included in the probability that "the die shows an even number" and also in the probability that "the die shows a number 4 or less." Just adding the two probabilities together means we're double-counting the probability that we'll get a 2 or a 4.

To correct for this, we've got to subtract one of these double-counts. Since the probability of getting a 2 or a 4 is one-third, we have to subtract that from our total. That gives one-half plus two-thirds minus one-third, which equals five-sixths.

In this example, there's another way to find the answer. The probability that the die will show an even number *or* a number of 4 or less (or both of these events) is the probability that it shows a 1, 2, 3, 4, or 6. And that is just five out of the six equally likely possibilities; it is, as we have just seen, five-sixths.

In general, when we calculate the disjunction of two events, we must check to see if they have anything in common. Then, to avoid double-counting the probability of that common part, we must subtract one of those double-counts.

Events often have nothing in common. That makes calculating the disjunction easy, since then the common part has a probability of zero, so nothing has to be subtracted. For example, what's the probability of the disjunction of the event "The die will show 2 or less" and "The die will show 5 or more"? Or to put it another way, what's the probability that the die will show "2 or less," "5 or more," or both "2 or less" and "5 or more"? Clearly the probability that the die shows *both* "2 or less" and "5 or more" is zero: it can't show "2 or less" *and* "5 or more" at the same time. So we can simply add together the probability that "the die will show 2 or less" and the probability that "the die will show 5 or more."

When events have nothing in common they're said to be *exclusive* or *incompatible*. If two events are exclusive, then their conjunction has a probability of zero: they can't occur together.

So now I can give the full form of the addition rule: *The probability of the disjunction of two events is the sum of their separate probabilities, minus the probability that both of them occur.* The probability that both of them occur is the probability of the conjunction of the events.

Since the joint occurrence of events is what lies at the heart of coincidences, let's look at conjunctions in more detail. Here's another example, slightly different from the earlier one: What's the probability of the conjunction of the two events "The die shows an even number" and "The die shows a number 3 or less"? Well, the probability that the die shows an even number is just one-half (three of the six faces are even: faces 2, 4, and 6). Then, *among those three faces,* one-third of them (face 2) shows a number 3 or less. So the overall probability that "the die shows an even number" *and* "the die shows a number 3 or less" is just one-third of one-half. That is, one-sixth. That this result is right is easy to check, as we can get at it directly. Only one of the six faces, that numbered 2, satisfies both the conditions "The die shows an even number" and "The die shows a number 3 or less." One out of six is one-sixth.

This example uses *conditional probability.* This is simply the probability that one event will occur when you know that some other event occurred. In our example, *among the even-numbered faces* (that is, *given* that an even number came up), one-third showed a number 3 or less. We say that, *conditional on* an even number showing, one-third had a number 3 or less.

So, more generally, we find the probability of a conjunction of two events by multiplying the probability of one of them by the probability of the other, *given* that the first occurred, or "conditional on the fact that the first occurred."

Knowing that something else has happened doesn't always change the probabilities of events: sometimes probabilities are the same *whether or not another event occurred.* The probability that a die will show a number 4 or less is two-thirds. And the probability that it will show a number 4 or less *given* that you know it shows an even number is also two-thirds.

When the probability of one event is the same whether or not another event occurs, the two events are said to be *independent.* In such cases we can find the probability that both events occur, that is, the conjunction of the events, by simply multiplying together the separate probabilities of the events. The probability that "the die shows an even number" is just one-half; the probability that "the die shows a number 4 or less" is just two-thirds, regardless of whether the number is restricted to the even numbers or not; and the *joint* probability that *both* events occur is just one-half times two-thirds, or one-third.

If the probability of one event *does* depend on whether or not another occurs, the two are not independent—they're said to be *dependent.* Returning to our example of the two events "The die shows an even number" and "The die shows a number 3 or less," what happens if we simply multiply together the separate probabilities of these events? We get one-half times one-half, which is one-quarter. But, as we've already seen, the conjunction of these events, both of them occurring together, happens only when the 2 face shows. The probability that this particular face will show is just one-sixth. So the probability of both events occurring is actually one-sixth, not one-quarter.

What's gone wrong is that the two events aren't independent. Here, the probability that the die showed a number 3 or less, *given that it showed an even number,* is just one-third, whereas the probability that the die showed a value 3 or less, *given that it did not show an even number,* is two-thirds. So the probability of the die showing a number 3 or less is not the same regardless of whether the die shows an even number.

This illustrates the *multiplication rule* of probability: the probability of two events both occurring (the conjunction of those two events) is the probability of one multiplied by the probability of the other when you know that the first has occurred. And if two events are independent the occurrence of the first doesn't affect the probability of the second, so the rule becomes merely the product of the probabilities of the two events.

Notes

EPIGRAPH

1. Quoted by Lisa Belkin, "The Odds of That," *The New York Times*, August 11, 2002.

1. THE MYSTERY

1. fUSION Anomaly, *"The Girl from Petrovka,"* last modified August 1, 2001, http://fusionanomaly.net/girlfrompetrovka.html.
2. Carl G. Jung, *Synchronicity: An Acausal Connecting Principle*, trans. R.F.C. Hull, Bollingen Series XX (Princeton, NJ: Princeton University Press, 1960), 15.
3. N. Bunyan, "Double Hole-in-One," *The Telegraph*, September 28, 2005.
4. Émile Borel, *Probabilities and Life*, trans. Maurice Baudin (New York: Dover Publications, 1962), 2–3.
5. An early mechanical form of word processor, in which the keys were directly linked to small metal hammers which struck an ink-soaked ribbon to leave imprints of letters on the page.
6. Borel, *Probabilities and Life*, 3.
7. Ibid., 2–3.
8. Ibid., 26.
9. Antoine-Augustin Cournot, *Exposition de la théorie des chances et des probabilités* (Paris, Librairies de L. Hachette, 1843).
10. Karl Popper, *The Logic of Scientific Discovery*, Routledge Classics (London: Routledge, 2002), 195. First published 1935 by Springer, Vienna.
11. Borel, *Probabilities and Life*, 5–6.
12. Brian Greene, "5 Strange Things You Didn't Know About Kim Jong-Il," *U.S. News & World Report*, December 19, 2011, www.usnews.com/news /articles/2011/12/19/5-strange-things-you-didnt-know-about-kim-jong-il.

2. A CAPRICIOUS UNIVERSE

1. This was a classic British comedy from the 1920s and '30s. www.you tube.com/watch?v=8U22hYXUIvw.
2. B. F. Skinner, "'Superstition' in the Pigeon," *Journal of Experimental Psychology* 38 (1948): 168–72.
3. It's interesting that more superstitions seem to be associated with bad luck than with good. It may be an evolutionary consequence of the need for caution: you're more likely to survive if you can spot potential threats.
4. Francis Bacon, *The New Organon: or True Directions Concerning the Interpretation of Nature* (1620), Aphorisms, Book One, XLVI.
5. Robert K. Merton, *On Social Structure and Science* (Chicago: University of Chicago Press, 1996), 196.
6. Robert L. Snow, *Deadly Cults: The Crimes of True Believers* (Westport, CT: Praeger Publishers, 2003), 112.
7. David Hume, *An Enquiry Concerning Human Understanding*, 2nd ed. (Indianapolis, IN: Hackett Publishing 1993), 77. First published 1777.
8. Daniel Druckman and John A. Swets, eds., *Enhancing Human Performance: Issues, Theories, and Techniques* (Washington, DC: The National Academies Press, 1988).
9. John Scarne, *Scarne on Dice* (Harrisburg, PA: Stackpole Books, 1974), 65.
10. Holger Bösch, Fiona Steinkamp, and Emil Boller, "Examining Psychokinesis: The Interaction of Human Intention with Random Number Generators—A Meta-Analysis," *Psychological Bulletin* 132 (2006): 497–523.
11. Scarne, *Scarne on Dice*, 63.
12. J. B. Rhine, "A New Case of Experimenter Unreliability," *Journal of Parapsychology* 38 (1974): 215–25; Louisa E. Rhine, *Something Hidden* (Jefferson, NC: McFarland and Co., 2011).
13. Peter Brugger and Kirsten I. Taylor, "ESP: Extrasensory Perception or Effect of Subjective Probability?" *Journal of Consciousness Studies* 10, no. 6–7 (2003): 221–46.
14. James Randi Educational Foundation, "One Million Dollar Paranormal Challenge," accessed March 1, 2012, www.randi.org/site/index.php/1m -challenge.html.
15. Carl G. Jung, *Synchronicity: An Acausal Connecting Principle*, trans. R.F.C. Hull, Bollingen Series XX (Princeton, NJ: Princeton University Press, 1960), 19.
16. Jung, *Synchronicity*, 25; on the topic of Jung's coining of the term "synchronicity," Arthur Koestler remarked on p. 95 of his 1972 book *The Roots of Coincidence*: "One wonders why Jung created these unnecessary complications by coining a term which implies simultaneity, and then explaining that it does not mean what it means. But this kind of obscurity combined with verbosity runs through much of Jung's writing."
17. Jung, *Synchronicity*, 22–23.

18. Paul Kammerer, *Das Gesetz der Serie: Eine Lehre von den Wiederholungen im Lebens- und im Weltgeschehen* (Stuttgart and Berlin: Deutsche Verlags-Anstalt, 1919).

19. Rupert Sheldrake, *The Presence of the Past: Morphic Resonance and the Habits of Nature* (New York: Crown Publishing, 1988).

20. Pierre-Simon Laplace, *Essai philosophique sur les probabilités* (Paris: Courcier, 1814).

3. WHAT IS CHANCE?

1. Persi Diaconis and Frederick Mosteller, "Methods for studying coincidences," *Journal of the American Statistical Association* 84, no. 408 (1989): 853–61.

2. John J. Lumpkin, "Agency Planned Exercise on Sept. 11 Built around a Plane Crashing Into a Building," Associated Press, August 21, 2001, www.prisonplanet.com/agency_planned_exercise_on_sept_11_built _around_a_plane_crashing_into_a_building.htm.

3. Leonard J. Savage, *The Foundations of Statistics* (New York: John Wiley & Sons, 1954), 2.

4. Edward Gibbon, *The History of the Decline and Fall of the Roman Empire, Volume 2* (London: Strahan and Cadell, 1781), chapter XXIV, part V, footnote.

5. *La logique, ou l'art de penser* was published anonymously in 1662 by Antoine Arnauld and Pierre Nicole. Blaise Pascal was probably also a contributor.

6. Legend has it that Lorenz wrote this on a piece of paper when he was visiting Professor Eugenia Kalnay at the University of Maryland.

7. Although, in his book *The Emergence of Probability*, the philosopher Ian Hacking describes an afternoon spent rolling dice in the Cairo Museum of Antiquities and discovering that those dice appeared to be "exquisitely well balanced." He says, "Indeed a couple of rather irregular looking ones were so well balanced as to suggest that they had been filed off at this or that corner just to make them equiprobable" (that is, to make it equally probable that each of the faces would show, or as near to it as one could tell from an afternoon rolling them).

8. Øystein Ore, "Pascal and the Invention of Probability Theory," *The American Mathematical Monthly* 67, no. 5 (1960): 409–19.

9. Luca Pacioli, *Summa de Arithmetica, Geometria, Proportioni et Proportionalità* (Venice, 1494).

10. Giovanni Francesco Peverone, *Due Brevi e Facili Trattati, il Primo d'Arithmetica, l'Altro di Geometria* (Lyon, 1558).

11. David Napley, "Lawyers and Statisticians," *Journal of the Royal Statistical Society, Series A* 145, no. 4 (1982): 422–38.

12. Adolphe Quetelet, *A Treatise on Man, and the Development of his Faculties* (Edinburgh: William and Robert Chambers, 1842; New York: Burt Franklin, 1968), 80.
13. Bruno de Finetti, *Theory of Probability: A Critical Introductory Treatment* (New York: John Wiley & Sons, 1974–75).
14. Girolamo Cardana, *Liber de ludo aleae* (*The Book on Games of Chance*) (1663).
15. Francis Galton, *Natural Inheritance* (London: Macmillan, 1889).
16. Theodore Micceri, "The Unicorn, the Normal Curve, and Other Improbable Creatures," *Psychological Bulletin* 105, no. 1 (1989): 156–66.
17. Henri Poincaré, *Science and Method*, trans. Francis Maitland (London: Thomas Nelson, 1914), chapter 4.
18. Lewis Campbell and William Garnett, *The Life of James Clerk Maxwell: With a Selection from His Correspondence and Occasional Writings and a Sketch of His Contributions to Science* (London: Macmillan, 1882; Cambridge: Cambridge University Press, 2010), 442.
19. http://archive.org/details/TheBornEinsteinLetters.

4. THE LAW OF INEVITABILITY

1. Lottery slogans are a genre in their own right. The Massachusetts State Lottery only slightly bent the truth with "Someone's gotta win" (forgetting that perhaps no one bought the winning ticket). The Oregon Lottery moved onto dubious moral ground with "It does good things." Colorado's lottery kept to the simple "Don't forget to play." North Carolina stuck to the unvarnished truth with "Gotta be in it to win it." And so it goes on.

5. THE LAW OF TRULY LARGE NUMBERS

1. Augustus De Morgan, "Supplement to the Budget of Paradoxes," *The Athenaeum* no. 2017 (1866): 836.
2. J. E. Littlewood, *A Mathematician's Miscellany* (London: Methuen and Co., 1953), 105.
3. Ellen Goodstein, "Unlucky in Riches," November 17, 2004, http://lottoreport.com/AOLSadbuttrue.htm.
4. The lottery changed from a 6/39 to a 6/42 lottery over this period. The one-in-a-trillion figure then assumes that Ms. Adams bought one ticket each week for a four-month period.
5. Christina Ng, "Virginia Woman Wins $1 Million Lottery Twice on Same Day," Good Morning America, April 23, 2012, http://gma.yahoo.com/virginia-woman-wins-1-million-lottery-twice-same-160709882--abc-news-topstories.html.

6. "Identical Lottery Draw Was Coincidence," Reuters, September 18, 2009, www.reuters.com/article/2009/09/18/us-lottery-idUSTRE58H4AM 20090918.

7. R. D. Clarke, "An Application of the Poisson Distribution," *Journal of the Institute of Actuaries* 72 (1946): 481.

8. Nicholas Miriello and Catherine Pearson, "42 Disease Clusters in 13 U.S. States Identified," *The Huffington Post*, last updated May 31, 2011, www .huffingtonpost.com/2011/03/31/disease-clusters-us-states_n_842529 .html#s259789title=Arkansas.

9. Uri Geller, "11.11," September 17, 2010, http://site.uri-geller.com/11_11.

10. Ibid.

11. The word "random" here is used in a rather special sense. What it means is that each of the ten digits occurs one-tenth of the time, any pair of digits occurs one-hundredth of the time, any triple occurs one-thousandth of the time, etc. Its digits run on forever and never repeat in cycles.

12. If you want to find where the digits of your own birthday occur, look at the wonderful Web page www.angio.net/pi/piquery.

13. Mark Ronan, *Symmetry and the Monster: One of the Greatest Quests of Mathematics* (Oxford: Oxford University Press, 2006).

14. R. L. Holle, "Annual Rates of Lightning Fatalities by Country," Preprints, 20th International Lightning Detection Conference, April 21–23, 2008, Tucson, Arizona.

15. www.pga.com/pga-america/hole-one.

16. www.holeinonesociety.org/pages/home.aspx.

17. *The Times*, May 24, 2007.

18. Tim Reid, "Two Holes in One—And It's the Same Hole," *The Times*, August 2, 2006.

19. "Hunstanton, England," Top 100 Golf Courses of the World, accessed June 9, 2013, www.top100golfcourses.co.uk/htmlsite/productdetails.asp ?id=75.

20. Mick Power, *Adieu to God: Why Psychology Leads to Atheism* (Chichester, UK: Wiley-Blackwell, 2012).

21. Thomas H. Jordan et al., "Operational Earthquake Forecasting: State of Knowledge and Guidelines for Utilization," Report by the International Commission on Earthquake Forecasting for Civil Protection, *Annals of Geophysics* 54, no. 4 (2011): 315–91, doi:10.4401/ag-5350. www.earth -prints.org/bitstream/2122/7442/1/AG_jordan_etal_11.pdf.

22. Richard Wiseman, *Paranormality: Why We Believe the Impossible* (London: Macmillan, 2011), www.richardwiseman.com/ParaWeb/Inside_intro.shtml.

23. Martin Plimmer and Brian King, *Beyond Coincidence* (Cambridge, UK: Icon Books, 2004).

6. THE LAW OF SELECTION

1. Charles Forelle and James Bandler, "The Perfect Payday," *The Wall Street Journal*, March 18, 2006, http://online.wsj.com/article/SB1142 65075068802118.html.
2. Erik Lie, "On the Timing of CEO Stock Option Awards," *Management Science* 51, no. 5 (2005): 802–12. www.biz.uiowa.edu/faculty/elie/Grants -MS.pdf.
3. Ward Hill Lamon, *Recollections of Abraham Lincoln 1847–1865*, ed. Dorothy Lamon Teillard (Cambridge, MA: The University Press, 1895 / rev. and exp. 1911; Lincoln, NE: University of Nebraska Press, 1994).
4. Francis Bacon, *The New Organon: or True Directions Concerning the Interpretation of Nature* (1620), paragraph XLVI.
5. The phrase "regression to the mean" is the origin of the use of the word "regression" in statistics.
6. Linda Mountain, "Safety Cameras: Stealth Tax or Life-Savers?" *Significance* 3, no. 3 (2006): 111–13.
7. Arthur Koestler, *The Roots of Coincidence* (London: Pan Books Ltd., 1974).
8. Daniel Kahneman, *Thinking, Fast and Slow* (New York: Farrar, Straus and Giroux, 2011).
9. William Withering, *An Account of the Foxglove, and Some of Its Medical Uses: With Practical Remarks on Dropsy, and Other Diseases* (Birmingham, England: G.G.J. and J. Robinson, 1785).
10. David J. Hand, *Information Generation: How Data Rule Our World* (Oxford: Oneworld Publications, 2007).
11. Horace Freeland Judson, *The Great Betrayal: Fraud in Science* (Orlando, FL: Houghton Mifflin Harcourt, 2004).
12. John P. A. Ioannidis, "Why Most Published Research Findings Are False," *PloS Medicine* 2, no. 8 (2005): e124.

7. THE LAW OF THE PROBABILITY LEVER

1. Sebastian Mallaby, *More Money Than God: Hedge Funds and the Making of a New Elite* (New York: The Penguin Press, 2010), chapter 4.
2. S. Machin and T. Pekkarinen "Global Sex Differences in Test Score Variability," *Science* 322 (2008): 1331–32.
3. Roger Lowenstein, *When Genius Failed: The Rise and Fall of Long-Term Capital Management* (New York: Random House, 2000).
4. Bill Bonner, "25 Standard Deviations in a Blue Moon," *MoneyWeek*, November 13, 2007, www.moneyweek.com/news-and-charts/economics/25 -standard-deviations-in-a-blue-moon.
5. Izabella Kaminska, " 'A 12th "Sigma" Event If There Is Such a Thing,' " *FTAlphaville*, May 7, 2010, http://ftalphaville.ft.com/blog/2010/05/07 /223821/a-12th-sigma-event-if-there-is-such-a-thing.

6. Carmen M. Reinhart and Kenneth S. Rogoff, *This Time Is Different: Eight Centuries of Financial Folly* (Princeton, NJ: Princeton University Press, 2009).

7. In Figure 7.2, the normal distribution has mean 0 and spread 1, and the Cauchy distribution has mean and scale parameter 1.

8. M. V. Berry, "Regular and Irregular Motion," in *Topics in Nonlinear Dynamics: A Tribute to Sir Edward Bullard*, American Institute of Physics Conference Proceedings 46 (La Jolla, CA: American Institute of Physics, 1978), 16–120.

9. Alister Hardy, Robert Harvie, and Arthur Koestler, *The Challenge of Chance: Experiments and Speculations* (London: Hutchinson, 1973).

10. Ibid., 25.

11. Persi Diaconis and Frederick Mosteller, "Methods for studying Coincidences," *Journal of the American Statistical Association* 84, no. 408 (1989): 853–61.

12. Ray Hill, "Multiple Sudden Infant Deaths—Coincidence or Beyond Coincidence?" *Paediatric and Perinatal Epidemiology* 18 (2004): 320–26.

8. THE LAW OF NEAR ENOUGH

1. Carl G. Jung, *Synchronicity: An Acausal Connecting Principle*, trans. R.F.C. Hull (Princeton, NJ: Princeton University Press, 1973), 22.

2. Ibid., 21.

3. Alister Hardy, Robert Harvie, and Arthur Koestler, *The Challenge of Chance: Experiments and Speculations* (London: Hutchinson, 1973), 34.

4. Zener cards were designed in the early 1930s by Karl Zener, an associate of J. B. Rhine, specifically for ESP experiments. There are twenty-five cards in a deck, with five of each of five types. Each type has a different line drawing: a circle, a Greek cross, three vertical wavy lines, a square, or a five-pointed star.

5. Arthur Koestler, *The Roots of Coincidence* (London: Pan Books Ltd., 1974), 39–40.

6. The concept of "statistical significance" is described in detail in chapter 11.

7. Koestler, *Roots of Coincidence*, 39.

8. They can be thought of as the lengths of the sides of right-angled triangles. Pythagoras's Theorem tells us that the sum of the squared lengths of the sides adjacent to the right angle is equal to the squared length of the other side. So a triangle with side lengths 3, 4, and 5, for which $3^2 + 4^2 = 5^2$, is a right-angled triangle.

9. I'm indebted to Mike Crowe for this example.

10. Here are three other examples:

$e^\pi - \pi = 19.9991 \ldots$, near enough to the integer 20 for many purposes;

$\sin (2017 \times 2^{\frac{1}{3}}) = -0.9999999999999999785 \ldots$, very close to -1; $\pi^9 / e^8 = 9.9998 \ldots$ very close to 1.

11. Charles Piazzi Smyth, *The Great Pyramid: Its Secrets and Mysteries Revealed* (also titled *Our Inheritance in the Great Pyramid*) (London: Isbister and Co., 1874).

12. Charles Dickens, *The Old Curiosity Shop* (London: Chapman and Hall, 1841), chapter 39.

9. THE HUMAN MIND

1. P. P. Wakker, *Prospect Theory for Risk and Ambiguity* (Cambridge: Cambridge University Press, 2010).

2. Thomas Gilovich, Robert Vallone, and Amos Tversky, "The Hot Hand in Basketball: On the Misperception of Random Sequences," *Cognitive Psychology* 17 (1985): 295–314.

3. S. Christian Albright, "A Statistical Analysis of Hitting Streaks in Baseball," *Journal of the American Statistical Association* 88, no. 424 (1993): 1175–83.

4. Jim Albert, "A Statistical Analysis of Hitting Streaks in Baseball: Comment," *Journal of the American Statistical Association* 88, no. 424 (1993), 1184–88.

5. C. G. Jung, *Memories, Dreams, Reflections*, rec. and ed. Aniela Jaffé, trans. Richard and Clara Winston (London: Collins and Routledge & Kegan Paul, 1963).

6. Ibid., 136.

7. Ibid., 188–89.

8. "Is this Britain's luckiest woman?" *Mail Online*, updated June 28, 2011, www.dailymail.co.uk/news/article-2008648/Is-Britains-luckiest-woman -Former-bank-worker-earns-living-winning-competitions.html.

9. Richard K. Guy, "The Strong Law of Small Numbers," *The American Mathematical Monthly* 95, no. 8 (1988): 697–712.

10. The first conjecture is false, but the second is true.

11. Nevil Maskelyne, "The Art in Magic," *The Magic Circular*, June 1908, 25.

12. Leonard Mlodinow, *The Drunkard's Walk: How Randomness Rules Our Lives* (New York: Pantheon, 2008).

13. E. H. Carr, *What Is History? The George Macaulay Trevelyan Lectures Delivered in the University of Cambridge*, Penguin History (Cambridge: Cambridge University Press, 1961; London: Penguin Books, 1990).

10. LIFE, THE UNIVERSE, AND EVERYTHING

1. Richard Dawkins, *Climbing Mount Improbable* (London: Penguin Books, 1996), 66.

2. William Paley, *Natural Theology; or, Evidence of the Existence and Attributes of the Deity, Collected from the Appearances of Nature* (London: R. Faulder, 1802).

3. Tim H. Sparks et al., "Increased Migration of Lepidoptera Linked to Climate Change," *European Journal of Entomology* 104 (2007): 139–43.

4. Mark Ridley, *The Problems of Evolution* (Oxford: Oxford University Press, 1985), 5.

5. Charles Darwin, *On the Origin of Species by Means of Natural Selection, or the Preservation of Favoured Races in the Struggle for Life* (London: John Murray, 1859), 127.

6. Victor J. Stenger, "Where Do the Laws of Physics Come From?" preprint, PhilSci Archive, 2007, http://philsci-archive.pitt.edu/3662.

7. http://physics.nist.gov/cgi-bin/cuu/Value?mnsmp|search_for=neutron -proton+mass+ratio.

8. Fred C. Adams, "Stars in Other Universes: Stellar Structure with Different Fundamental Constants," *Journal of Cosmology and Astroparticle Physics* 2008, no. 8 (2008): 010.

9. John D. Barrow and Frank J. Tipler, *The Anthropic Cosmological Principle* (Oxford: Oxford University Press, 1988), 16.

10. Ibid., 28.

11. Martin Gardner, "WAP, SAP, PAP, and FAP," *The New York Review of Books 23*, no. 8 (May 8, 1986): 22–25.

12. Barrow and Tipler, *The Anthropic Cosmological Principle*.

11. HOW TO USE THE IMPROBABILITY PRINCIPLE

1. Paul J. Nahin, *Duelling Idiots and Other Probability Puzzlers* (Princeton, NJ: Princeton University Press, 2000; reissue ed., 2012).

2. B. F. Skinner, "The Alliteration in Shakespeare's Sonnets: A Study in Literary Behavior," *The Psychological Record* 3 (1939): 186–92.

3. Since there is such a wealth of literary scholarship about Shakespeare's works, it would be too much to expect Skinner's conclusions to remain unchallenged. Ulrich Goldsmith explored the matter further, and said "[Skinner] not only ignores the historical aspect of alliteration in the sonnets, but denies the presence of artistic purpose in the poet's alliterative practice." Ulrich K. Goldsmith, "Words Out of a Hat? Alliteration and Assonance in Shakespeare's Sonnets," *The Journal of English and Germanic Philology* 49, no. 1 (1950): 33–48.

4. Arthur Conan Doyle, *The Sign of the Four*, chapter 6, in *Lippincott's Monthly Magazine*, February 1890.

5. David Hume, *An Enquiry Concerning Human Understanding*, 2nd ed. (Indianapolis, IN: Hackett Publishing, 1993), 77.

6. This name is perhaps a little unfortunate, since Bayes's theorem is just a

mathematical way of calculating probabilities, and *all* statisticians use it to calculate probabilities, not merely those who hold the degree-of-belief interpretation of probability.

EPILOGUE

1. *The Times,* July 12, 2007.
2. James A. Hanley, "Jumping to Coincidences: Defying Odds in the Realm of the Preposterous," *The American Statistician* 46, no. 3 (1992): 197–202.
3. *The Telegraph,* December 21, 2008.
4. *Fortean Times* 153 (December 2001): 6.
5. Mike Perry, "Scrabble Coincidence from a South African Artist," *67 Not Out: Coincidence, Synchronicity and Other Mysteries of Life,* www.67notout .com/2010/10/scrabble-coincidence-from-south-african.html.
6. *The Times,* January 2, 2012; http://news.yahoo.com/wedding-ring-lost-16 -years-found-growing-garden-230706338.html.

APPENDIX A

1. Legend has it that the name of the Internet search company Google was a misspelling of the word "googol."

Index

Page numbers in *italics* refer to figures and tables.

A NOTE ABOUT THE AUTHOR

David J. Hand is an emeritus professor of mathematics and a senior research investigator at Imperial College London. He is the former president of the Royal Statistical Society and the chief scientific adviser to Winton Capital Management, one of Europe's most successful algorithmic-trading hedge funds. He is the author of seven books, including *Information Generation: How Data Rule Our World* and *Statistics: A Very Short Introduction*, and has published more than three hundred scientific papers. Hand lives in London, England.